D1556939

We'll Laugh about
This . . . Someday

We'll Laugh about This . . . Someday

ANN COMBS

Atheneum   1983   NEW YORK

Library of Congress Cataloging in Publication Data

Combs, Ann, ———
    We'll laugh about this—someday.

    1. Family—United States—Case studies. I.—Title
HQ536.C72 1983   306.8'7'0924   83-45067
ISBN 0-689-11393-5

To Lee

GOD, KID, I MISS YOU

৯►Contents

WE'LL LAUGH ABOUT THIS . . . SOMEDAY

PROLOGUE 3

AND THEN THERE WERE SIX 14

NEXT THERE'LL BE A SWARM OF LOCUSTS 34

AND MILES TO GO BEFORE I SLEEP 51

YOU CALL THIS FULFILLMENT? 70

FROM PILLAR TO POST 83

BATTERIES NOT INCLUDED 94

FROM DR. DENTONS TO CALVIN KLEINS 109

AND THE SOUND OF THE SCHOOL BUS
IS HEARD IN THE LAND 122

GO BACK TO BED, YOU'RE SUPPOSED
TO BE SICK 136

YOU'LL BE AS GOOD AS NEW   152

LOOK WHAT FOLLOWED ME HOME   174

ADVICE AND DISSENT   186

I'LL DO IT, I'LL DO IT...AS SOON

AS I FINISH THIS   199

UP IN THE MORNING, OUT ON THE ROUTE   214

'TWIXT TWELVE AND TWENTY   226

OH, MY STARS   254

ISN'T IT TIME YOU BROUGHT HOME

A SLICE OF THE BACON?   268

WHO SAYS PRACTICE MAKES PERFECT?   284

DID I JUST HEAR SOMEONE GO OUT

THE BACK DOOR?   298

THERE'S ALWAYS SOMEONE WHO

BLINKS FIRST   310

ন⋙ We'll Laugh about This... Someday

SOME PEOPLE attack life as if it were a closet begging to be cleaned. They organize and rearrange. They work from left to right. If a hatbox falls off the shelf or a Christmas angel drops to the floor and shatters, they grumble briefly. But they dust the box. They sweep up the broken wings, and they put things right again. Then they go to the next challenge.

Others march through their days like Crusaders stumbling across twelfth-century Europe. They endure plague and pestilence, long nights and bleak days. But they never complain and they never give in. "This is my lot in life," they murmur, "and I'll endure it."

Not me. I lurch through life tripping over rocks, stepping knee-deep into puddles and often falling flat on my face. And when the furnace is billowing soot or the pipes are frozen or the dog has taken a nip out of the neighbor's wife, I take a deep breath, clench my teeth, and mutter, "Hang in there, girl. We'll laugh about this... someday."

We'll Laugh about This . . . Someday

ॐ Prologue

GO AHEAD, exalt Mother Nature. Tell me in hushed tones how she paints the western sky at sunset, how she dusts the barren landscape with the first snow, and how she's responsible for roses, mist, and summer breezes. As far as I'm concerned, she's a whimsical old broad, and she's not to be trusted.

One minute she flits around, fluffing up clouds and stringing spider webs like angel hair in the branches of the hemlock, and the next thing you know she's decided to detonate a volcano and send several million cubic feet of dust and debris circling the globe. One minute she's skipping over the water, filling a sail here and gliding with a sea gull there, and half an hour later she's changed her mind, whipped up a storm, and swamped a fleet of trawlers.

She delights in practical jokes. She turns lovable, fat puppies into huge, undisciplined dogs and teaches them to leap up on your mother-in-law and to bury the children's tennis shoes in the tulip bed. She hangs the fattest blackberries on the bush just beyond the poison oak. She covers up the scenery with clouds when Aunt Lou and Uncle Warren come to town for their annual visit. And during a winter storm she fells the poplar and slaps it across the garage roof instead of dropping it on the lawn, where all it would do is crush the crab grass.

She's never fair. She lavishes wealth on someone who already has ash blond hair, brown eyes, and a body that sends writers scrambling to their dictionaries for more superlatives. She doles out the set of piano legs to the girl who's also saddled with an overbite, a concave bust, and sallow skin. Then just for fun she makes them sisters.

And every now and then, when she's bored, she simply gives the world a vicious spin. Then she sits back and chortles while old rules tumble, old customs shatter, and we all scramble around, saying, "What happened? Where did we go wrong?"

I suspect she was bored back in the days when my husband, Joe, and I first were married. She must have been, for something in the world went haywire right about then, and I know I didn't touch anything.

It was in the late 1950s. Life was simple. Mount Everest had finally been conquered. Joe McCarthy had come, done his damage, and gone. Elvis had rocked onto the musical scene, and parents were shaking their heads and muttering, "obscene." A description of Adlai Stevenson had introduced *egghead* into the nation's vocabulary. Pink plastic flamingos stalked suburban lawns. Chlorophyll dog food promised Rover clean, fresh breath. For $11.50 you could buy a paint-by-numbers Last Supper complete with a gold frame.

Young girls dreamed of looking like Jon Whitcomb illustrations. Boys had crew cuts and wore letterman's sweaters. Folks were reading *Peyton Place, The Catcher in the Rye*, and, *Kids Say the Darndest Things!* Huntley and Brinkley were the final word in news. Willie Mays was the idol of every Little League outfielder. Dinah Shore advised us all to "See the U.S.A. in your Chevrolet." And Tom Lehrer sang, "Let's find love while we may, /Because I know I'll hate you, /When you are old and gray."

T-shirts had yet to become billboards. Banks had yet to become our pals. The generations had yet to gap.

Sports figures were still heroes. Movie stars were still glamorous. An upper was still the top berth in a Pullman car. And maintenance engineers were still janitors.

Folks had yet to discover cellulite, alfalfa sprouts, and polyester pantsuits. Onion soup dip was still a novelty and still tasted good. Men and women still danced cheek to cheek. Songs still had melodies. Running was something you did only when the bus was about to pull away without you. Pot was what Cousin Harry had gone to after Lucy left him to run off with a shoe salesman. And people still shuddered at the grammar of "Winston Tastes Good Like a Cigarette Should." "You know" had yet to be invented.

Families were still popular then, too. Everyone aspired to have one of his or her own, and Joe and I were no exception.

"Let's see," we said when we were engaged and like a couple surrounded by travel posters, still in the planning stage, "how many children do you think we should have?"

"I dunno...three? Four?"

"Not three. They say middle children suffer when there are three."

"All right then, two or four."

"How about six?" The ban on frivolous begetting had yet to be nailed to the bedroom door, and like other

children of the Depression who came from small families
but had read *Cheaper by the Dozen*, I envisioned happiness as a big house in the country with hordes of laughing children tumbling down the stairs on Christmas
morning.

"Gee, I don't know. Six is a lot."

"Oh, I think it would be fun. It would be just like
'Father Knows Best' with twice the children."

Of course, at the time "Father Knows Best" was thought
to be a fairly realistic portrayal of everyone's ideal family.
Things are different now. Fathers don't come home from
work, hang up their coats, put on sweaters, and settle
down to read the paper anymore. Now they jog home,
and after five minutes of cool-down exercises when they
look as if they were trying to move the house off its
foundation, they stumble in the front door and head for
the shower.

The children don't run to greet them anymore either.
There's no "Daddy, Daddy, can you help me with my
algebra?" or "Say, Dad, I need to talk to you. I'm having
a little problem, and I want your advice." Algebra these
days, with its quadratic equations and polynomials, is
like a foreign language to fathers who were brought up
on x's and y's, and no teen-ager in his right mind would
ever ask for advice from anyone in a three-piece suit. If
he's lucky, the modern father will get a nod and an unintelligible grunt. But as a rule he hears a sigh and a
"Sounds like *he's* home again."

Mothers are different these days, too. Margaret An-
derson always wore a freshly ironed dress, nylon stockings, and heels. Today lipstick and a clean sweat shirt
mean you're expecting company. She never hauled out
a box of Hamburger Helper or said, "Hand me the tofu
and the hoisin sauce, someone. Tonight we're woking
it," either.

Margaret put a roast in the oven in the afternoon before she donned her hat and gloves and went to a parents' tea at school. She shelled the peas and mashed the potatoes when she got home. She reminded Betty, "Be sure to put a clean tablecloth on tonight"—plastic place mats shaped like Snoopy and Donald Duck were still a ways off. And she never poured herself a double martini or tossed down a couple of Valiums, saying, "You can't imagine what a day I've had."

But then she didn't have to. Life was kinder to mothers back then. Their days didn't start with a breakfast where the cereal was coated with artificial sweeteners that cause cancer in laboratory rats, the eggs were laden with cholesterol, the toast lacked fiber, the bacon was full of nitrites, the coffee was bad for the pancreas, and the sugar in the coffee caused tooth decay and hyperactivity. The morning paper didn't have the latest statistics on eight-year-old alcoholics or an article about the alarming increase in the number of unwed teen-age mothers.

In Margaret's world Bud hadn't dropped out of high school. Betty wasn't threatening to run off with a rock musician. And she didn't want to shave her head, join the Hare Krishna, and sell flowers at the airport. Kathy didn't come home from school in the afternoon and explain away flunking her history test by saying, "I never could keep all those fucking presidents straight." And husband Jim wasn't going through the male menopause. He wasn't mixing it up in a motel with the boss's daughter, and he hadn't traded in his double-breasted suit for a fishnet shirt, tight jeans, and a necklace.

No one insisted Margaret brush up on her parenting skills and learn how to communicate effectively. No one said she'd stifled Kathy's creativity because she hadn't let her draw pictures on the walls as a toddler. And no one insinuated that Bud's hostile behavior was the result of having been bottle-fed instead of nursed as a baby.

But then Bud wasn't hostile. He went to school, did his homework, and put on a coat and tie when company was coming. He also mowed the lawn, took out the trash, and helped carry in the groceries. True, he often left his clothes on the floor. He also teased his sisters and put off doing his book report till Sunday night. But he spoke when he was spoken to. He laughed more than he groused. He allowed himself to be seen in public with his parents. And when he rebelled, it was rarely anything more than a pitiful "Aw, gee, Dad, do I have to?"

Betty wasn't hostile either. In fact, she was downright affable. She helped around the house and actually volunteered to start dinner or finish up the dishes. She initiated conversations with people over thirty...even over forty. She brought her dates clear into the house and introduced them to everyone. She went with the family to the county fair and had a wonderful time. She helped Kathy with her homework and listened sympathetically to Bud's problems. And she never tried to grow marijuana in her window box.

Kathy, the little one, was happy, too. Like other pre-teens, she didn't seem to mind that her measurements were 28"- 28"- 28". She wore her hair in pigtails and didn't plead for an Afro. She played house, had tea parties, and learned to ride a bike. She thought boys were dumb but adored her father. She hated spinach but ate it anyway, gulping huge mouthfuls and washing them down with milk. And when she turned ten, she didn't demand a training bra or try to pierce her ears with a hot safety pin. In other words, she was a typical child growing up in a normal everyday family.

They all were typical because that's how life was in the forties and fifties. Families consisted of one father, one mother, and several children. Fathers came home from work at the same time every day. Mothers seemed to be content with their lot, and they professed to enjoy canning peaches and making new curtains for the kitchen. Children...well, we were simply children; awkward, stumbling, unsure, gullible, supersensitive, impressionable children.

We weren't expected to be very bright, and that is why everyone told us, "Clean your plate, remember the starving Armenians," and "Don't pick up that frog, you'll get warts," and "Eat your carrots, they'll help you see in the dark." And we were expected to do as we were told. So we cleaned our plates and wondered how much postage it would take to mail a package of liver and onions to Armenia. We dropped the frog and stared at our hands, sure we could see warts forming in clusters on our knuckles. And we ate our carrots, shut ourselves in closets, and tried to read the phone book in the dark.

We went to school except when we were sick, and we never managed to convince anyone we were sick when we had a math test second period. We studied our lessons. We learned about subordinate clauses and the subjunctive case. We memorized our geometry theorems and Hamlet's soliloquy. We drew diagrams of the Bessemer furnace, conjugated Latin verbs, and dissected all manner of formaldehyde-preserved specimens. We wrote reports on Oliver Cromwell. And though we hated Miss Brasselle and referred to her as "the chinless wonder," we never argued with her, never chewed gum in her class, and never were late with one of her assignments.

At home we all had chores, and for the most part we did them. I cleaned the bathrooms, vacuumed the stairs, and helped with the dishes. I think I was given the bathroom duty because that's where I went when it was time to do the dishes.

We also did our homework and remembered that spell-

ing, punctuation, and neatness counted. We said "please,"
"thank you," and even "you're welcome." We stayed at
the dinner table till everyone was through, though in
emergencies we were allowed a "Please may I be excused? I have to call Marilyn and get the history assignment." We stood up when our elders entered a room. We
opened doors and let others go in first. We shook hands.
We willingly talked to our parents' friends. We always
tried to look our best since we believed those who told
us, "If you can't be beautiful, at least be neat and clean."
And for some reason we assumed that our parents, though
admittedly old-fashioned and stodgy, had all the answers.

Our motivation was fear—not terror, just a nagging
uneasiness that whispered, "What will people
think?...What will people think if you flunk biology and
have to take it over?...What will people think if they
see dust balls on the stairs?...What will people think if
you don't lose weight before the dance?...What will people think if you wear that sweater instead of something
less revealing?" And, "Oh, my Lord, what will Leroy
think if you let him hold your hand or kiss you on the
first date?" It was a powerful motivation. It kept us in
line and made us live up to expectations. There were a
lot to live up to.

For one thing, we were expected to finish high school,
so we did. We were expected to go on to college, so we
did; and we girls remembered we weren't being prepared for a career in executive management, nor were
we headed off to law school. That future was reserved
for male cousins, boyfriends, and brothers. But we consoled ourselves with the maxim "Educate a man and you
educate an individual. Educate a woman and you educate
a family."

After college we were expected to get married and have

children. So we did. Joe and I got married in 1957. We promised each other "for richer, for poorer, for better, for worse." We sipped champagne. We were showered with rice. And we settled down and prepared to raise our own family and realize our own expectations.

I expected to have children who'd grow up much as I had. I was an Episcopal clergyman's daughter and the product of a semi-British upbringing—Mother came from a mill town in Oregon, but Daddy was a second generation Englishman complete with high tea and trifle. Since he'd spent most of his adult life as a missionary in China and the Philippines, he not only avoided the noonday sun but also held to the tenet, popular with those abroad, where amahs were a fixture, that children were not simply little adults and should therefore be civilized before being allowed in the living room or invited to sit at the dinner table. I expected to carry on the tradition, though in a modified form.

I expected my children would be sensitive, friendly, and well behaved. They wouldn't, for instance, make fun of Mrs. Herklotz, who blinked a lot and stuttered, and they'd let her tell them about her grandson's kitten without interrupting or saying, "You told me that last time."

They'd be imaginative. Of course, I thought of *imaginative* as invisible friends, homemade tree houses, and birthday poems, not exploding chemistry sets, salt in the sugar bowl, or little sisters' being dared to eat worms. They'd be bright and enthusiastic. The girls would giggle at the mere mention of boyfriends or kissing or padded bras. The boys would roar at ancient knock-knock jokes. They'd learn to whistle through a blade of grass and spend endless hours reading the latest Tom Swift book. And they'd all rush home after school to tell me what Mr. Fenton did when Cindy Wentworth threw up in biology.

They'd have friends: someone to mess around with on a boring Saturday afternoon, someone to talk to about life and diets and Mindy Dimmer's older brother, and someone to ride bikes and go swimming with. Their friends would come and go and help themselves to a handful of cookies. They'd stop and talk to Joe or me without looking as if the pain were unbearable. They'd help haul in the groceries. And they'd stay for dinner if we weren't having sautéed mushrooms or cauliflower soup.

Because I'd spent a total of nine years at boarding school and college, I expected some enthusiasm toward schoolwork. I looked forward to seeing F. Scott Fitzgerald and Hemingway discovered once again. I relished the idea of dinner conversations about infinity and life on Mars. And I hoped for at least one child who'd be able to explain the use of the semicolon to me.

Of course, I knew better than to expect perfection. I knew there'd be occasional rebellion, defiance, and insubordination. I knew there'd be long nights waiting for fevers to break and equally painful hours waiting for the sound of the car coming up the driveway, followed by a tap on the bedroom door and an "I'm home."

I knew the days of uniforms and starched white shirts were waning. Undoubtedly there'd be torn pants and muddy knees and grass stains. There'd be jackets slung into the back of the car and socks dragged out from under the bed. And there'd be constant reminders: "Don't forget to comb your hair and brush your teeth." But I hoped for a suit and tie at Christmas dinner or in church. I hoped, though little girls rarely wore smocked pinafores and patent leather shoes anymore, there'd be long gowns and corsages at the junior prom. And I hoped for at least a semblance of neatness and style on a day-to-day basis.

Joe was less concerned with matching socks and tucked-in shirttails. What he expected was diligence: beds made; lawns mowed; firewood chopped and stacked. As a child he'd proved his worth through manual labor. He'd fed the chickens, milked the cow, swept the floors, and started dinner. He'd polished brass, vacuumed rugs, raked leaves, and buffed the kitchen floor. Consequently he expected his children would do the same, and with a minimum of grumbling.

Ah...the things we both expected. It was going to be a wonderful twenty years or so. Of course, at the time we didn't know Mother Nature was bored and was about to turn the world on its ear.

We'd learn soon enough, we and everyone else.

❧ And Then There Were Six

IT ALL STARTED OUT SIMPLY ENOUGH, but then doesn't everything?

A cake starts out simply with flour, salt, sugar, and shortening. True, it often ends up lumpy or lopsided or stuck to the pan, but it starts out simply. A dress starts out simply, too, with material, a pattern, and a spool of thread. Things may get complicated along the way when the pattern tears, the bobbin jams, or a gusset puckers. But it starts out simply.

So it once was with marriage and raising a family. It started out simply, with two people who were entranced with each other. She was sure he had the most beautiful eyes she'd ever seen. He couldn't get over the adorable tilt of her nose. She told all her friends that when he laughed, it was like listening to bells. He told all his friends he couldn't believe a goddess like that could actually love him. He sent flowers. She knitted socks. He sat in the living room and talked to her father. She asked his mother for the apple crisp recipe. And neither of them could remember ever having been so much in love.

So they booked a church and sent out invitations. He threw away the pictures of Barbara and Angela and Becky Sue. She burned her letters from Wally and Ogden and Leonard, the poet. And they got married and settled down to what they knew was going to be the one perfect marriage of all time.

Today a couple lives together for a while because they feel the vibes but aren't sure they want to make a commitment. He likes her ass. She says he's great in bed. He tells his friends he couldn't swing the rent alone. She tells her friends it beats living at home, where she had to keep her room clean. He asks his father to lend him $100 so he can pay off his stereo. She asks her mother to let them have the old dresser from the guest room.

After the birth of their second child, whom they decide to name Moses or God, she taps Dad for a big wedding, they make it legal, and his daughter from a previous marriage comes to live with them.

Joe and I had been taught to gasp or at the very least snicker at the mention of "living in sin, without benefit of clergy." So we fell in love, got married, and settled down at Sheppard Air Force Base in Wichita Falls, Texas. He was a first lieutenant, a student, and later an instructor at the Photo-Radar Intelligence school there. We were two thousand miles from Bainbridge, the small wooded island in Puget Sound that we called home. And though we would have preferred an assignment in northern California or Oregon, the Air Force had requested the honor of Joe's presence in Texas. So there we were, and there is where we started out, simply enough, "to love and to cherish till death us do part" and to raise a family.

We weren't as prompt about the latter project as was the custom then. Nine months and twenty minutes after I'd said, "I do," I wasn't lying in the labor room, breathing deeply and bearing down. None of my wedding notes said, "I just know Joe and I and the little stranger, who's due in the fall, are going to get a lot of use out of the lovely fish server you sent us." And our first fight wasn't cut short because I got nauseated and had to dash to the bathroom.

I waited a full eight months before trading in my going-away outfit for a smock and a skirt with a hole cut out of the front. Of course, nowadays people who are pregnant after only eight months are asked, "What's the matter? Did you forget to take the Pill?" But things were different then. Motherhood was meant to follow the wedding vows the way "Come in" follows a knock at the door.

As a result, when Joe and I came home on vacation with no big news, no "Guess who's going to be a grand-mother?" and no "I think I felt a kick last night," we became objects of some concern.

"Has Ann tried everything?" my loving but clinical and terribly modern friend Betty asked Joe during a cocktail party in our honor.

"Everything?" He was still a relative stranger to my friends and not prepared for frank discussions with the very married.

"Yes, you know what I mean. Has she tried the various postsex positions...to encourage conception?"

Joe took a gulp of his martini, toyed with the idea of saying no, but decided against it when he sensed a neg-ative reply would call for graphic elaboration. "Oh, yes" he stammered, "yes, of course."

"Good." She put her hand on his arm and gave it a reassuring squeeze. "Then I guess the best thing you two can do is relax and be patient."

"Oh, you're right," Joe agreed. "You're absolutely right."

As it happened, Betty's gymnastics weren't necessary.

Several months later, when we were back in Wichita Falls, I came home from a visit to a local obstetrician and announced that our family, or the first additional member of it, was on the way.

"How about that?" I said to Joe after we'd gone through the "Really?"'s and the "Are you sure?"'s. "You and I are going to be parents." I sighed, then sat up straight. "Oh, Lord," I said, "I hope I don't get milk leg."

"You hope you don't get what?"

"Milk leg."

"What is it?"

"I'm not exactly sure. All I know is Mother said she always worried about getting milk leg when she was pregnant with Geoff and me."

He shook his head. "I don't think they're concerned about that anymore," he said. "I could be wrong, but my sister's had three children, and I've never heard her mention milk leg."

He was right, of course. Milk leg, like the vapors, belonged to generations past. This was modern times with modern ways and modern apprehensions. True, these modern ways, like hemlines and hats, would change with time. In twenty years obstetricians would be delivering babies in dimly lit rooms with strains of Mantovani in the background. Husbands would be yanked out of the waiting room and invited to share in the delivery. They'd bring along their Minoltas and their Polaroid One Steps. They'd snap candid shots of the doctor, the nurses, the lights, the walls, their wives, and their new sons or daughters.

Labor rooms would fill up with anxious mothers and mothers-in-law passing the time with horror stories about their own thirty-six-hour agonies and their own terrifying deliveries. And anesthetics would become an abomination used only by the callous and the cowardly, not interested in experiencing "every phase of the miracle of birth."

Pregnancies would change, too. Anything mildly pleasurable would be outlawed. Doctors would rail against a gin and tonic with dinner, a cigarette with the morning paper, and second helpings of blueberry cheesecake. They'd insist on long walks in the rain and half an hour of knee bends and leg lifts in the morning and at bedtime. And every Thursday night would call for "parenting" classes in the basement of the Lutheran church.

But this was the 1950s. This was our today, and those of us staggering around in stretch slacks, gathered overblouses, and our husband's boxer shorts were the latest thing in the world of motherhood.

We were the Spartan generation. Where our mothers had been confined to bed for three weeks after giving birth, we were routed out of the recovery room after eight hours and told to "go on down the hall to your ward." Two days later we were sent home, the only restriction being "Don't lift the couch and don't load bricks for a while."

While our mothers had been encouraged to "eat for two" and our daughters would be told to gain at least twenty-four pounds, we were warned that six or eight pounds over the baby's weight was quite sufficient and more was intolerable. As a result, we subsisted on cottage cheese and celery sticks. We wore summer clothing to all our doctors' appointments, and we threw our coats on the floor and leaped out of our shoes before we stepped on the scales.

Our mothers had been instructed to follow the Alice in Wonderland "he-only-does-it-to-annoy-because-he-knows-it-teases" school of child rearing. So they'd slavishly adhered to rigid schedules: "bathtime, 10:30 A.M.; feeding time, every four hours; bedtime, 6:00 P.M. and *do not* pick up your baby simply because he's crying."

Our daughters would join breast-feeding societies and nurse on the bus or at the ballet. They'd strap two-week-old infants to their chests and take them to Safeway to check out the sale on spaghetti squash. And after six weeks they'd drop Junior off at the day care center and go back to work.

We in the middle were told to feed on demand. We could bathe our children when we chose as long as we kept to some sort of schedule. Though daily outings in the fresh air were sanctioned, we were admonished not to expose the little one to crowds for the first few months. And we were not even to consider getting a job till the youngest was in college.

Of course, all these contradictory rules caused no end of trouble when mother and daughter joined forces and prepared to take care of the new infant. When Mother flew down to Wichita Falls after David was born, the subject was bellybands.

"Where do you keep your bellybands?" she asked, bare minutes after she arrived.

"My what?"

"Your bellybands."

"I didn't know there was such an animal."

"You mean you don't have any?"

"How could I? I don't even know what they are."

"They're strips of cloth you wrap around the baby's stomach."

"Why?"

"To keep him from catching a cold."

"In his stomach?"

"Yes, in his stomach."

"Oh, come now, Mother, you can't be serious."

"Of course I'm serious. Newborn babies need protection from the cold."

"But it's May...in Texas. He couldn't get a cold if he tried."

Oh, but he could, she insisted, and the next day she went off in search of bellybands. I would have sworn she'd never find any; but she did, and naturally she bought half a dozen. So for the next two weeks David wore bellybands. Of course, once she was back on the plane headed north, I stuffed them into a drawer and forgot about them. I did haul them out again for a few days when he finally did get his first cold. But that was only because Mother phoned and said, "He would have gotten one sooner if he hadn't been wearing those bellybands I bought." It was also because I run on guilt.

David didn't care either way. He was happy no matter what happened. But then why shouldn't he be? He was the adored object of our affection. Life was daily baths in the kitchen sink with a washcloth to suck on and a rubber tugboat that squeaked. It was rides in the stroller after sunset and conversations with neighbors, their children, and their dogs. It was puréed lamb and peaches heated to the perfect temperature and a bottle of milk to go. It was long sessions sitting on Joe's lap in the rocking chair. It was games of peekaboo with me stretched out on the floor next to the playpen with a blanket over my head. And it was listening to stories about Muffin, "the little dog with a cinder in his eye."

There'd be time enough for "the thousand natural shocks that flesh is heir to" later. When he was on his feet and tottering around the neighborhood, for instance, he'd learn that Willie Muntz liked to bop people on the head for no particular reason. In kindergarten he'd be told he needed extra work at home if he planned to pass skipping. And he'd learn how it hurts to be the last one picked when they're choosing sides.

Eventually he'd wonder about the advantages of being the oldest in a family of six, and he'd suspect he was being used as a guinea pig to test out the untried theories of inexperienced parents. In time he'd question the necessity of sisters, and he'd discover that while good grades and diligence impress parents and teachers, they annoy siblings and make classmates hostile. Finally, he'd learn that mothers are woefully inadequate when it comes to making small talk about computers.

But that was in the future. For the time being pajamas were soft and warm, grass tickled the feet, soap bubbles had rainbows in them, mashed bananas tasted cool and sweet, and life was grand.

David was the ideal first child. He was the shill, the one who lulled us into thinking parenthood was uncomplicated. He slept late, giving me time to have a cup of coffee and to get Joe his breakfast before I had to tend to formula and cereal and soggy diapers. He enjoyed being put in the playpen with assorted rubber balls and blocks and rattles and bears. He didn't eat his bathrobe tie. He didn't rip out Teddy's eyes and stuff them in his ear or swallow them. He didn't hang on the bars and howl for freedom.

When I was busy in the kitchen, he entertained himself. He pulled out the pots and pans, crashed the lids together, and squealed with delight at the sound. He rolled tomato sauce cans across the floor, then rolled them back again when it was pickup time. And he stood at the screen door and babbled incoherent greetings to the neighbor's dogs, to robins in search of worms, and to passing cars and trucks.

Once he was ambulatory, he didn't bolt out the door and head straight for the street.

"Streets are for cars and trucks and buses," we told him, and he echoed the statement. He even spread the word, standing safely on the grass while Willie Muntz and Debbie and the Randolph sisters cavorted in the carport. "Streets are for cars and trucks and buses," he shouted at them, banging his toy mower on the ground. "Get out of the street."

They, of course, ignored him. Willie even stuck out his tongue and called him a "stupey dumb dumb." But David stood by his principles, and later, when a cow happened to wander up the main thoroughfare in the base housing unit, he added cows to his list. "Streets are for cars and trucks and buses and cows."

David's days started with a smile and a greeting that meant, "So what are we doing today?" They went on to include trips accompanying me to the clothesline, where we played tag, dodging in and out between the sheets and the diapers. He paid daily visits to Marilyn's house, where on cue he made a few clever statements and was rewarded as usual with a cookie. At noon he pressed his nose to the front window and watched for Joe. And when Daddy came home, they discussed their respective mornings while I got lunch.

After naptime we filled up the wading pool, and he and Joe and half the neighborhood played Moby Dick for an hour or two. Then it was dinner, sitting on Daddy's lap to watch Huntley and Brinkley, a bath, a story or two, and bed. This parenthood thing was a snap, and by the time we'd been at it for fifteen months we were thoroughly spoiled. We didn't realize this, of course. As far as we were concerned, things were going along precisely as expected.

But then this was still the fifties. The livin' was still easy, and "Father Knows Best" was still an attainable goal. Ike, everyone's benevolent grandfather, was president, and the country smiled at pictures in the evening paper that showed him putting golf balls on the White House lawn. The Sunday barbecue was all the rage, with hamburgers and foil-wrapped ears of corn slapped on every grill in the neighborhood. On Tuesday nights Jack Webb solved crimes with "Just the facts, ma'am." And folks, awed, amazed, and shocked that the Russians had beaten us to it, scanned the evening skies for a glimpse of Sputnik.

While David was stringing his first words together, college students still majored in liberal arts. While he lounged in his playpen, they stuffed themselves into VW bugs and phone booths. And while he shared his teething biscuit with Teddy, they called home to plead, "Send money."

The change would come. Like the Santa Ana wind, the sixties would roar across the country with a hot fury and leave the charred remains of what had been. But how were we to know? We were still cool and comfortable in our own decade.

Then Sylvia arrived. She was our first clue that heads, traditions, Mom, and apple pie were about to roll. She breezed into our lives like Halley's comet with a sound track. There was no more of this tidy living, with a time for everything and everything at its time. Sylvia made her own schedule.

"Eat, you say?" she seemed to chortle every four hours or so. "Well...maybe just a taste. But don't close the kitchen. I might like a little more in another ten minutes or so.

"And about this going to bed at seven-thirty," she added,

"you have to be kidding. Why should I hit the hay when you two are out there laughing it up, watching 'Masquerade Party' and 'Dobie Gillis'? Can't you understand it's boring in here? I want out."

She greeted the day with a bellow. She raced through the morning, flinging toys out of the playpen and staggering into the bedroom to roll cans under the bed, where they remained till Meat Loaf Tijuana called for a splash of tomato sauce and I had to burrow under the slats to retrieve them. In the wading pool, which was too deep to sit in, she bobbed around in her life jacket like a jubilant cork. At dinner she beat on her highchair with the flat of her hand and laughed uproariously as the remainder of her spinach kangarooed to the edge and flopped over onto the floor.

She adored David, though her way of showing it was sometimes debatable. She pelted him with wet diapers and kicked at the towers he'd carefully built out of blocks and Lincoln logs and wooden arches. She tried to flip the pages to the good part when he was lying on the floor reading *Sam and the Firefly* from memory. And when he tried to sleep at naptime, she said, "Look, Davey, look," then flopped down on her back with a pacifier upside down over each eye and another in her mouth. If he wouldn't look, she threw them at him.

Sylvia was the original girl with the curl right in the middle of her forehead. Cross her and it was like poking a lion with a stick. She howled. She cried. She wet her pants and let her nose run. If she was being removed from a store where I was not about to buy her a bag of malt balls or a musical goat, she went limp, like a bag of wet sand, and had to be hauled out while shoppers clucked and whispered, "Poor little thing." If she objected to wearing boots, she stiffened up and dared me to go ahead and try to shove them on.

And when I'd had enough and plunked her down on a chair, saying, "Sit! Here! Now! I'll set the timer for twenty minutes, and don't you move till it goes off," she roared and sniveled and sobbed. But she also sat. And when the timer went off, she wiped her nose on her sleeve, hopped off the chair, and skipped away, humming.

"She's something," I told Joe. "She's a delight one minute and a terror the next." I patted my once again expanding abdomen. "I hope whoever is waiting in line here is a tad less volatile. I sure could use the rest."

I meant it. I could have used the rest. I didn't get it, though. Jenny was born in transit, the summer we left Texas, when we were on our way to four years in Japan and had stopped en route to spend some time at home on the island.

She arrived when we were living out of suitcases. She arrived when all but our bare essentials were packed, crated, and in a warehouse somewhere, waiting to be shipped overseas. And she arrived in an examining room in the local clinic since it was the middle of the night and the last ferry to Seattle had just pulled away from the dock.

By the time she came, however, I was into the swing of things. I no longer panicked when she hiccuped or broke out in a rash. Guilt no longer lay on my shoulders like a sodden bath towel when I discovered she actually was hungry and not simply fretting as I'd insisted. And I no longer leaped out of bed at the first sound of a midnight whimper. If I couldn't outsmart Joe and shame him into taking the feeding, I struggled to my feet and mumbled, "I'm coming. I'm coming. Hold your horses."

I think Jenny sensed this. Either that or she was simply a good baby. But then she had to be. By the time she was three months old—David was three years and Sylvia

two—she'd flown from Seattle to San Francisco, rebelling only at the takeoff from Seattle when she threw up
all over my mother-in-law. She'd made two car trips from
San Francisco to Travis Air Force Base in a converted
dog basket. And she'd flown across the Pacific to Tachikawa, an air force base outside Tokyo. I suspect when
she finally hit a bed that wasn't gaining altitude, slowing
down for a freeway exit, or preparing to land, she was so
relieved she decided to be a model child and not risk
another move.

She needn't have worried. Now that we were in the
land of inexpensive maids and houseboys and someone
to do the ironing, I wasn't about to let them send us back.
Besides, who's going to exile a dainty and adorable red-
head? When you have a brother and sister working their
bedroom window out of its frame till it crashes to the
ground, shears off the outside faucet, and floods the
neighborhood, who's going to be anything but thrilled
with a child who masters going downstairs—backwards
and on her knees—after only two lessons?

True, Jenny sat around with her feet in the *benjó*—the
Japanese toilet built into the floor—but it was only because David and Sylvia convinced her it was a foot bath.
She crawled over to the furnace—also in the floor at the
bottom of the stairs—and had to be grabbed by the feet
and dragged away by whoever was closest to it, but it
was only because she was trying to get from the living
room to the dining room. And she slithered out of my lap
and tottered off on her own when she was barely nine
months old, but only because she was anxious to meet
the neighbors.

Jenny was the family's ambassador. In her smocked
dress, her hooded sweat shirt, and her bright red leotards,
she tiptoed through the neighborhood picking up a discarded toy here and giving it back to its owner with a

"Here...say thank you," stopping there to watch Pammy's mom paint her toenails, and wandering over to see what the big kids were up to.

She didn't join David and Sylvia, who were learning to ride a bicycle "without any training wheels." While David wheeled around the Konvalinkas' house and made a successful pass through the "chute" and Sylvia, who'd learned everything but how to stop and get off, circled the court, bellowing, "Help, someone. Come get me," Jenny sat in Mrs. Konvalinka's dining room, having a second cup of cambric tea.

She didn't rush outside with them to cavort in the rain and slide through giant puddles either. Why should she? I'd let her play with some of my earrings and drape herself with scarves and pop-it bead necklaces. Who needed to get wet and muddy when there was a chance of having perfume dabbed on your wrists and behind your ears?

Jenny was the lady, the party girl, the little mother. And when she wasn't out visiting, she was home ordering Geoffrey to drink his milk and stop throwing his teething ring onto the floor.

Geoffrey had sneaked into her life and into the other crib in her room when she was barely a year old. He arrived on Sylvia's third birthday. It was a month before he was due, but it was all right by me. I'm not the sort that thrives on children's birthday parties. In fact, Sylvia's party, held a day early, on a Sunday so Joe could be there, was the reason Geoffrey came ahead of schedule.

It had to be. I'd gotten up at five-thirty to make a green rabbit cake complete with floppy ears and coconut whiskers. Green rabbit cakes were big in those days. We'd invited five of the children in the neighborhood to join in the festivities, and twenty-five had showed up. And Sylvia was so wound up it took three "Can I have a glass of water?"'s, two "There's a mosquito in my room"'s and an "I can't sleep I'm too hot" before I could get her to sign off for the night. Consequently, when Geoffrey arrived the next morning, my first thought was: Thank God. Now we can consolidate the birthday parties.

Geoffrey was another good baby. In fact, he was almost too good. He didn't get up on his hands and knees and bang his crib against the wall for hours at a time. He didn't twist and turn and make pinning on a clean diaper a gymnastic exercise. He didn't even turn from his back onto his front till he was ten months old.

Joe, who'd taken eighteen months himself to learn how to walk, thought he was a chip off the old block. I was afraid he was slow. Mother, in Tokyo for a couple of months on her way to Hong Kong, Bangkok, and the Philippines, was convinced he was blind. And she lay awake nights wondering how to tell me I had a child who would never see snow falling, never know what grass looked like, and never be able to recognize his mother's face.

As it turned out, he was perfectly normal. He simply had no reason to turn over. Joe and I had decorated his crib with an origami bird mobile, a bouncing clown on a spring, and a musical mobile that whirled colored streamers around and around and tinkled out a mechanical version of "The Blue Danube." No baby in his right mind is going to struggle to flip to his stomach and stare at a wet sheet when a show like that's in progress.

Once we took away a couple of the mobiles, he turned over, sat up. and crawled, all in the space of a week. Future pediatricians would nod wisely when I told them what had happened, and they'd say, "It's a classic example of a stubborn personality." They'd be right.

Before he was a year old, however, and before I had my first chance at consolidated birthday parties, we moved again. The '64 Summer Olympics were coming to Tokyo, and Washington Heights, where we lived, had been tapped to house Russian weight lifters, Ethiopian marathoners, and a whole platoon of swimmers. So we were loaded up and trucked out into the country, to Johnson Air Base.

We didn't mind. Johnson was glorious. The housing area was spacious and rolling with cherry trees rimming the premises. Johnson also brought us Fusako-san, a multitalented Japanese girl who knitted, sewed, hammered, sawed, and, just for the fun of it, painted daisies on the scrub bucket. She made paintings with pulverized eggshells. She made a sweater and two pairs of socks from the yarn in a castoff knit suit. And she made exquisite flower arrangements. She was in her seventh year of *ikebana*, and in her hands three tulips and a pine branch made a Mother's Day bouquet from FTD look garish.

Fusako-san introduced me to broiled eel and showed me how to make sushi. She taught me how to make origami roosters and chickens and we turned David and Sylvia's bedroom wall into a barnyard. We went on junking expeditions together. She helped me refinish tea chests, chow tables, and all the assorted clocks I bought for 200 yen ($.75) each. And she alone gets the credit for Geoffrey's basic neatness.

I had nothing to do with it. It was she who said, "Come on *boku-chan* ['little boy']. First we pick up your toys; *then* we have lunch." She was the one who handed him the sponge when his orange juice had spilled on the kitchen floor. And it was she who convinced him that a coat on the hook is worth two on the floor.

It was too late for the other children. They'd been under my care too long. Geoffrey, however, was still pliable. So while David rode his bike around the block or went across the street to hit fly balls to Joe, while Sylvia lay prone on a skateboard and paddled down the sidewalk like an oversize turtle, and while Jenny was next door having coffee and rice crackers with Michiko-san, Geoffrey toddled after Fusako-san, helping her hang out the laundry, keeping her company while she did the dishes, and threading in and out between the grocery sacks.

At times the others objected to his precision. "Come on, Geoffrey, hurry up," they howled on Christmas morning as he unwrapped his presents slowly, one at a time, and played with each for a while before going on.

"Let's go," Jenny pleaded on the days she joined us as we sauntered down the street and stopped to inspect an ant here, a dandelion there, and a clutch of pebbles over there. "Don't stop again. Let's go."

But Geoffrey would not be hurried. While the others thundered past him down the stairs to be the first outside and in the car, he took his time, knowing full well that he who hesitates is usually carried. And while they wolfed down their sugar cookies, he nibbled his and still had half to go when they were through and craving more.

Geoffrey was supposed to complete the family. He was the fourth child and that was certainly sufficient. But as I said, the Pill was still chemicals in a test tube. And lectures on finite resources, if they were being held, were being held six thousand miles away out of our earshot. Consequently, before we could throw our second consolidated birthday party, I was at the obstetrician's door again, listening to snide remarks about my Episcopalian upbringing and my Roman Catholic sex habits.

No mention was made about the possibility of twins, however. And since I'm not the sort whose heart beats a little faster at the thought of matching outfits and "cute" names that rhyme or sound like something produced in an echo chamber, the thought of two for the price of one never occurred to me. Still, twins arrived, Robbie first and Joan eight minutes later. And by the time I flaunted my ignorance by asking the doctor, "Are they identical?" and heard him reply, "No, dummy, one's a boy and one's a girl," I rather liked the idea.

Naturally Sylvia and Jenny were ecstatic—live dolls of their very own. What could be more exciting? David's interest was detached. After all, he was a first grader who'd put smelly diapers and soggy bibs behind him. Now he was learning to add, subtract, and write "cursive." Not even twins could rival that. Geoffrey was noncommittal. Later, when it was his lot to share a room with his younger brother and sister, he'd voice an opinion, but for the time being he simply ignored them and concentrated on charming Fusako-san out of her last piece of breakfast bacon.

Robbie and Joan weren't easy to ignore, though. I found this out in June 1965, when they were barely four months old and the Air Force shouted, "Time's up. It's back to the States and the real world for all of you."

Unfortunately I also found out that the real world had tilted some since we'd last glimpsed the famous purple mountain's majesty and amber waves of grain. It was a shock. It shouldn't have been, but it was. Four years of *ikebana*, bending with the bamboo, and dinner at the Officers' Club had led me to believe the tranquil fifties had renewed their lease.

Naturally some word of change had filtered through. We knew the Beatles were what Frank Sinatra had been to our older sisters and what Elvis had been to those following on our heels. We knew that parents in San Diego and Milwaukee were shaking their heads over the emergence of boys in shaggy haircuts. But Japanese schoolboys weren't of the crew cut ilk either. So we shrugged and said, "So what?"

Naturally we'd been stunned and sickened by the news of John Kennedy's assassination. But with details coming weeks later in the usual backlog of magazines and with no marathon television coverage of Jackie's face frozen in anguish, John John's salute, or the riderless horse, the pain subsided long before it might have.

We read the papers of course: *Stars and Stripes*, the *Asahi Evening News*, and the *Yomiuri Shimbun*, English edition. But in six or eight pages we got a headline story of a political demonstration on the Ginza. There were pictures of Prince Hiro going to school and on page two the latest report on when the cherries were expected to bloom. Western columnists told about finding their way around Tokyo without benefit of street signs: "Turn right at the soba shop. Go straight till you see the place with the refrigerator out in front. Then three-tenths of a mile and you're there." And there was always our Japanese lesson and today's sentence, *Omizu-o ippai kudasai masenka*? ["Please may I have a glass of water?"]. But it hardly kept us current with life back home.

So when we moved into a house in Hillcrest Heights, Maryland, Dr. Spock was still a pediatrician as far as I was concerned. George Wallace was a vague, distasteful name attached to an even vaguer face. William Miller was a defeated candidate we wouldn't have known if he'd come to the door selling vegetable brushes.

We knew about Vietnam, of course, but living in a military atmosphere, we saw it still as a wobbly domino in a row that went around the Pacific basin. We'd also seen pictures of protests and civil rights demonstrations spilling from one page to another in *Life* and *Time*, but time and distance had taken away some of their urgency.

Bed races and piano-wrecking competitions were new. I had yet to be introduced to Julia Child's irreverent approach to the soufflé. And Betty Friedan's confirmation of what I'd suspected all along—that woman's work is not only never done but rarely rewarded and seldom uplifting—had yet to reach my ears.

So the return home in the mid-sixties was like picking up a book I'd put down only to find that the middle chapters had been removed. In a while I'd figure out the plot again, but I'd never quite understand why the hero left home and why the heroine was so upset.

There was also the domestic shock of life without Fusako-san but *with* three more children than I'd had when I left. Though I'd hardly spent our overseas tour playing bridge and sipping gimlets at wives' club luncheons, I had got used to having someone with whom to divide my labor, and I'd certainly gotten used to a helper with this new experience—twins.

That was gone, however, and now suddenly laundry grew and multiplied like mold on old leftovers. Mealtime, with six impatient diners, two waiting to be fed simultaneously by one mother while one father supervised the other four, was an exercise in patting your head and rubbing your stomach. Simple family trips across town meant at least three hours of advance preparation. And the ironing was a week late and two blouses short.

I stumbled along, though, and when Robbie rejected spinach after the fact, or Joan woke up in the middle of the night and howled for company, I sighed and remembered the first precarious months when their simple survival was in doubt.

❧ Next There'll Be a Swarm of Locusts

ROBBIE AND JOAN, like most of the rest of the clan, arrived at night. It was February 8, 1965. They'd threatened to make their entrance all day. But it was past ten when Joe finally pulled up to the gate at Tachikawa, paused, then headed for the hospital.

Since this was my fifth such excursion and since I was in no pain, I didn't clutch at the dashboard and he didn't have the standard "Oh, my God, we'll never make it" look on his face. In fact, we both were so casual one would have thought we were on our way home after a movie.

We hadn't said much during the ride from Johnson. Johnny Carson was on armed forces radio, and we'd concentrated on "How cold *is* it?" But now as we approached the hospital, I remembered why we were there and what lay ahead.

"You know something?" I said finally.

"What?"

"If this isn't a false alarm and the baby's really coming tonight, I'm at the end of approximately thirty-nine months of my life spent in maternity clothes."

"Ye gods."

I shrugged. "Oh, well, at least that's thirty-nine months when I haven't had to worry about holding my stomach in. And at least I know the nurses will be glad to see me this time."

"They will? Why?"

"Because if there's one thing hospital personnel love, it's the sight of a prospective mother who's been through all this before."

"They do?"

"Heavens, yes. I think it's because they know we're not going to leap off the delivery table or get silly and say things like 'Hasn't anyone called the doctor yet?'"

"Aw, come on."

"I'm right...wait and see."

And I was. When I first waddled into the ob/gyn clinic, the nurse eyed me with the steely glare of a drill sergeant sizing up a new recruit. But the minute I divulged the fact that this was my fifth delivery, she broke into a warm, welcoming smile.

"Oh, please...sit down," she said, leaping to her feet. "And here, let me get a chair for your husband. Would you like some coffee, sir?"

"Thank you. That would be nice."

I winked at Joe.

"Now let's see," she said, settling down again. "When is it you're due?" She glanced at my obvious and protruding girth. "Was it last week or last month?"

I shook my head. "Actually not till the middle of March."

"Good Lord. " She gasped. "Are you expecting twins?"

"The doctor says no; but I haven't been able to tie my shoes since Thanksgiving, and I have a hunch he's wrong."

"I wouldn't be surprised." She lowered her voice. "And it wouldn't be the first time either."

She then took my vital statistics. She added them to my file and flashed me an encouraging smile. "Now let me see if I can find someone to help you."

With that she called another nurse to take us into the communal labor room, and she disappeared. I found out later where she went. She went to round up spectators. They do this sort of thing in the military when they have a batch of orderlies sitting around the lounge, drinking coffee and reading *Playboy*. It's called "Find busy work for the enlisted men." It always ensures a good crowd at routine deliveries.

Apparently they didn't consider this routine, though, for when they wheeled me into the delivery room, it was as if "Dr. Kildare has consented to demonstrate surgical slipknots." The walls were lined with capped, gowned, and masked figures, and at least ten pairs of eyes stared at me as I made the ungainly transfer to the delivery table.

Good Lord, I thought, they must have gone out and dragged people in off the streets. They hadn't, as I soon found out. These were Japanese interns observing "Large *gaijin* lady having many babies." And I gather they enjoyed the show, for every now and then the masks sucked in as one and I heard the strains of *"Ah-h-h so deska"* and *"Hanto yo."*

It wasn't something I would have requested had I been in charge of things, but I must admit it added a certain drama to the proceedings. And when I obliged by effortlessly producing Robbie and Joan, it was as if I'd just come over the brow at the summit of Mount Fuji. Heads bobbed. Eyes crinkled with delight. Everyone chattered excitedly. Even the nurse joined in the merriment, hugging me and telling me, "You were wonderful."

I had to agree. Giving birth to twins who weighed four

pounds two ounces each seemed to me like a good day's work. Besides, by having a boy and a girl, I'd kept the family ratio even, meaning that when we went back to the States we wouldn't necessarily need a house with a fourth bedroom.

I pointed this out to Joe when he greeted me in the hall as I was being transferred to a bed in the ward. "How about that?" I said. "I may be producing in litters now, but at least I'm keeping the genders balanced."

He beamed. "You did well, honey," he said. "Now get some rest, and I'll see you tomorrow." Again he grinned and shook his head in amazement. "Wait till the rest of the tribe hears the news."

As expected, they were delighted. Of course, there was a certain amount of grumbling when, a couple of days later, I came home without the twins, but as I explained, "They're both still in incubators, and the hospital won't send them home till they weigh at least five pounds."

Frankly I was glad for the extra time. There was lots to be done, and even with Fusako-san helping it was going to take awhile to rearrange the tiny sewing room and turn it into a nursery for two. Besides, with the promise of strenuous days and less than sleep-filled nights ahead, I was thankful for any chance, however brief, to get to rest and visit friends one more time before I disappeared forever under a mountain of diapers and multiple feedings.

For several days Fusako-san and I worked feverishly. We moved cribs. We stacked diapers. We filled a chest of drawers with receiving blankets and tiny undershirts—the bellybands had long since been disposed of. Then Fusako-san took her day off. I did, too.

After I'd made the beds and done the breakfast dishes, I bundled Jenny and Geoffrey up, and we three set out to see Anne Long, a friend who'd stayed with the older children the night the twins were born.

It was a cold, clear day and not far to Anne's house. The dry yellow grass crackled under our feet, and I had no trouble keeping up with the children as they bounded off ahead of me. But on the way back, when we were about halfway home, suddenly something felt very wrong. My vital organs seemed to be letting go. I slowed my pace and adopted a geisha-in-tight-kimono gait.

"Wait up," I called to Jenny, who had Geoffrey by the hand and was dragging him behind her.

She stopped. "Go faster," she yelled.

"I can't."

"Sure you can. Come on." With that, she danced off again, Geoffrey still in tow and bumping along behind her like a balloon on a string.

By now I could see our back door, so I let her run on ahead, and I shuffled after her as best I could, praying that when I got there, Joe would be home for lunch. He was. When I tottered into the kitchen, he was already slapping sandwiches together and pouring the children's milk.

When I minced in, he looked up. "Hi," he said. "What kept you?"

I shuffled past. This was no time to stop and talk. I had to get upstairs. "Something's strange," I muttered.

He followed me. "What do you mean something's strange?"

"Well, it's this way..." I explained what was wrong as we climbed the stairs.

"Good God," he said, "I'd better get you up to the dispensary."

"But you can't. Who'll watch Jenny and Geoffrey?"

"I'll call Anne." He reached for the phone.

"No. I was over there just now and she said she didn't feel good."

"How about Jean next door?"

"Well, you might see if she's home."

"OK. Now you lie down and don't move till I get back."

He raced off, and I lay there wondering: What now?

Minutes later he was back. Jean was with him.

"Of course I'll take care of the kids," she said as she helped me sit up. "I'll take Jenny and Geoffrey over to my house now. And when David and Sylvia come home from school, they can come over, too. Don't you worry about a thing."

I put my coat back on and stood up. "I owe you one," I said as I followed Joe down the hall. "I won't forget."

"Oh, don't be silly. Now get on with you."

Joe had explained what was going on to the children. So I gave them each a hug, told them to be good, and we were off.

The first stop was the clinic on our base. The clinic was always the first stop. It was where they separated the wheat from the chaff, the flu from the bronchial pneumonia, and the indigestion from the ulcer. If your complaint called for simple bed rest and could be cured with cough syrup or aspirin, you were whisked through in a mere hour or two and sent on your way. Acute pain and profuse bleeding called for the forty-minute trip to Tachikawa.

Business was brisk when we got to the clinic. It always was around noon. Captains on their lunch hours stopped by to refill allergy prescriptions. Sergeants brought their two-year-olds in for DPT (diphtheria-pertussis-tetanus) booster shots, and mothers who'd insisted, "You'll be fine...once your math test is over," were in with their fifth graders to see if they actually did have the measles.

We spied Ben Noguchi right away. Ben was a doctor at the clinic. He was also a friend.

"Hi," he called out, "I'll be with you in a minute," and he turned back to a small boy with a cast on his arm.

"I'm going to tell him this is an emergency," Joe said. I held onto his arm. "No, don't. He won't be long."

But he was. The boy with the cast had a mother who wanted Chuckie to tell nice Dr. Noguchi he'd stop banging his cast on the radiator. She wanted Chuckie to tell nice Dr. Noguchi he'd stop dipping his cast in the bathtub, too. And she wondered if there wasn't something she should do about the funny patch of rough skin on her arm. Finally she left, and Ben hurried over. He was not pleased when he took me into the examining room and found out what was wrong.

"Why in God's name didn't you say something?" he asked.

"I don't know. I guess I didn't think it was that serious."

"Well, it is. You're hemorrhaging, and I'm going to have to send you to Tachikawa. Now get dressed again, and I'll go arrange for an ambulance."

"Oh, please, Ben, not an ambulance. Couldn't Joe drive me down?"

"Well..."

"It'll be fine, really."

"Oh, all right, but only if you promise you'll get in the back seat, lie down, and stay lying down. I'll call ahead, so they'll be expecting you."

He left the room, and when I was ready to go, he walked me to the front door, where Joe waited with the car.

"I mean it now," he said as I got into the back and lay down. "You stay quiet."

"I will. I will. I promise."

"All right. Now get going. And, Joe," he said, "you drive carefully."

Joe nodded, waved, and put the car in gear. Forty minutes later we pulled into the parking lot at Tachikawa.

"I guess we go in that door over there," Joe said, pointing to the entrance to the women's ward. "Can you make it, or do you want me to drive right up to the door?"

"Oh, I can make it."

"Are you sure? It's been about three hours since all this first started, and you've lost quite a bit of blood, you know."

"I'm sure. Besides, I want you with me, not off parking the car somewhere."

"OK, let's go."

So we went. I shuffled along as quickly as I could, and Joe scurried on ahead to get the door. Except for the murmur of the nurses having their afternoon coffee break in the examining room, the ward was quiet.

Joe cleared his throat. "Excuse me," he said as they looked up. "I'm Captain Combs, and this is my wife, Ann."

Three faces looked blank as if to say, "So?"

"I believe Dr. Noguchi from the clinic at Johnson called to say we were coming?"

"Nope." A tall, steely Florence Nightingale rose to her feet and moved to block the door in case we had any thoughts of penetrating any farther. I could see my warm reception in maternity did not extend to this ward. "No one's called," she said, "and your wife can't come here till she's gone to admittance."

"Admittance?" Joe gasped. "But that's clear over by the main entrance and my wife is hemorrhaging."

Florence shook her head. "Sorry, that's the rules."

Joe sighed disgustedly to let her know what he thought of the rules. She was unimpressed. "Well, does she have to admit herself, or can I do it?" he asked.

She shrugged. "You can do it."

"And my wife can stay here till I get back?"

"Sure." She turned back to her coffee and to the cigarette that had burned down to the filter and was teetering on the edge of the ashtray, about to fall on the floor.

Joe cleared his throat again. "Do you at least have a chair she can sit on?"

"A chair? Oh...yeah, there's one in that room across the hall."

So I sat in the chair across the hall and waited while Joe went down the full length of the ward, out into the main hall, right for a city block or so, and left again to the main desk. When he came back, I was officially admitted, so we braved Florence and her cohorts again.

This time she couldn't avoid us. "All right." She sighed. "You go down to supplies with Marge. Change into hospital pajamas. Then come back here. I'll see if I can find the doctor."

I followed Marge to supplies at the other end of the ward. "It's lucky I'm only hemorrhaging," I muttered.

"Huh?"

"I'd hate to have to drag a broken leg or a disjointed hip back and forth, up and down this hall."

Marge looked at me quizzically, then decided to pretend she understood. "Oh...right," she said.

By the time I'd changed and trekked down the hall once more Dr. Zirbel had arrived. I remembered him. He'd delivered Geoffrey three years before, but since military doctors come and go like conventioneers in New York City, I hadn't expected to see him again.

Apparently he hadn't expected to see me either. But there I was, and there it seemed I would stay. Once he'd examined me, confirmed Ben's original diagnosis, and commented uncharitably about nurses who insist on going by the book, he told Florence to find a room for me and get me to bed.

"I already have a bed waiting." She sniffed. Then she helped me down off the examining table and steered me out into the hall. "Mrs. Combs," she said as she raised her hand to gesture.

"I know, I know," I interrupted. "Go on down to the other end of the ward. Come on, Joe." I took his arm. "If we log at least one more mile, we should be able to collect for travel expenses."

"It's the last room on the left," Florence called out. "Take the empty bed, and I'll be right there to hook up your IV."

I took the empty bed—once I found it, that is. The room, like a submarine waiting for the German armada to pass overhead, was pitch-black, and there were five other beds in there, all occupied. Luckily mine was next to the door. So while Joe stood out in the hall, I crawled in.

When Florence came to hook me up and get me settled, he went over to the nursery to check on Robbie and Joan. I myself was able to visit them when they let me up on the second day. In the meantime, however, I was confined to bed.

We all were. Jan, across from me, was recovering from an appendectomy. Nita, against the far wall, was in traction; she'd slipped on her son's skateboard and fallen down the basement stairs. Wilma, next to me, was undergoing tests of some sort and was constantly linked to some tube or other. Teri, in the corner, had had a hysterectomy. And Beth, in the other corner, had pneumonia.

Of the six of us, only Beth was ambulatory. And since none of us was allowed the luxury of a buzzer to summon the nurse, it was Beth who got up to find Teri a couple of aspirin, Beth who checked to see what had happened to Wilma's dinner, and Beth who cranked up Jan's bed.

When Beth was asleep, I summoned help by whistling through my teeth. It didn't wake her. She was used to noise. Of course, it didn't bring Florence on the run either. But then nothing brought Florence on the run. I think she figured we'd get well faster if we weren't coddled.

She may have been right. I know I concentrated all my energies on rehabilitation. I lay still when I should. I slept when I should. I ate what I should. And after three days Dr. Zirbel signed my release. Joe and I took one more walk down the length of the ward, and this time we kept on going. We stopped off to see Robbie and Joan again; to tap on the nursery window and comment that they looked like newly hatched sparrows as they lay there all arms and legs and tummies. Then we went home.

It was Wednesday.

On Friday after dinner, when all four older children were in the tub together and I was on my knees, doing my best to scrub elbows and ears and still keep dry, the phone rang. Joe answered it. I couldn't hear the conversation, but when he came back into the bathroom, he seemed puzzled.

"That was the hospital," he said. "They said Robbie has a slight fever. They want me to come down right away."

I struggled to my feet. "I'm coming, too. Call Jean and ask her if she'll watch the children one more time."

"No, you stay here."

"What do you mean, stay here? I'm coming."

"No, you're not. You just got out of the hospital yourself, and you need to rest. The doctor said so."

"What doctor?"

"The one I just talked to. He said I was to come and you were to stay home and rest." He put his arm around me. "Don't worry, honey. It's just a fever. I'll call you when I find out what's wrong, and I'll be back as soon as I can."

I did worry, though. While I rubbed David down with a big bath towel, while I buttoned up Sylvia's nightgown, and while I put pajamas on Jenny and Geoffrey, something in the back of my head whispered, "Why would they want Joe to drive clear to Tachikawa if it's only a slight fever and there's nothing to be concerned about?"

Why doesn't Joe call? I thought as I read *The Noisy Book* to Jenny and Geoffrey and did my best to imitate the sounds of "people's feet" and "an awning in the wind." He should be there by now.

I tucked them in, kissed them good-night, and turned out their light. I wish to hell he'd hurry up and call, I thought as I proceeded to David and Sylvia's room and Chapter 5 of *Mary Poppins*. It isn't as if he doesn't know I'm waiting for some word.

"You skipped a part," Sylvia said.

"Sorry. I thought maybe you wouldn't notice."

She snuggled up against me. "I can read," she said.

"She can't read," David protested. "She just knows this part by heart."

"I can too read."

Just then the phone rang. I jumped up and ran into my room to answer it. It was Joe, and I could tell from the sound of his voice something was very wrong.

"Honey," he said, "I'm here in Dr. Tubergen's office."

"What's the matter? What's wrong with Robbie?"

"Well." I heard him take a deep breath. "Apparently he has spinal meningitis."

"Spinal meningitis?" My mind raced as I tried to remember what, if anything, I knew about spinal meningitis. "Isn't that what all those soldiers died from awhile back?" I asked.

"Just a minute," Joe said. "I'll let Dr. Tubergen explain it all to you."

There was a pause while I, like someone in the path of an avalanche, waited to be mowed down.

"Hello, Mrs. Combs?" The voice was gentle, reassuring even, but deadly serious. "This is David Tubergen."

That's odd, I thought in the split second it took him to take a breath. He didn't refer to himself as Dr. Tubergen. I wonder if it's SOP to use your first name when the news is bad.

"Let me see if I can explain what we're dealing with here."

I listened, memorizing for later, when I'd go over it again and again in my mind. There was talk of a jaundiced condition which had led the nurses to suspect there was something wrong. Dr. Tubergen had taken a spinal tap. He'd also noticed a "very slight convulsion." The essence of it all was Robbie was critically ill and had one chance in four of living through the night.

"The next twelve hours are critical," he said finally. "If he makes it through the night, he should have it made, period. Now I'll let you talk to your husband again."

"Honey?" Joe said. "Listen, I'm going to stay here tonight. Will you be all right?"

"Oh, yes. Don't worry about me. How about you? Are you OK?"

"Sure. I'm fine...but sweetheart, I don't want to tie up the doctor's phone. So I'd better say good-bye. I'll call back later. In fact, I'll call every hour...or if there's any change. All right?"

"All right."

I hung up the phone and stood there for a moment. The radio was on. Petula Clark had just discovered the bright lights "Downtown." But all I could think was: Robbie can't die. I've never even held him. He can't die if I've never held him, can he?

"Mom?" David called from the other room. "Aren't you going to finish the chapter?"

"What?" I wanted time to think, to absorb it all. But life doesn't work that way. The world doesn't stop to let you catch your breath. Like an escalator, it keeps on moving, even when you've just dropped two packages and your purse. While you scramble around trying to pick everything up, it keeps on moving.

"I'm coming," I called. Then I went in and tried calmly to explain what was wrong.

They seemed to understand. And when I suggested we finish *Mary Poppins* another time, they agreed and promptly snuggled down under the covers.

"I hope Robbie's better tomorrow," David said as I kissed him good-night.

"Me, too," Sylvia echoed. "And, Mommy?"

"What, honey?"

"I can too read."

"All right. Now go to sleep."

I turned out their light and went downstairs to heat up some coffee and wait for Joe's next call. Suddenly I wanted to call someone—anyone. I wanted to say, "Come talk to me. Help me keep my mind off what's going on down there in the incubator at Tachikawa." But I didn't know how to go about it.

"Besides," I said to myself, "at this time of night people are busy with their own lives."

I should have known better.

I had just poured myself a cup of coffee and sat down at the dining room table to try to keep busy with a cross-word puzzle when the phone rang. It was Margaret Fuller, the colonel's wife. She'd called to invite me to a shower—for me—but something in my voice made her ask, "What's wrong?" When I told her, she said, "I'm coming down."

It was like that all evening. Pat Noguchi, Ben's wife, came over. Anna Friend, who'd been bowling and got home late, came by. Jean left the kids with her husband and brought over some cookies and another pot of coffee. Even Hank Schibi called for Joe. They worked in the same office, and he wanted to discuss some military business. When I told him where Joe was and why, he paused. "I think I'll go down to Tachikawa and keep him company," he said, and hung up.

And Mary Jo, our neighbor from Washington Heights who now lived in another housing area, called. "I know it's late," she said when I answered the phone. "And I know you were probably asleep, but for some reason I simply had to call and see how you were."

It was uncanny, and it helped. It helped to talk about nothing in particular: recipes; Lyndon Johnson's election; the latest sumo matches. It helped to forget for a while and to laugh at Anna's retelling of the day she wore her dress backward. It also helped when the phone rang and I knew it was Joe to have someone there assuring me, "Don't worry, it'll be all right. He's only checking in."

At ten o'clock, when he called, he said they'd found an Episcopal clergyman who'd just finished baptizing both Robbie and Joan.

"His name is Bishop Vial," he told me. "And guess what? He knows your father. I'm not exactly sure from where, but when I introduced myself and mentioned you and your father, he said, 'Oh, sure. I know Vincent Gowen.'"

Suddenly I knew everything was going to be all right. I can't say why I felt that way. There was certainly no logical explanation for it. But there it was. I was still concerned, still anxious even, but way down deep, where fear and terror lie in wait, I wasn't worried anymore.

At midnight Joe said he wouldn't call again till morning. "There hasn't been any change in the last couple of hours," he said, "and now I want you to try and get some sleep."

"All right," I promised. "I'll try."

And I did. After everyone had gone home, I took the radio upstairs, checked the children one more time, and crawled into bed. I left the radio on since I couldn't bring myself to turn it off. I didn't sleep, but I did rest.

Around seven, just as the children were beginning to stir, Joe called again. This was it. Either Robbie had made it or he hadn't. I took a deep breath, held it, and picked up the phone.

"He made it," Joe exulted. "Dr. Tubergen just checked him, and he says he thinks the crisis has passed."

I exhaled slowly, carefully. "Are you sure?"

"That's what he says, and he's been here all night. In fact, he just told me, 'Joe, it looks as if you've got a fighter there.'"

"Oh...thank God."

"You said it. One thing, though, honey." His voice was subdued again.

"What?"

"Well, Dr. Tubergen says that apparently Robbie also has a slight heart murmur and a hernia."

I waited for the hollow "Oh, no, please, no" feeling. It didn't come. Somehow, since Robbie had made it through the night, I knew he'd make it through anything else that came along. We all would. I knew it. And I kept on knowing it.

The next week when Joan, who was still at the hospital, too, seemed unable to keep any food down and her doctor couldn't figure out why, I knew there was nothing to worry about.

In fact, I even offered him one of my "mother knows best" diagnoses. "I bet it's pyloric stenosis," I said. "David, our oldest, had the same trouble at the same age, and the symptoms were similar."

"It is a possibility," he agreed, "but a remote one."

After he'd operated on her—for pyloric stenosis—and she was recovering nicely, I accepted his reluctant congratulations and told him, "I knew that was it, and I knew everything was going to be fine."

When further tests revealed that both Robbie and Joan had had, and recovered from, a recently discovered and little-understood condition called cytomegalic inclusion disease, and when Dr. Tubergen said, "It may have left them both mentally and physically retarded. We can't tell. You'll have to wait and see," I still didn't panic.

And I didn't fall apart when, as a last straw, David, Sylvia, Jenny, and Geoffrey took turns having chicken pox at home.

Six months later, when everyone was well and we all were back in the States, living in a house of our own on the outskirts of Washington, D.C., I saw a television drama one night. When Eddie Albert, playing the part of a pediatrician, kept an all-night vigil with a newborn baby, I burst into tears and sobbed for a solid hour.

But then I always was a little slow on the uptake.

੬ And Miles to Go Before I Sleep

ASK THE MAN who's pedaling a unicycle across a tightrope and juggling a couple of raw eggs at the same time. He'll tell you. The only way you'll make it is if you keep going and don't stop to think about what you're doing.

The same is true when you're up to your rafters in children, laundry, unmade beds, dirty dishes, Tinkertoys, diapers, and highchairs. If you pause, even for a moment, and say to yourself, "How do I do it?" things start to blur, and you find yourself crawling back into bed with the firm intention of staying there for a decade at the very least.

I tried to avoid taking stock the first year we were a family of eight, with David only seven and the twins still counting their ages in months. I also tried to avoid reading about Ethel Kennedy, who seemed to manage her eight or ten children without so much as taking a deep breath. It wasn't easy. The junior senator from New York and his family were a never-ending source of journalistic interest in the Washington, D.C., area, and a day without a story on the latest touch football game at Bobby's place was like a day without the weather report.

"It's not that I dislike the lady," I told Joe one night when I finally got around to reading the morning paper and happened on another account of the goings on at Hickory Hill. "I don't. In fact, I admire her. But you'll have to admit it's depressing knowing there's someone right across the Potomac who has more children than we do and still manages to get outside and play tennis and touch football. It's discouraging knowing she thinks nothing of throwing a dinner party for the prime minister of England and forty or fifty other dignitaries. And I can do without realizing that she's never stumbled through the day only to realize at the end that she forgot to comb her hair and that she's wearing shoes that don't match."

"Now, now," Joe murmured as he tends to do when he's buried in the NBA statistics and I'm ranting again.

"No, I mean it," I wailed. "I haven't been outside in so long I almost fainted yesterday when I saw that the leaves had fallen off the trees. The last game I played was Cootie. Sylvia talked me into that, and she beat me by two ears and a tongue. I spend so much time in the basement doing laundry I feel like a Welsh coal miner. And the few times I manage to have guests for dinner I have to remind myself not to say, 'Sit up straight and stop playing with your salad,' or, 'No dessert till you finish your broccoli.'"

"Now, now," Joe said again. "It's not that bad. You're just tired."

He was wrong. It was that bad, at least when I stopped to think about it. Luckily I rarely had time to stop and/ or think about it.

My day began around five-thirty when the alarm intruded on dreams of summer afternoons which I spent in a lawn chair under the trees, sipping lemonade and reading novels. I didn't have to get up at five-thirty. It would be a good forty-five minutes before anyone else in the house stirred. At the time, however, I was still aiming for perfection, and the perfect mother never burrows down under the covers while her babies howl and her children eat their cereal out of a cut glass candy dish. The perfect wife doesn't pad into the kitchen looking like a donation to the Goodwill either.

"After all," as I'd heard and read time and time again, "your husband's last glimpse of you is the image he'll carry with him through the day."

So I got up at five-thirty. I dressed, washed my face, and brushed my teeth. Then I tiptoed downstairs, made a pot of coffee, and ate the grapefruit, dry toast, and soft-boiled egg prescribed by my latest diet.

On good days Jenny, Geoffrey, and the twins slept until Joe had left for work and David and Sylvia were safely on the bus to school. On bad days everyone got up at once. We had about as many good days that year as we had total eclipses of the sun. As a rule, the breakfast hour was only slightly less frantic than a "One day only... going out of business... half price... bargain basement" sale.

Joe fended for himself. He threaded his way past Geoffrey, who was sitting on the stairs in his pajamas with Eeyore, his stuffed donkey, clutched in his hand. He skirted Jenny, who'd been routed out of bed by Sylvia. He veered off in time to miss a collision with David, who was heading out of the kitchen and into the dining room. He backed up so Sylvia could run down to the basement and get her sweater out of the dryer. And he edged his way around the twins and me.

We were on the floor. Robbie and Joan were in what we called their bouncing chairs—wrought-iron frames covered with a canvas sling. I sat cross-legged in front

of them and dished out oatmeal and puréed apricots like
a Las Vegas blackjack dealer. I could have put them up
on the table, I suppose, but I didn't dare. The chances
were good that at some point I'd have to get up to find
Sylvia's shoe or mop up a glass of spilled milk or go for
a washcloth when Robbie gave me the Bronx cheer and
sprayed us all with cereal, and I didn't want them vaulting off the table while I was gone. Later they'd graduate
to highchairs, and I, too, would surface; but we'd still be
part of the obstacle course.

To add to the din, Hugh Downs, Barbara Walters, and
Frank Blair muttered in the background. It probably
would have been less confusing without them, but they
were my link with the outside world. It was they who
told me Hurricane Betsy had veered off into the Gulf of
Mexico. They described the crowds gathered at Yankee
Stadium to greet Pope Paul VI. They kept me up-to-date
on President Johnson's gall bladder operation and showed
me his scar. It was they who provided me with ringside
seats for battles in the highlands of Vietnam, they who
showed me my first demonstrations against the war, and
they who told me about all the New Yorkers who'd been
stranded in elevators during the blackout.

True, I missed hearing how many home runs Willie
Mays had hit in 1965 because David chose that moment
to ask me if I'd signed the permission slip saying he could
go on the class trip to the Smithsonian. And Joan was
howling when they announced who'd won the Nobel
Prize for Literature. But it didn't matter. Joe would fill
me in on Willie Mays later. In fact, if I let him, he'd give
me Carl Yastrzemski's batting average and Mickey Man-
tle's shirt size, too. As for the Nobel Prize, it always
seemed to go to someone who'd renounced the world
years ago and was now living and writing poetry in a

cave in the mountains of Bolivia. So I hadn't missed much. Besides, I appreciated what I had managed to hear.

Of course, social critics and those who claimed they spent their leisure hours rereading *Tristram Shandy* and conjugating Latin verbs deplored the fact that we housewives watched television and listened to the radio while we scrubbed and dusted and sorted the laundry.

"You're ruining your minds," they said. "You're filling your lives with nothing but game shows, soap operas, and trivia."

Perhaps so, but I ignored them. What did they know? They weren't confined to quarters till further notice. They'd have turned the TV on, too, if it meant having something to occupy their minds while they folded six loads of laundry. And they'd have snatched at the chance to hear MacDonald Carey utter complete sentences on "Days of Our Lives" if they'd had to spend the better part of every day conversing with preschoolers.

When one has to go through ten or twenty "Guess what?" "What?" "That's what"s in an hour, Monty Hall starts sounding like Eric Sevareid. If you spend a morning discussing all the dogs Grandmother has had and are asked to describe how each died, you find yourself counting the minutes till the midday news. And if you listen to "Jenny's a poop." "I am not." "Are too." "Am not." "Are too" for any length of time, you'll gladly sell your soul to hear someone answer the jackpot question, "What was Queen Elizabeth's maiden name?" That, quite simply, is how it is on the home front.

Once Joe had grabbed the car keys and headed off to work and I'd shooed David and Sylvia out the door with their mittens, their lunch boxes, and ten cents for milk, it was time to feed Jenny and Geoffrey and get Jenny ready for kindergarten. Robbie and Joan by now were either in their playpen or trying to scale the barrier at the top of the stairs to the basement.

They were an adventurous twosome, and they were fast on their hands and knees. He could skitter out of the kitchen and be stirring the dead ashes in the fireplace before I realized he was no longer at my feet. She could scramble into the bathroom, pull herself up, and be busily dipping Jenny's slippers into the toilet before I knew she was gone. And both could be in Sylvia's room, rifling through her drawers in the time it takes to say, "Does anyone know where the twins are?"

Consequently, all the bedroom and bathroom doors were shut, all the stairways were blocked with accordion fences, and all the lower cupboards were tied shut with rope, dishtowels and, on occasion, an apron or my wool scarf. It complicated things a bit. The bedrooms and the bathroom on the first floor, the last stop on our central heating system, were icy in the winter. Answering the phone in another room sometimes meant I had to vault over the latest barricade. A trip up from the basement with Joe's socks, a load of bath towels, and six shirts on hangers, left me working the fence open with my teeth. And getting dinner was the equivalent of earning a merit badge in square knots.

The other children helped me keep track of Robbie and Joan; but it was a full-time occupation, and they were easily distracted by their own pursuits. Geoffrey, for instance, had trucks to roar around the living room, fortresses to build with the couch cushions. He had pictures to draw—our art department included finger paints, coffee cans full of broken crayons, chalkboards, pencils, usually with the erasers carefully pried out of the ends, and rolls of butcher paper for long illustrated stories about adventurous freight trains.

And he had things of his own to get into. A favorite was the Band-Aid can. It beckoned the way a pint of muscatel beckons a wino. Why I don't know. Maybe it was the satisfying snap of the lid on the box. Maybe it was all those red strings begging to be pulled. It might even have been the sympathy you get when a knee or an elbow is swathed in bandages. Whatever the attraction, I knew that any unexplained silence probably meant Geoffrey was upstairs in the bathroom, getting into the Band-Aids again.

Usually he exercised restraint, with one round patch on his arm and only one or two small strips on his forehead. One day, however, he went whole hog. I was talking to the mailman at the time. I always talk to mailmen. When you're a shut-in, you talk to anyone who'll talk back: the mailman; the meter reader; the guy who's pouring concrete for your neighbor's patio—anyone. On this particular day Mr. Brewster and I were discussing color. Joe and I had just painted the kitchen blue, and Mr. Brewster said he'd read an article recently that claimed blue and green kitchens make people eat more.

"That's all I need." I groaned, indicating I'd eaten quite enough already.

He chuckled. "I know what you mean," he said. Then suddenly his gaze shifted, and his mouth fell open.

"Good Lord," he said with a gasp.

I turned around. Geoffrey was halfway down the stairs, and he looked as if he'd been caught in an adhesive tape explosion. He had Band-Aids on his arms, his legs, and his chin. Two huge pads covered his knees. A little one was wrapped around his thumb. And a couple more peered out through the gap between the bottom of his shirt and the top of his pants.

I looked back at Mr. Brewster. I could see thoughts of

"child beater," "brutal mother," even "overweight brutal mother" tiptoeing across his mind.

"You mean him?" I said, gesturing casually at the wounded warrior behind me.

"Yes. What happened to him?"

"What happened is he got into the Band-Aid box."

"Oh." The sigh of relief was audible. "Oh. I see."

I don't think he did. And I noticed he was never quite as friendly after that. He also made a point of asking, "How's the little fellow?" every time Geoffrey wasn't right there hanging onto my skirt. But he needn't have worried. The little fellow was fine. They all were. Their mother was frazzled, but they all were fine.

As a rule, the mornings raced by. The first order of business, once the commuters were off, was the laundry. There was always laundry. Mother tried, on her various visits, to convince me I needn't spend the best years of my life washing, rinsing, and tumble drying in the basement.

"If you'd simply teach the children to fold or hang up the clothes that aren't really dirty—" she intoned.

"Sure, sure," I said. "And while I'm at it, I'll teach them conversational French, too."

"You needn't be sarcastic."

"I'm not really. It's just that I have my hands full, trying to get them to pick up their toys and stop leaving their shoes under the couch. If I also have to conduct a 'This Sweater Was Worn Only to School and Back. It Has No Dried Spaghetti Sauce on the Front, No Grass Stains on the Elbow, and No Mud on the Sleeve. Therefore, It Is Not Really Dirty' seminar, I'll take to drink."

She didn't understand, and nothing I could say would convince her it was simply easier to grab up anything that wasn't in a drawer or on a hanger and stuff it into the washing machine.

True, six loads a day required more than a minibasket, but that's how it was. And with a little organization and a timer I managed.

The timer was one of those clever key chain affairs. It was supposed to sit in my purse while I lunched with the girls or took in a matinee. Then, when the parking meter needed another dime, it was supposed to buzz like a captive bumblebee and send me galloping out to the car before I got a ticket. The chances of my lunching with the girls or taking in a matinee were negligible, however, so I clipped the timer onto my belt and set it for two minutes short of the average heavy duty cycle. When it went off, I dropped my mop or broom or coffee cup and raced downstairs to pull the clothes out of the dryer and dump them on the folding table, to yank the clothes out of the washer and toss them into the dryer, and to stuff the next load into the washer. It was a precision act, and John Philip Sousa could easily have set it to music if he'd been alive. He wasn't, though, so I did my eurhythmics unaccompanied.

I did most everything unaccompanied. Oh, I had small children trailing after me, saying, "Whatcha doin' now, Mom?" But no one dropped by for a cup of coffee or the latest details on the Wiggins' divorce. I'd invited the only two women I knew in the neighborhood to come by any-time. But after one brief visit they insisted, "Now it's your turn to come see me," and that was something only slightly less complicated than moving to another city.

For one thing, the twins were now too heavy for me to carry both at once. This meant hauling out the stroller, which would have been fine if Hillcrest Heights had had sidewalks or if our house had been on a level with the street. But there were no sidewalks, and our house was perched on a hill. So if I was to get the stroller to the street, I either had to bounce it down the stairs, a feat which wasn't possible since the stairs were narrow and a twin stroller isn't, or I could rush headlong down the hill and pray for a break in traffic when we skittered out into the middle of the street.

Then, too, by the time I'd changed the twins; dressed them; put on their coats and hats; packed a bag with extra diapers, a couple of bottles of juice, and some toys; and had stuffed Geoffrey into his traveling clothes they were wet again, the morning was over, and it was time for lunch.

After lunch we gave the all-American nap a try, and while the children slept or pretended to, I ironed. Ordinarily I wouldn't have, and I gave it up the minute permanent press was invented. But at the time ironing was on the "required activities" list, and there was no way of getting out of it.

Believe me, I'd tried. There were shirts at the bottom of the basket that belonged to David, fit Geoffrey, but wouldn't surface till Robbie entered high school. Unfortunately there were also Joe's uniforms at the top, and for some strange reason he didn't go along with my idea that we press them by laying them out between the mattress and the box spring of our bed. So I ironed.

Of course, I stopped when Jenny bounded in the front door. I also heaved a sigh and pulled the plug when the slightest noise from upstairs suggested naptime was over. After all, I rationalized, it's not safe to iron when there are toddlers and babies crawling around underfoot. And if I'm too busy with a yoke or a gusset to listen to the latest news from school, I'll never hear what Randy did with his milk and crackers or learn why Miss Gavin was fired.

I was right. Children just home from school were full of wild tales and information. But wait an hour or so, and

I'd be lucky to get a "Huh? The spelling test? Oh, it was fine."

Jenny, fresh from kindergarten, could hardly wait to tell me, "Jerry Stillman put a whole slug of paper towels down the toilet and it overflowed and Mrs. Reiker had to call the janitor and have him mop everything up and Jerry had to go to the principal's office and boy, is he in trouble." But later, if I asked her to repeat the story for Joe, she usually shrugged and said, "You tell him, Mom."

When David came in and plunked his lunch box down on the counter, I couldn't have kept him from explaining how to use an abacus if I'd wanted to. "What you have to remember, Mom," he'd say as he followed me down to the basement, where another load of diapers waited to be folded, "is that each row of beads stands for a certain number...fives...tens...hundreds."

Hours later, over dinner, his enthusiasm had abated and he was more interested in telling how he and Mike and Danny had gone over to the hills after school and played hide-and-seek with their walkie-talkies.

Sylvia always had news, and her recitation of who had fallen off the monkey bars at recess and why, of what colors you had to mix to make barn brown, and of how many Oreos Leroy could stuff in his mouth at once couldn't wait for another time.

So I gladly put away the ironing and turned my attention to the latest bulletins. It wasn't my full attention. I couldn't afford that luxury. Part of me had to translate the muffled noises filtering down from upstairs. Was the rhythmic thumping Joan vaulting her crib across the room, or was it Robbie whapping the wall with his teddy bear? Were all three of them laughing because they'd just wakened and were rested and cheerful, or was the hilarity due to the fact that they thought it was funny to pull feathers out of Geoffrey's pillow and blow them around the room?

Another part of me had to remember that the hamburger was still in the freezer. I mustn't forget I had to call Joe before he left the office and ask him to pick up some lettuce and a pound of margarine. I could see a button on David's coat was loose, and I thought: I'd better sew that back on before he loses it. Jenny needed to be reminded she'd left her tea set out in the tree house and it was starting to rain. I spied Robbie's shoes under the dining room table and remembered I ought to take them with me when I went upstairs to get him up from his nap. And it occurred to me Sylvia's bangs could use a trimming. Other than that, I was all ears.

By the time Joe came home I'd had my fill of listening. I'd refereed a couple of fights between Sylvia and Jenny, who'd undressed Sylvia's Madame Alexander doll and lost the tie to the velvet cape. Robbie had bopped Joan on the head with a copy of *How Hippo!* and I'd had to stop everything and comfort her. One of the potatoes I'd thrown into the oven to bake with the meat loaf had exploded, and bits of it, lying on the coil, kept catching fire. Jenny had spilled grape juice on her shirt, and I'd had to strip her down and pour boiling water through the stain. Someone had left the bathroom door open, and Robbie, lurking in the shadows, had crawled in and poured shampoo all over the rug. And Geoffrey had accidentally kicked down a tower David was building.

So when I heard the car pull up down on the street, it was all I could do to keep from flinging open the front door and shouting, "You've come. You've come. At last you've come."

Joe, on the other hand, had had a hard day. Classified documents had been misplaced. A sergeant had failed to come back from his coffee break and had later been found lapping up the suds at a local bowling alley. A briefing session had gone badly, and all he asked for now was a martini, a peaceful dinner, and a chance to relax.

Was it ever thus. By the time the sun does its number in the west Mom has had it with home and hearth. Dad hasn't. From his side of the fence, life away from the marketplace seems safe, secure, and uncomplicated. So while she wants sympathy, he wants to check the mail. While she wants to tell him what happened when the sink backed up, he wants to read the paper. And while she wants him to entertain the children and keep them out of her hair while she gets dinner, he wants her to entertain the children till he's had a chance to unwind. It's a no-win situation, one that keeps psychiatrists and marriage counselors in cashmere coats and Gucci loafers.

I understood the mechanics of it all. I also remembered Mother's admonition: "Wait until after he's had his dinner. Don't present problems to a man with an empty stomach." But it didn't stop me.

"Boy, am I glad you're home," I'd blather before he even had a chance to take off his coat. "You can't imagine what a day I've had."

"Oh?"

"Yes, it's simply been one thing after another."

"Hm."

"I tell you. Sometimes I think if I hear, 'Mom? Hey, Mom?' one more time, I'll scream."

By now he was usually looking for the martini pitcher and searching through the kitchen drawer for the ice pick.

"Did anything interesting happen at the office today?" I was starved for details from what I considered Joe's fascinating life out there in the world.

"Nope."

"Nothing at all?" He didn't realize I'd settle for anything. Even the news that the traffic light at Marlow Heights was out and cars were backed up to the D.C. line sounded exciting to me.

"Nothing at all."

"How's Barney Metz?"

"Oh...he's OK."

"But I thought I heard his house had burned to the ground and he and Mary and the kids were living in temporary quarters with their only possessions the clothes they had on their backs."

"Yeah, they are."

"Well, tell me about it."

"What's there to tell?"

"What's there to tell?" I'd shriek. "Well, for openers, how did the fire start...who discovered it...was anyone hurt?"

At this point one of the twins usually howled or Geoffrey clomped into the kitchen to wail, "When are we going to eat?" So I turned my attention back to dinner and the green beans simmering at the back of the stove. Joe went to check the turmoil in the living room.

After dinner—and I still maintain dinner is a mistake since it gives renewed vigor to small children who God knows should be winding down—we had a family hour of sorts. It wasn't the sort of thing that would have sent Longfellow scrambling for his rhyming dictionary. Joe didn't sit in a wing chair and chuck David under the chin, nor did he pat Sylvia's golden hair. Actually it was more of a melee.

In the winter we hauled out our seven-year accumulation of building blocks and had contests to see who could build the highest tower or the longest bridge. Sometimes we lined up the long, skinny ones domino fashion, and if Jenny didn't accidentally kick one and Robbie didn't crawl over and set them off, we wound them around the coffee table, past the couch, and out to the front door. Then someone pushed the first one, and down they went, one after the other…flap…flap… flap…flap.

Most of the time, though, Joe lay on the living room floor and the children took turns using him to play Superman. They made him lie on his back like a dead beetle while they grabbed his hands and balanced themselves on his upturned feet. They hopped, skipped, then jumped over him. And they walked up and down on his back.

I was on the floor, too, but I was the training table, for beginners only. While the others rolled over Joe or tumbled and squealed with delight as he sailed them through the air, Robbie and Joan crawled back and forth over my inert form.

In the summer we went outside.

Joe and the older children trotted down to the median, the approximately thirty-foot-wide strip between the two halves of Twenty-eighth Parkway. There they played catch, flew kites, held three-legged races, and drew stares from passing motorists. The twins stayed with me. I let them crawl around on the front lawn, and I kept them from their favorite pastime: scrambling up the back hill, easing their way through the hole in the fence, and galloping out into the street above us.

We had a marvelous time, but we were the only ones. We certainly never saw anyone else out there mixing it up with his kids. And one night a man going by was so amazed at the sight of a father playing tag with his children that he almost drove over the curb.

But Joe loved it, and the children loved it. Even when a modified ball game ended in tears because the others

yelled at Jenny, who refused to slide into second base
and get her dress dirty, they loved it. On more than one
occasion Sylvia stomped back across the street, saying,
"Daddy throws the ball too hard," or David quit when,
as he claimed, "Sylvia cheated." But sure enough, after
dinner the next night there they all were chanting, "Come
on, Daddy. Let's go play in the median."

Besides, it was worth the trouble just to wear them out
before bathtime, and Lord knows, when you have to run
six small bodies through the suds, it helps to have several
of them played out. Otherwise they squirt the soap at
each other. They cup their hands into makeshift water
pistols. And you end up looking like the last survivor
hauled into the lifeboat.

David, Sylvia, and Jenny took their own baths. Joe
stood by to reach another towel or help button a pair of
pajamas. He scrubbed backs, dried hair, and made sure
Jenny's slippers were on the right feet.

I was the overlord for the upstairs crew. They were a
boisterous lot. They brought rubber frogs, Ping-Pong balls,
and plastic boats with windup paddle wheels in with
them. They splashed the water with the flats of their
hands. They sucked on the washcloths and dared me to
rip them out of their clenched teeth. And they called
each other poopoo and weewee and roared with laughter
at their own impudence.

I knelt by the side of the tub and did my best to scrub
the flailing arms and legs and feet. Then one by one I
hoisted them out, dried them off, and carried them into
my room, where our king-size bed acted as a giant changing table. The logistics of this last maneuver were complicated, especially during the first year, when the twins
were too little to be left in the tub alone even for a few
seconds. If Sylvia was still up and hadn't taken her bath

yet, I called on her to act as a sentinel. Otherwise Joe helped me. He held out a towel. I handed him a wet, slippery body. He wrapped it up and took it into our room.

It was like a bucket brigade, and once we had them all safely on the bed, I grabbed for undershirts and diapers. I wrestled with whoever was closest, crammed arms into sleeves, and forced legs into pajama bottoms. And while I fumbled with snaps and reached out to snatch at a foot and drag back an escapee, the others giggled and chortled and bounced up and down on the bed like an Olympic trampoline team.

With baths completed we settled down for storytime. David was by now on his own, reading *Tom Swift* and *The Rover Boys* to himself. Sylvia and Jenny had graduated to stories with a minimum of illustrations. But the twins and Geoffrey and I stretched out on our stomachs on my bed, and for at least the thousandth time we marveled at "Emmeline who's not been seen for more than a week." We chanted about green eggs and ham, and bellowed, "I do not like them Sam I am." And we mourned the sad fate of *The Giving Tree*.

Then, like a theater crowd dispersing, it was off to bed. Geoffrey and Robbie went peacefully, and the minute they were safely tucked in they nodded off. Joan was less willing to give in, especially when the sounds from downstairs told her we hadn't closed up shop for the night. Sometimes she howled till one or the other of us clambered up the stairs to rock her for a while and try to calm her down. We knew we were breaking some written or unwritten rule of child rearing, but prolonged sobbing and choking in the background tend to make one weak. Sometimes we brought her downstairs for a few minutes, and she sniffled a couple of times, rubbed at her eyes with her fist, then grinned the sly grin that says, "Well, I won this round." Other times we simply let her cry.

On Friday nights, with no school the next day, we let David, Sylvia and Jenny stay up till nine o'clock or so. Jenny rarely made it past eight-thirty, but David and Sylvia were wide-awake and dying to play parcheesi or Probe or any of the other games we'd accumulated along the way. The Marquis of Queensberry rules were not always strictly observed. At times one or another of the players stormed off to bed in a huff after having been cleverly edged out of a victory. There were occasional impassioned pleas to start over "because I'll never catch up." And every once in a while I had to drop out simply because I couldn't play and take care of Joan, too.

Mother, on her visits, was horrified by the fierceness of the competition. She was the sort that let raging opponents win in order to keep peace. So when Joe slipped his man past David and David burst into tears, she protested, "You're being cruel." But Joe argued that you couldn't let a child win all the time and then send him out into a world that doesn't care if he bursts into tears or not. And though I myself had been taught to defer to others, I had to agree with him. So we played for blood, and only occasionally, when I was sure I wouldn't get caught, did I hold back and let one of the children take advantage of me.

On week nights, when taps sounded early, Joe and I filled the remaining hours of the day with projects. We sat on the floor and made a rug for the dining room by sewing together remnant hunks of carpeting I'd bought from a company that remodeled real estate offices. Either that or we refinished furniture, built shelves, and papered the bathroom walls.

Finally we stumbled up to our room to crawl into bed

and watch TV on the tiny set that perched on a wobbly stand near the door. Down the hall Joan bellowed one last time, and Joe and I fought for the privilege of being the one allowed to ignore her and stay in bed. I usually lost.

And sometime during the late news or halfway through Johnny Carson's monologue I wound the clock, set it for five-thirty and turned out my light. Luckily no one was there to ask, "Say, Ann, how do you do it?" I wouldn't have had an answer. Come to think of it, I still don't. I haven't the faintest idea how I did it.

ᥛ You Call This Fulfillment?

As a rule, I'm not the envious sort. If you have a new red Ferrari and I'm limping to the grocery store in an old station wagon that got its first dent the day they broke into the Watergate, you won't find me sulking and saying, "Did you know red cars are involved in more accidents than any other color?"

If you're going to Hawaii for two weeks in January and I haven't been farther than Discount City since last August, I won't snarl and mutter something about the aging effects of too much sun and surf. I'm delighted when you tell me your husband's been promoted for the third time this year. I applaud your son who got a full scholarship to Yale. And the fact that you've lost twenty pounds and are now a perfect size eight pleases me as much as it pleases you...most of the time.

But if I find out you're one of those people who enjoys housework, if someone tells me you clean out your vegetable drawers even when your mother-in-law isn't expected at any moment, and if I discover you've never had mildew in your shower stall, then I'm sorry, friend, you're on my list, and I'll do my best to locate a dust ball under your couch or some fingerprints on your toaster. I may even be forced to interrupt a formal dinner with "Excuse me, Gloria. Do you have another fork? This one seems to have some dried peanut butter on it."

I'm not proud of this flaw in my character. I'd love to be able to overlook the fact that your cookie sheets shine and your potholders aren't scorched, but I can't. I just can't.

You see, I'm one of those unfortunate souls whose talent for housekeeping is only slightly stronger than her talent for symphonic composition. In other words, I can walk by a Christmas candle in February and never have the urge to rush it up to the attic, where the other decorations are carefully sorted and put away. And I can stare at cobwebs that are older than most fine wines. I can admire the way they swoop from the corner of the ceiling down to the lamp and then over to the window. I can even watch them as they flutter when the furnace turns on and circulates the air. But guilt (and only guilt) moves me to whisk them away with a broom.

So when, on our return to the States, I heard that Betty Friedan and others were speaking up, actually saying out loud that housework isn't the ultimate in creative expression for women, I cheered.

"See," I told Joe and Mother and anyone else who would listen, "it's just as I said. Housework is dull and repetitious, and I should be doing better things with my time."

They agreed...with reservations. Joe pitched in and helped. He mopped the kitchen floor, vacuumed the living room, and changed his fair share of diapers. But when there was laundry to fold, when the dresser drawers had to be sorted and rearranged, and when David's coat pocket had a hole in it or Sylvia needed a button sewn on her sweater, he pleaded no talent and begged off.

Mother agreed, too. But her visits were still sprinkled with "These blinds really ought to be washed" and "When was the last time you polished the children's shoes?" and "The refrigerator door wouldn't be so gummy if you'd just get in the habit of wiping it every time you do the dishes."

The media—television, magazines, and the morning paper—didn't agree at all. "Don't you care that your wash isn't as bright as it should be?" they railed. "Your toilet tank's a disgrace," they added. "And what's more, all your neighbors say your furniture's dull and lifeless."

They were probably right there, since fate, chance, and the patron saints of home and hearth continually bring me neighbors who dust their refrigerator coils, iron their dishtowels, and change their shelf paper twice a week. But though I doubted my neighbors wasted their time worrying about my dingy coffee table, and though I continually preached the doctrine of liberation, the guilt and the knowledge that my performance was substandard prevailed.

I'd tried to emulate these paragons of polishing. When Joe and I were first married and I was still entranced with the idea of being a model housewife, I could hardly wait to spring out of bed in the morning to tackle the breakfast dishes, scrub the sinks and the bathtub, sweep the floors, and whirl around our small apartment, brandishing my dustcloth. This lasted for a week.

Then my enthusiasm diminished. I no longer delighted in the fact that a sinkful of hot, sudsy water works miracles on hardened egg yolks and the scorched remnants of beef stew. A shiny tub lost its appeal when I realized bending over to clean it gave me a crick in the back, squatting beside it hurt my knees, and rinsing the gritty cleanser away took half the morning. As for dusting, it suddenly occurred to me I'd rather watch traffic or count dots in an acoustical ceiling than wipe off the Venetian blinds every day, day after day.

So I postponed my housework. "I'll get to it in a bit," I told myself, "just as soon as I finish this."

"This" varied. Some days it was a letter to Mother. Some days it was a book I had to finish because it was due back at the library. Most of the time "this" was some aimless occupation seized upon because anything is more interesting than housework. I got caught up in the vital statistics in the paper. I looked through my cookbooks and tried to decide if I should attempt to make marsh-mallows. Or else I flipped through the dictionary and checked out word origins.

In the panic-stricken moments before Joe came home I flew around the house like a domestic dervish. And when the back door opened, I was blowing the last of the dust off the window sill and muttering, "Tomorrow I'll get this all done before noon."

Once the children started arriving like selections from the Book-of-the-Month Club, my fascination with house-work deteriorated even further. For now, in addition to my regular janitorial duties, I had loads of diapers to contend with. I had small socks that insisted on parting company with their mates, bibs that required presoaking, and grass-stained playsuits to scrub.

Rattles and blocks flung out of the crib with infantile exuberance had to be picked up. Bottles had to be ster-ilized. Floors needed more frequent mopping. And the jigsaw puzzles we'd left out to be finished when we found that last piece of the Arc de Triomphe had to be put away before Geoffrey found it for us and ate it.

Of course, motherhood had its advantages. It gave me a legitimate excuse for putting off till tomorrow the scouring I should have done today.

"David was fussy all afternoon," I could say. "He wouldn't let me put him down for a minute. That's why I didn't get the windows washed.

"I thought the children needed to get out in the fresh air for a change, so instead of polishing the brass lamp I took them out for a walk.

"I know I promised to clean the oven today. But Sylvia didn't take her nap, and the way she gets around these days it was simply too dangerous to try."

I could also blame the tribe for the lack of order in the living room or the bedroom or the linen closet.

"I had everything neat as a pin this morning, but you know how it is with toddlers.

"Little boys certainly do leave monumental rings in the bathtub, don't they?

"Would you believe I had all the sheets and blankets sorted according to size a week ago? I guess that'll teach me not to let Sylvia and Jenny build tents in their room."

Excuses, however failed to impress Mother, the media, and almost anyone who crossed our threshold. Josephine the plumber waved her can of Comet and assured me there was no reason to have blueberry stains in our sink. Fashion models dressed for high tea at the very least pirouetted past their end tables and chastised me for not feeding my furniture. *Better Homes and Gardens*, appalled by the fact that Sylvia's raincoat was hanging on the banister, David had lost one of his mittens, and Jenny had kicked her boots down the basement stairs, suggested I make life easy for myself and spend three hours building a "back hall coat catcher."

I answered that I didn't have a back hall and added

that its last project, a toy chest that was supposed to take a weekend to assemble, had occupied our lives for half of an April and most of a May.

Comments from neighbors and friends were veiled but not totally concealed, and I knew that "I admire you. You're so easygoing," really meant, "How can you stand to live with all this confusion?"

"Could you watch my kids for a couple of hours while I wax the kitchen and buff the dining room floor?" translated into "What do you care if you have two more? Your house is a mess anyway."

"I'll bet you were an English major in college" was a nice way of saying, "Apparently they didn't offer home ec at Smith."

Even Mother's "While you were out getting the twins their booster shots, I cleaned the grating in the fan over the stove. I hope you don't mind" had an underlying "God knows, somebody had to do it" tone about it.

And I did try to improve...constantly. I made up schedules and followed them religiously for a day or two. I read books by people who claimed to be slobs but lied. Periodically I announced, "I've turned over a new leaf, and this is how it's going to be from now on."

The reaction was minimal, but every now and then one of the children groaned, "Oh, no, not again."

Still, I kept at it. I even collected Hints from Heloise the way a repentant sinner collects old Billy Graham sermons. And I tried them, too. When she suggested I hang unironed clothes out on the line overnight so the dew could dampen them, I stumbled out into the darkness and carefully pinned them up like headless ghosts. Of course, I forgot to bring them in till after they'd dried the next day. But I kept at it till Joe asked me whatever happened to his new white shirt and I was forced to drag it in, sprinkle it the regular way, and iron it.

I tried her broken walnut idea, too. I bought a bag of walnuts, broke them in half, and rubbed them over the scratches in our furniture. It worked like a charm even if I did use the whole bag and even if I did get so caught up in the whole project I forgot to defrost any chicken and dinner was two hours late.

I admit I balked at her suggestion that I save old hot-water bags so I could slice them up and make my own rubber bands. And I simply didn't have the inclination or the energy to put plastic bowl covers on the wheels of the stroller every time I brought it inside.

I knew I should. Betty Friedan aside, all the propaganda I heard and foolishly believed still told me that every woman not in traction was ecstatically embracing this new counteroffensive in the war against dirt. But somehow I simply couldn't work myself into a frenzy over it. That's just how it was with me. I knew what was expected of housewives. And I knew I was falling far short of the goal. But while I agonized over my shortcomings, I was only sporadically nudged into action. Besides, who wants to vacuum the living room when she can sit out on the lawn and show a little girl how to make daisy chains and acorn dolls instead?

"It'll be easier when the children are older," I told myself. "Then they'll be able to help around the house more. I know they try now. Sylvia wants to iron handkerchiefs. Jenny thinks folding towels is fun. And Geoffrey keeps trying to wield the broom and sweep the kitchen floor. But they're still a little short on dexterity. Once their skills catch up with their enthusiasm, it'll be a snap."

Naturally I was wrong. One of the basic truths, though no one ever repeats it to mothers of young children lest it cause them to run screaming into the street, is that a child's proficiency increases at the same rate his or her enthusiasm decreases. This leaves twenty minutes or so somewhere during the twelfth year when he or she is both willing and able.

Unfortunately I was usually out of the house at the time.

So though I was there the day Jenny did the laundry and vacuumed the dining room, but accidentally threw my only cashmere sweater into the washer with a load of sweat socks; though I was working out in the yard when she polished every flat surface in sight, but left a wet rag on the buffet where it created a white stain that looks like a cross between the outline of Massachusetts and a pregnant scorpion; and though I was cleaning the bathroom when she did all the dishes, but dropped a sterling silver spoon down the garbage disposal, I was gone when her ability caught up with her eagerness.

And the next day, when she could have boned a chicken and stuffed it whole—she was that clever—she decided to sleep on top of her bed so she wouldn't have to make it so often, and she dumped half a cup of grease down the sink with the explanation "Putting stuff away's not my job. And if Geoffrey left the grease in the pan, it's his fault."

I tried to nudge everyone into domestic responsibility. I nagged when I found a spongy bar of soap glued to the bottom of the tub and towels draped over everything but the towel rack. I reminded all and sundry that apple cores tossed in the general direction of the wastebasket should be picked up when they hit the wall and rebound into a shoe. And I harangued those who clogged the laundry chute with books, track shoes, and anything else that happened to be on their floor when I bellowed, "Clean up your room...now." I also had a few words to say about the clothes that were returned to me still folded after they had failed to make the great leap forward from the dryer to the chest of drawers.

It didn't do much good. Coats continued to lounge over the banister and across the backs of chairs. Muddy footprints continued to march in the back door and head for the refrigerator. And stacks of books, magazines, school reports, pencils, and pens continued to gather like conventioneers on the kitchen counters.

And though I still made periodic stabs at renewing my own vow to find a dusted place for everything and keep everything neatly in its place, reform never really took hold.

I agree I have a natural disinclination toward neatness. I also admit I consider trying to keep the house clean when there are six children around on a par with shoveling snow in a blizzard. But in my own defense, I must say things might be easier if all the labor-saving devices we have didn't refuse to save labor.

I don't know what's the matter. I don't mistreat them or speak ill of them in front of strangers. But they constantly rebel. The washer lurches across the utility room floor like a tethered bull, and the moment I hear it I have to dash in, turn it off, and shove it back against the wall before it rips out all the pipes. The dryer likes to keep spinning even when the door's open. So "tumble dry" shirts have to be snatched out on the downward swing of the tumble, and we all have to duck out of the way when tennis shoes sail across the room like hand grenades.

The stove turned off its oven light the first month we had it. I didn't mind since no one really wants a clear and lighted view of the inside of my oven. But I did object when it as much as said, "If you like that, wait till you see what else I can do," and proceeded to short out one burner and turn another to either a permanent simmer or off. I also found it cumbersome when the handle on the oven door dropped off. Now if I want to rescue the soufflé before it collapses, I have to pry the door open with gloved hands. And even Julia Child, who's in favor of "keeping it simple," would agree that cooking wasn't meant to be a handicap sport.

We've had several toasters over the years. We've had two-holers. We've had four-holers. We've had the ones with the little drawers that claim they're baby ovens and lead you to believe three-course meals have been baked in them. And we've had ones that say they "never, never, never need service." Perhaps they don't. One thing's for certain. You can never, ever, ever find someone who will service them. Or any of the other toasters either for that matter.

I know. I've tried. I tried to get someone to look at the toaster that heated one side and one side only. I went to three places with the one that carefully burned the toast, then tossed it up, out, and onto the floor. And I had a friend take a look at the one that barely warmed the bread. They all said the same thing: "It'll cost more to fix it than it would to buy a new toaster."

But the toasters were models of efficiency compared to the dishwasher. Joe bought it after the twins were born. I think he thought of it as a reward, a memorial in honor of my having survived the first month back in the States without Fusako-san. Whatever his intent, I was delighted, even if it was a portable model that hooked up to the sink and spent the rest of the day in the way.

Shortly after he got it, though, it turned eccentric like all our other appliances. First it worked its hose loose. Its debut performance came the day I went outside to plant some bulbs while the dishes were running through their various cycles. While I was gone, the dishwasher grunted and groaned till the intake hose broke free. Then it shot a stream of hot water across the kitchen and down the basement stairs.

Of course I'd stored all our camping equipment—the tents, the lanterns, the portable stove, and our considerable collection of sleeping bags—under the stairs. By the time I came back in the house and slid over to the sink to turn the faucet off, water was cascading down the stairs like a salmon ladder, and enough moisture had seeped through to soak even the badminton net on the bottom.

After we got the hose fixed, the timer went. I noticed it the morning the rinse cycle lasted for an hour. Naturally I sent out an immediate call for a repairman. He came...eventually. I suspect he had trouble with the directions I gave him on how to get to the house. I know he had trouble with the timer's directions. But only after he'd gone did I realize how much trouble he'd had. That was when I discovered he'd put the timer in backward so the wash cycle rinsed, the rinse cycle washed, and the soap cups sprinkled detergent over everything at the end.

We lived with this. And we made do. But then the motor lost interest, and I had to stand by to urge it along its appointed rounds. That eventually—I don't give up easily—is when we parted company.

I'd long since parted company with my ironing board. It was a miracle of modern design with legs that bowed out to allow the drudge at the controls to sit while she pressed. Though the idea was innovative, left-handers like me faced legs that bowed in, and after an hour or two at the controls we walked like a strolling band of lady cellists.

I'd also disposed of a homicidal electric knife. I'd given a marauding eggbeater up for adoption. And I'd destroyed a sponge mop that disintegrated in soap and water. Of course, as fast as each nonfunctioning appliance departs, progress sends another to take its place. So I remain a casual housekeeper with absolutely no chance of being named Homemaker of the Year.

But after all these years I've finally made peace with my inadequacies. I've learned not to dive under my desk when I hear a car door slam and remember Judy said she was going to stop by and pick up our extension ladder. I no longer apologize for the stack of books next to my bed or the condition of Robbie's room. I've stopped staring at the baseboards and saying to myself, "I should go at those with a toothbrush and a vat of cleanser."

And though I still sweep all the unfolded clothes into the dryer when company is due, though I still try to maintain a semblance of neatness in a majority of the rooms, and though I've finally trained myself to make my bed before I do anything else, I don't go into a decline and scrub for a week before every dinner party. I don't flog myself because I know someone who irons her husband's socks. And I don't compare myself to the two brothers who collected so much clutter it took the authorities two weeks to find them after they died.

I think it was the remodeling that made me stop trying to keep up with the Joneses' cleaning lady. Three years of knocking out walls, sanding plasterboard, and wading through sawdust will do that for you. Suddenly you discover no one faints if you have to move a stack of tiles off a chair so he or she can sit down. Headlines in the local paper don't scream, "Hostess Neglected to Dust," when you serve up a potluck supper in a half-finished dining room. And children aren't traumatized when they have to help build their own rooms or throw their own clothes in the washer because you're under the house, putting in heating ducts.

Then I discovered another basic truth. I found out that teen-age sons and daughters, while they may no longer volunteer to help Mommy vacuum the den, will do anything to earn enough money for a silk blouse or a stereo. So when the children were old enough, and it was obvious I'd never be able to live up to the housekeeping standards that still prevail even though women are now working outside the home and have little time left over for waxing and buffing, I hired them.

While their wardrobes grew and their record collection expanded, I looked out at the world through clean windows. I hung my coat in a neat and rearranged closet. And I came home to a shiny kitchen floor.

❧ From Pillar to Post

THE MOVING VAN wasn't the national truck when I was growing up. No one was singing, "My momma done told me. We're moving to Cleveland." And Christopher Robin wasn't patting Piglet on the head, saying, "Daddy's been made district manager in charge of personnel, so we're selling the Hundred Acre Wood and buying a split-level in Tucson."

Children grew up in the town where their parents had grown up. They sat in school desks carved with their cousins' initials, rode Dad's old bike to Saturday matinees, and skied down Miller's Hill on Granddad's old skis. The same teacher who'd given their sister a "Perfect" in spelling shook her head over their "ocasional" and "recieve." The same druggist who'd told their brother, "No, I won't let Prince Albert out of the can," told them, "No, I'm not moving the store because it's on the bus line and the bus is coming."

Children knew all their relatives when I was a girl. They knew that Uncle Walter was senile, so everyone gave him presents on his birthday and took them away the next day. They knew Aunt Bella had once been in love with a poet, and they giggled because she always stuffed handkerchiefs up her sleeve and down her considerable cleavage. And they had contests imitating Uncle George, who sounded like a bathtub draining when he laughed.

Children went to high school with the kids who'd been in their kindergarten class. Girls married boys they'd hated when they were six. And boys married the police chiefs' daughters or their best friends' little sisters.

Back in the 1940s and early 1950s houses weren't put up for sale every three or four years. Friends' mothers weren't real estate agents and didn't wear gold jackets. June wasn't the month for throwing going-away parties. Kids didn't spend July asking, "Any mail for me?" because their friends had moved to Tucumcari or were on a trip to Mexico. All their friends lived down the street, and Aunt Martha sent a card only on birthdays. Summers meant nights sleeping out in the clubhouse. It meant making a new raft because the old one had floated away in a winter storm. And it meant a Mickey Mouse watch bought with money earned by picking blackberries. No one went to Disneyland in June or flew to Santa Barbara in August to visit grandparents.

The universe was about ten miles wide in those days, and it was the rule rather than the exception to find yourself on your twenty-first birthday never having traveled farther than the state line.

In fact, I, a transplant from the Philippines who'd been relocated courtesy of World War II, was considered an oddity, a sort of "Children from Faraway Lands" in the flesh. A less theatrical ten-year-old would have cringed at such attention. Not I. I enjoyed my status as one of a kind. I even played it up.

"You mean you really lived in a village with headhunters?" friends who'd never been past the edge of town would say with a gasp.

"You bet."

"And you spent almost three years in a Japanese internment camp?"

"Right."

"Weren't you hungry?"

"Sure we were."

"What did you get to eat?"

"Oh, bananas...okra...rice." I struck a pose of studied nonchalance and added, "Of course, the rice usually had weevils in it."

This always got a big reaction, an "Oooo...yuck" at the very least, and it gave me a chance to slip in my zinger: "It wasn't so bad. Besides, the weevils gave us protein."

I was quite the attraction there for a while.

But time passed. Men who'd fought in Burma and spent a week in San Francisco before shipping out were no longer content to come home and settle down on a small farm in Iowa. Wives who'd waited out the war in San Diego were reluctant to go back to the cold of South Dakota's winters. And children born on a base in Florida were no longer curiosities in the second grade back in Topeka.

When bomber production gave way to Chevrolets and Studebakers, Americans packed their bags and, like the bear, drove over the mountain to see what they could see. And by the time I grew up and Joe and I got married people were folding their tents and moving on with regularity.

No one, however, moved more often than those of us in the military. We pulled up stakes at the drop of a transfer order. We got vaccinations for diseases our grandparents had never heard of. We settled down in towns we never knew existed. We sampled tacos, bagels, jambalaya, pizza, sukiyaki, macadamia nuts, and other strange delicacies. We added *y'all* and *so deska* to our vocabularies as automatically as we now mention polyunsaturated fats. And we traveled farther going home on one leave than many of our parents had in a lifetime. It may not have been a settled and stable existence, but it certainly made for variety.

The children seemed to thrive on all these comings and goings. They raced through each new house, checked out attics and basements for treasures left by former owners, and roared back to show me a one-legged doll or a truck or, in one instance, a set of his-and-hers bedpans.

They traded roommates. David shucked Sylvia and moved into delicious solitary confinement when Jenny emerged from the toddler stage. Geoffrey drew Robbie when a five-bedroom house gave Sylvia her own basement enclave and the arrangements upstairs were divided according to sex. And Joan remained under Jenny's fearsome tutelage till Joe retired and we built her a room of her own.

Like jet-setters who lunch in Paris and go on to London for dinner, they were casual about their travels:

"Oh, this slide of yours is all right. But nothing beats the marble slabs on either side of the stairs leading up to the Lincoln Memorial. Now those were slides."

"You think you have a neat Christmas tree, do you? Well, let me tell you about the national Christmas tree. It was something else with trees from all the different states on either side of it."

"You better not play with that. That's Dad's Fuji stick, from the first time he climbed Mount Fuji."

"You want to stay for dinner? Mom's making sushi."

On dull Sunday afternoons, when there was nothing

else to argue about, they fought over who was born in the best place:

"Don't think you're so smart, David? You were born in Texas."

"What do you know about Texas? You've never even been there."

"I know it's not as good as being born on Bainbridge Island."

"It is, too. Texas has tornadoes and neat thunderstorms. Bainbridge Island just has dumb old rain."

"I like rain. Besides, there aren't many people who were born on the island. Most of them had to go into Seattle. So I'm special."

"You think you're special? How about those of us who were born in Japan? We're Japanese."

"You are not, dummy."

"Are too."

"Are not."

The battles went on for hours, and kids from next door or up the street stood by with their mouths open, not daring to mention their births had taken place in the hospital across town.

But the older they got, the more they accumulated friends who were also world travelers and the more global the arguments became. Chuck, whose father was an engineer, had spent a couple of years in Teheran. Amy's family had bicycled through Europe two summers in a row. And Beth had been in seven schools in four years.

So after a while they went back to the time-honored "My brother's taller than your brother" and "Our dog's smarter than your dog" and "Bet you can't stuff a whole banana in your mouth."

It was better that way. Being the freaky new kid isn't so bad if it happens only once or twice. But if every couple of years you're the lone Dalmatian in a kennel of Saint Bernards, life can be tough. So it helped that more and more Americans were paraphrasing Horace Greeley and going west, south, east, north and "growing up with the country." It helped that other children had shallow roots, too.

Speaking for myself, I loved the nomad existence. For one thing, we were never anywhere long enough for the PTA to catch up with me and suggest I head the band uniform bake sale. For another, moving every couple of years gave me a chance to whip out old stories without having to worry that anyone but Joe would shift uncomfortably and mutter, "My God, that's the third time she's told that ridiculous tale about traveling across country with a monkey."

It was also a pleasure, on occasion, to shake the dust of a neighbor who hid behind curtained windows and rapped on the glass when one of the children took a shortcut across her property or a baseball sailed over the fence into her backyard. And I shed no tears when we said good-bye to our vertical front lawn either.

Of course, six of one neighbor was usually half a dozen of another and six of one lawn was half a dozen of another, too. When we bade farewell to the friends of David and Sylvia who wet the bed whenever they slept over, we said hello to a three-year-old with a hairdo that sprouted out of the top of her head like an atomic explosion. And we said hello to her every morning at six, when she turned up at our front door.

When we left the woman who liked to confide, "I don't have anything on under my muumuu, and it drives Vergil wild with desire," we gained Clara, who finished people's sentences for them.

Ah, Clara. A conversation with her was like trying to load a shaky mousetrap.

"Hi there," I'd say, "I just came back from—"

"The store."

"Right. Boy was it—"

"Crowded."

"Yeah, crowded. I could hardly—"

"Find a parking place."

My teeth would clench, and though a parking place was the thing I could hardly find, I'd do an immediate about-face and blurt, "No—a salesman. I could hardly find a—"

"Salesman."

Clara was quick, I'll say that for her. She inspired quickness, too. After I'd known her awhile, I found myself firing sentences at her, like rounds from a machine gun, in the vain hope I'd beat her to the period. I ran clauses together, leaped over parenthetical expressions, and changed pronouns in midstream. But it didn't do any good, and the only thing that saved my sanity was the fact that she eventually moved to a base in North Dakota.

As for lawns, when we left Hillcrest Heights and were finished with mowing the front grass alpine style—with pitons and a safety line around the waist—we gained irrigation problems. The altitude in Colorado Springs makes normal sprinkling a lesson in evaporation, and local gardeners recommend subterranean watering. So I rushed out and bought a contraption reminiscent of the pitchfork in Grant Wood's *American Gothic*, only in this instance the tines were hollow, with a hole at the point. When I got it home, I hooked the hose up to the bottom of the handle. Then I turned on the water, marched across the lawn, and, like someone searching for the septic tank, stabbed at the ground every couple of feet.

There was a certain fascination to the process. I liked watching the ground ripple and swell as I went along, and I never had to worry about the spray shooting in an open window. But if I didn't stab the sprinkler in at a precise angle or if I pulled it out carelessly, mud shot up at me. I spent whole summers looking as if I'd been in the front row when the gusher came in.

Still, in that move we'd gained sidewalks and a street that was safe for bicycling. We'd exchanged muggy summers when the air hung like steam in a sauna for Augusts with cool evenings and mornings that sparkled like ice in a water glass. And we'd traded the terrors of Washington, D.C., traffic: streets that came to a statue and vanished on the other side of General Somebody-or-other, intimidating tour buses, and the five o'clock rush on the Beltway for a left, a right, another left, and a straight shot to the center of town.

When Joe retired and we made the final move back to Bainbridge Island, though we left the sidewalks behind and though Joe swapped a three-mile drive to the office for thirty minutes on the ferry, we came into an acre of land, two apple trees, and only a couple of neighbors, one, because there's always one, who claimed we'd poisoned her well water when we built a toolshed out by the driveway.

Of course, there were disadvantages to moving about like balls of tumbleweed in the wind. The kitchen door never accumulated more than a few marks to show that David had grown an inch since March or Geoffrey was taller than Jenny had been a year ago. Robbie and Joan never got to spend an October weekend leaping off the tree house into a monumental pile of leaves because by the time they were old enough we'd left the tree house behind.

David never found another friend quite like Georgie, who brought him strawberries when he had the measles and shared his desk in the first grade. Sylvia missed out on a chance to be in the class that built miniature towns and wired them so streetlights shone and the garage looked as if someone were working late on a transmission job. And she had to give up the full scholarship to summer camp that she'd earned through a perfect attendance record in choir.

Jenny suffered, too. Though she moved away from Laura, a sometime friend who doled out her company like prizes in a Crackerjack box and was fond of saying, "I'm too busy to play with you today," and though she gained classmates who were more affable, they lived farther away than her bike was allowed.

Each child had his or her own regrets when we moved. Geoffrey missed the crabapple tree and remembered summer afternoons when he'd taken his lunch and sat under it. Sylvia hated leaving the mural, a girl with golden hair and a cat on her head, that her great-aunt Sylvia had painted on her bedroom wall. Jenny never got to accept first prize for the Bluebird who sold the most candy and nuts. Robbie had to say good-bye to Mrs. Keaton, who lived next door and had a cat that burrowed under the tablecloth like a giant mole. Joan had counted on walking to the first day of kindergarten with her brothers and sisters. And David's crush on Janet never had a chance to get past the "I can teach you how to add numbers in your head" stage.

Still, though the children couldn't count on growing up in the room they'd come home to at birth, though they'd forgotten their first-grade classmates by the time they hit the fourth grade, and though most of their relatives were virtual strangers whose faces blurred when they tried to remember them, some things remained constant.

Saturday morning always meant Joe would make pancakes and bacon and at least one child would be accused of using too much syrup. Bedtime always called for a story. I can still recite *The Story about Ping, Yo and the Yak, The Seashore Noisy Book, Wait Till the Moon Is Full,* and at least sixteen others by heart.

Thanksgiving always had the same menu, and each year another convert allowed as to how he was beginning to like green bean casserole. Each Christmas stockings always had a tangerine in the toe. The presents never went under the tree till Christmas Eve after everyone was asleep.

I always tried to make chocolate eggs for Easter and invariably added too much paraffin so they tasted like fat candles without a wick. And it always rained on Halloween.

Jenny always ate her breakfast with the Mickey Mouse fork and the Pluto spoon. We always had a special calendar in the kitchen, one that had stickers so you could put "Mom's Mean" on March 5 and "I Lost a Tooth" on August 3, and there was always a race to see who remembered to turn it when a new month began. Sylvia always split her Oreos and ate the filling first. Robbie always cleaned his room by dumping everything—shoes, sweaters, orange peels, old batteries, even bath towels—into the toy chest or his dresser drawer.

Geoffrey always carried Eeyore, his disintegrating donkey, with him. Joan always hated going to bed. David always got a puzzle in his Christmas stocking, and he always figured it out in five minutes or less. I always put silly poems and notes in everyone's lunch box. We always planted daffodil bulbs in the fall. We always looked for Orion high in the winter sky. And we always hated to see the leaves fall in the autumn.

That's because Joe always tried to organize family work

parties to rake them and always ended up more exhausted than anyone else, mainly because he'd done most of the work and had had to play foreman to a surly crew besides. The children's excuse was always: "But, Mom, if I do a good job, Daddy will make it mine forever." And he always answered by listing the chores he'd had to do as a child.

These constants were small. They didn't make up for best friends left behind, a good citizenship award lost in the last move, or awkward Septembers as the new kid in class. They didn't provide the security that comes with a fistful of summers mowing Mrs. Murphy's lawn, winters lying on the floor doing homework in front of the same fireplace, or springs looking in the woods for the same trilliums.

Still, when they're all home for Christmas and they're sitting in the kitchen long after dinner's over and I hear, "And then there was the time the movers packed Geoffrey's shoes and he traveled clear across the country barefoot. Boy, was Grandmother upset when she heard about it," they don't sound deprived.

≥ Batteries Not Included

MOTHER HAD A DOLLHOUSE when I was little, back when play was hard work and children were expected to do more than just sit there and watch Barbie and Ken develop a meaningful relationship.

It wasn't an elaborate structure. There were no fireplaces, no miniature Rubenses hanging on the living room wall, and no carpeted stairs. In fact, there were no stairs—period. The maid doll, complete with long black uniform, white apron, and starched white hat, had to leap through a hole in the upstairs floor when she'd finished making beds and wanted to get back to the kitchen.

But there were tiny chairs. There was a washing machine complete with a hand-cranked wringer. There were little silver forks and knives and spoons. There was a bowl of apples in the middle of the dining room table. And when I was allowed to play with it—the rules clearly stated that it belonged to Mother, not me—I thought it was the most glorious dollhouse in the world, and I could hardly wait to grow up and have one of my own just like it.

Of course, that was forty-some years ago. We all were apprentice housewives then. Boys—my brother, Geoff, included—got to climb trees, fly kites, dig for worms, get dirty, and, when no one was looking, spit through their teeth, but we girls played with dolls, cooked on toy stoves, made shapeless doll clothes on little sewing machines, and had carpet sweepers of our very own.

I was typical. Dolls lined my room like swallows on a telephone wire. I mixed up untold batches of flour and water biscuits, "baked" them in my oven, and fed them to Dick Deadeye, my pirate doll; to Emily, the "lady" doll with the china face and velvet cloak; to Kyoko, the Japanese baby; and to Heidi, the big rag doll I pretended was my sister. I ironed pinafores and pantaloons, swinging the iron back and forth to fan imaginary coals as I'd seen the amah do. And I cranked away on my toy sewing machine.

This palled after awhile, however, and though I continued to play with dolls, I now strapped them to the back of my tricycle and pedaled up and down the garden on an imaginary trip to Manila. I dragged Heidi with me when Geoff and I clambered down the narrow trail to walk along the edge of the rice terraces. Emily watched me crack walnuts by bashing them with my sewing machine. And I sat a couple of dolls in a chair while Geoff and I played pick-up-sticks or he taught me the rudiments of Monopoly.

When World War II interrupted the serenity of life in Luzon's Mountain Province and occupation troops herded us into internment camp, the toys and muffin pans and dolls, except for Heidi, stayed behind. It didn't matter. Mr. Ream, a genius at improvisation, made us girls sets of jacks out of twisted wire, and I learned "over the fence" and "into the well." He carved bamboo knitting needles, and we all made potholders and string bandannas for Christmas presents.

Hopscotch stones, of course, were free. The flagpole was always there as base for an impromptu game of hide-and-seek. And the bamboo rafters in the woodshed were perfect for hand-over-hand aerial tag.

On occasion we improvised. When a sudden tropical rainstorm drenched the parade ground, I, like the Pied Piper, led half the juvenile population of Camp Holmes outside to run and slide and roll in the mud till horrified mothers rushed out and dragged us to the showers. When simply seeing how high you could swing got dull, we gathered up pine needles, pumped as high as we could, then leaped off into them. And when I remembered Mother's dollhouse, I made a cardboard one of my own, with paper tables and chairs, rugs drawn on the floor in blue pencil, and one-dimensional dolls with arms that folded.

Like my other playthings, eventually it had to stay behind. And years later, when Joe and I got married, only Heidi, still in the dress Mother had made to match mine, was left to remind me that once upon a time little girls were mothers, little boys were cops and cowboys, and no one was in charge of remembering to get batteries.

C cells and D cells leaped out of the flashlight and into the toy chest somewhere around 1961, when Jenny was celebrating her first Christmas. Up till then life in my children's toyland was pretty much as I'd remembered it from my own childhood.

With his first steps David had staggered out the front door, dragging a wooden push mower with colored balls that rattled and bounced as he bumped along the sidewalk. The family power mower was still something only the Joneses had, and it would be a year or two before it filtered down to Fisher-Price and the air force base exchange toy department.

David had wakened from his naps to find various teddy bears and Big Fierce, a lion with a daisy in its mane, sitting in his crib, waiting to play. And for long trips to the end of the block he'd scooted along on his horse with wheels.

Of course, he had other toys. Assorted grandmothers, aunts, uncles, and cousins had sent him rattles, handmade biplanes, monkeys that swung on the railings and hung by their tails, and an inflated clown that always bounced back. But one can take only so much of an ever-grinning clown, especially when there's a whole world out there waiting to be felt, tasted, smelled, peered, and poked at. And when your mother is someone who doesn't want you to grow up without having rolled down a hill or felt mud squishing through your toes, you don't spend a lot of time punching a clown.

So the monkey swung by himself much of the time while David chased an ice cube around the tray of his highchair and watched it melt into a nondescript puddle. The plane stayed on the ground while he scrunched up cellophane and listened to it crackle or stuffed his finger down the hole in the playpen. The rattles were tossed aside because dry beans bouncing off each other were nothing compared to the glorious *WHAM* of a cookie sheet being dropped on the floor or two saucepan lids crashing together. And the clown stood neglected while toilets were inspected, grass was ripped up and flung at the dog, and Scotch tape was transferred back and forth from one finger to another.

By the time Sylvia arrived the toy chest was filling up. Stuffed animals lay under chalkboards and raveling Easter baskets. Wooden cars that clicked and snapped were thrown in with deflated beach balls and sand pails. A toy piano perched on top of a duck that quacked and flapped its wings when you pulled it after you across the room. And sprinkled through them all, like croutons in a tossed salad, were blocks. There were always blocks. They were the ultimate toy.

I tried to interest Sylvia in dolls, but she would have none of it. I can't say that I blame her. Rag dolls like Heidi were fading, and in their place was Chatty Cathy, nineteen inches of hard plastic and programmed conversation. You couldn't discuss fairy godmothers or a secret hiding place with Cathy the way I'd been able to with Heidi. She didn't want to hear anyone's problems. She wanted her blond rooted hair combed, and she wanted it combed now.

Ironing didn't excite Sylvia either. No doubt she'd heard me swearing over a dirndl skirt or a raglan sleeve. She might even have caught a few of Joe's comments as he viewed a refrigeratorful of damp unironed clothes. And as for tea sets with tiny cups and saucers, she invariably trundled them to the sandbox, where they were used to dig and scrape and help fill up David's dump truck. I shrugged my shoulders and vacuumed up the sand by the front door.

When Jenny came along, however, and woke up one morning to find that this was the Christmas Day everyone had talked about, we were in Tokyo, Santa's manufacturing plant, and the stack of presents under the tree looked as if Santa had emptied his entire bag at our house.

There were games and balls, bean-bags and sumo piggy banks. There were origami kits and trains, organ grinders and race cars, kokeshi dolls and china dishes, paints and storybooks. David got a sheriff set complete with hat and star. Still trying, I gave Sylvia a big cloth doll that had elastic on its shoes so you could slip its feet on yours and dance. Sylvia whirled around the floor once or twice and went to inspect David's Etch-a-sketch.

It was munificence at its height and though Playskool and Mattel were generously represented in the packages from home, the local offerings were made in Japan. Unfortunately, "Here you go. It's yours to play with" had been replaced with "Wait a minute, let me put in the batteries" and "Unh...unh...unh, don't touch."

"Wait a minute, let me put in the batteries," Joe said as David waited to get his hands on the new engine. "Don't touch," he added as he put the thing down on the floor and it whistled, blew smoke, and went around in circles.

"Here let me wind it up," I said as I cranked the key on the organ grinder's monkey. "Don't touch, you'll break it," I warned as I set it down and we stood back and watched it skate around and clap its cymbals together.

"Don't touch the robot," David barked as the flashing mechanical man stalked over to where Jenny was lying on the floor playing with a discarded box. "Just look at it."

"Don't touch, just look." That was the password that Christmas. It was also the phrase of the month the next Christmas, when Mother came to visit and spent December flashing yen in a toy store on Yoyogi Street.

But I'm no dummy. I noticed that after two or three days of standing by while the engine whistled and puffed and ran into the coffee table, David dumped it into the toy chest and forgot it. I didn't need any prompting to realize the thrill was gone when Sylvia let the monkey skate under her bed and left it there to entertain the gum wrapper and the old sock. And when the robot's batteries corroded and no one suggested we replace them, I didn't need a cue card to tell me they'd all lost interest.

So it was back to blocks and swings and hanging by your knees on the monkey bars. And by the time Jenny pulled herself to her feet and Geoffrey, the latest occupant in the playpen, was finally sitting I was over my brief infatuation with "battery-powered" and "wind clockwise."

It hadn't been a passionate affair. I'd known all along that a child's imagination is nothing to be trifled with. So now I ignored the chickens that laid eggs, the bathtub motorboats that tried to ram the drain, and the friction cars that refused to be driven over the sheets and around the pillow to Grandmother's house in the blankets.

I also let lie the host of coloring books and paint-by-number Little Bo Peeps. When freezing days and snowy afternoons kept everyone inside, I brought out rolls of butcher paper and they drew the route to Georgie's house or David's box kite in the wind. When night came early in the winter, I put up the card table, covered it with a blanket, and they all crawled into an igloo in Alaska. I let them sit in an empty bathtub and smear finger paint murals on the tiles. And when summer rains poured out of the sky, I remembered how it feels to run and slide through mammoth puddles and sent them out to try it for themselves.

Joe, who'd objected all along to being sent on various battery runs, relaxed again. He spent Saturday afternoons down in the hollow across the street, shagging balls and flying ten-centers (balsa wood airplanes) with David and his friends. He galloped after Sylvia when as a neophyte bicycler she wove in and out between the concrete clothesline poles and crashed into a bush. He caught Jenny and Geoffrey as they leaped off the picnic table and shrieked with delight at their own daring. And in the hot, muggy summer, when he came home from work, he joined them all in the giant wading pool and let them ride on his back as he circled underwater like a trained dolphin.

But when time and travel orders drove us back to the States, we discovered that "sit and watch" toys had journeyed across the Pacific in our absence. They were also big business, and on Saturday mornings, between segments of "George of the Jungle" and "The Road Runner," precocious children with straight teeth and professionally arranged freckles hawked eternal amusement and constant delight on television. The greed and desire they created were reinforced by the Christmas catalogue, known to its devotees as the Wish Book.

"Oooo, Mom, look at this," I'd hear thirty times a day from the first of November on. "Can I have one of these?" and "How about one of these?" and "Will you ask Grandmother to buy me one of these?"

The selection was enormous, and it certainly had caught up with the sixties. GI Joe, complete with scars, battle dress, and tiny hand grenades, was there for little boys who found news footage from Vietnam inspiring. Barbie had obviously read *The Feminine Mystique* and wasn't about to settle down with Ken in a split-level house in suburbia to raise hard plastic children with jointed hips. Of course, she wasn't out protesting on campuses either. Barbie's social conscience extended to her wardrobe. It went no farther.

Toys continued to keep up with the times, and the times were certainly achangin'. Each new television season brought a new set of dolls. Batman, Robin, and the Flintstones gave way to Mr. Spock and the starship *Enterprise*.

The realism that would develop into "telling it like it

is," and "letting it all hang out" took baby dolls that once had wet, closed their eyes, and wailed a passable "Mama," and taught them to wave, chew, pout, giggle, crawl, squirm, do somersaults and bleat non sequitur complaints. And when that grew commonplace, it had them consume large amounts of a "nontoxic gel" so they could have their disposable diapers changed.

Barbie acquired a tan. She moved into a house complete with a TV, louvered windows, a water bed, a pool, a barbecue grill, and potted rubber plants. And her closet was jammed with outfits for every sport with the possible exception of elk hunting. Ken grew his hair. He developed a five o'clock shadow and shaved it off before splashing on cologne. He flexed his "poseable wrists" and his one "gripping hand."

Make-believe kitchens, with food processors, dishwashers, microwave ovens, and water-dispensing refrigerators, now had more appliances than Betty Crocker ever dreamed of. Small cereal boxes, plastic butter, cheese, and cartons of eggs were now available for eight-year-olds who'd once made do with let's pretend and "Teddy, would you like another piece of pie?" And battery-operated vacuum cleaners, despite women's liberation, let little mothers clean the house while miniature dads pedaled along the sidewalk and shouted, "Breaker, breaker," on their little CBs.

I, however, turned a deaf ear to each new barrage of "Please, Mom, I won't ask for anything else, really I won't." I knew that Sissy Love a Lot, whose hair grew and retracted, most likely would be bald and ugly by spring. And I knew that games guaranteed to keep the whole family in a state of feverish excitement for hours would be tossed aside in favor of one "Hey, anyone want to play squashed sardines?"

I gave easels, paints, chalk, and colored pencils. I bought David puzzles, chemistry kits, Erector sets, and *Tom Swift* books. I went over the budget for carpenter tools for Geoffrey, who loved to help Joe build shelves. Sylvia and Jenny got knitting needles and yarn and tiny pans for thumbprint tarts. I gave them cookbooks and puppets and books that showed them how to make a TV set out of a cardboard box. And the twins got wooden boxes with odd-shaped holes and matching odd-shaped blocks. They got a pounding bench for whacking with a hammer, a wooden ark, and sacks of the prehistoric animals that had ignored Noah's "Yoo-hoo. The waters are rising. It's time to go."

For the most part my gifts were received without a great deal of enthusiasm. They were initially put aside in favor of the flashier offerings from Grandmother. By March, however, when Robbie had taken apart the genuine roadster, guaranteed to go three miles an hour and bash into cupboards, chairs, the lacquer table, and me, I noticed he was still marching tyrannosaurs through the shag and letting them swim in the bottom of the vaporizer. And when Sylvia had put the cat in Joan's stroller and collapsed it, and Jenny's high heels had snapped their elastic straps, they went back to making peanut butter cookies and putting on original plays.

"Face it, honey," Joe said, "you're simply someone who's appreciated after the fact."

Mother was less nonchalant. "I don't understand it," she grumbled. "Robbie told me he wanted that car more than anything in the world, and now look. It's in shambles, but he has yet to lose even one of those dinosaurs."

She also blamed me. "How could you let him do that?" she said. "That car cost twenty-nine ninety-five."

"Don't look at me," I protested. "I told you not to buy it."

"Still," she muttered, "you could have made sure he took care of it."

It was the "not quite dirty" clothes all over again. Mother, who'd had an amah to supervise Geoff and me when we were in the "Let's take it apart and see how it works" stage, didn't understand how it is when you have to clean, cook, chauffeur, wash, and unclog the drain as well as keep tabs on six boisterous children. And she didn't understand my contention that if you give a gift, you let it go and don't lurk in the shadows, monitoring its use.

"What it boils down to is this," I told her time and time again. "You should have known he'd get bored just sitting there, bouncing off the furniture, and sooner or later he'd try to dismantle it to see what made it go."

"Still..." she repeated, and the argument raged on.

It didn't matter, though. The older they got, the less they played with toys and the more they created their own amusements. True, Jenny craved a Barbie doll and eventually traded her roller skates for an extra one that her cousin Laura didn't want. But she also baked cakes and cookies in her Easy-Bake oven and on my birthday rushed in at the end of dinner to present me with two tiny apple pies.

When I vetoed the idea of a fish tank with undersea castles, coral rockeries, and a full complement of fish, she converted an old shoe box into an aquarium. She turned it on its side, threaded an assortment of fish through the top, glued rushes and seaweed to the bottom, and covered the front with plastic wrap.

David seemed delighted with the "improve your swing" tennis kit. He took it outside, put the weighted bag on the lawn, and swung at the tennis ball that was attached to a lengthy rubber band. But when the band pulled loose and the tennis ball sailed off into the blackberry bushes, he bagged it. He and Geoffrey chose instead to sink tuna fish cans into the grass and play golf with Joe's old clubs.

Sylvia played with her family of small dolls, sat them at their dining room table, and let them sleep in their beds. We even spent a whole day during spring vacation making a movie of *A Day in the Life of Sylvia's Dolls*. I manned the camera and lay prostrate on the living room floor, while Sylvia, Jenny, the rest of the family, and half the neighborhood moved arms, legs, heads and crash-landed a wooden plane.

But when that was over, she went back to making parachutes out of blankets so she could leap off the top of our VW bus. And she and Jenny, having watched Samantha wriggle her nose on "Bewitched," decided they, too, had supernatural powers. So they muttered secret incantations. They put hexes on everyone, especially me when I snarled, "Sit up straight and finish your dinner," or, "Go to your rooms...both of you...*NOW*." And when their friends tired of magic and potions and "eye of frog and hair of bat," they consoled themselves with the fact that "She wasn't a real witch anyway."

David and Geoffrey set up miles and miles of race tracks. When we remodeled our house and their rooms were separated only by bare studs, the tracks wove in and out from one room to the next and back again. When the walls went in, Geoffrey, who'd graduated from his carpenter set to Joe's hammer and circular saw, went outside and built clubhouses. Robbie and Joan helped him. They were drafted with only the promise "I'll let you sleep in it" as their reward.

They made several of them. One in the corner of the front yard had a loft. Another was carpeted with remnants donated by Grandmother. A third was thirty feet off the ground in the huge fir at the end of the driveway.

That was the one they later converted into a launching pad for their aerial tramway. They got the idea from Aunt Sylvia, who had one at her cabin on Whidbey island. My uncle Rupert furnished them with a pulley, and they strung three-quarter-inch line from the tree, across the road, over a patch of blackberries to a padded post in the clearing below. They worked on it for weeks. They tightened. They adjusted. They sent dummies zooming across the road.

Then came the day for the trial run. It was in the afternoon. Everyone else was off somewhere, and I was the sole spectator. In deference to the height of the launching pad they decided to take off from the top of a stepladder planted in the middle of the road. Robbie was first. Joan allowed as to how she'd wait till some future date for her turn.

While I held the ladder and Geoffrey hauled up the pulley with a towrope, Robbie scampered up and teetered on the top. Then he grabbed the pulley, leaped off into space, and sailed down to the meadow. We all yelled and cheered and danced in circles.

Then it was Geoffrey's turn. Again I held the ladder while he climbed up and reached for the pulley.

"Geronimo," he called as he jumped off, slid down the line, slowed, and came to a stop dangling over the blackberries.

He'd forgotten one thing. He hadn't taken into account the fact that three years Robbie's senior, he outweighed him by about twenty pounds.

"Mom...help," he cried, hanging there and trying not to lose his grip.

"Kick," I shouted. "See if you can edge yourself down farther."

But it was too late, and with a groan he dropped off and out of sight into the blackberries.

"Oh, Lord," I said with a gasp, "I have to do something, but what?"

What else? I had to play Supermom and rush in to rescue him. Since the bushes failed to part like the Red Sea, I collapsed the ladder and threw it over the bush in front of me. Then, while the spiny runners scratched my legs and tore at my blouse and my shorts, I balanced on the rungs and stumbled in to retrieve Geoffrey.

Finally I reached him. "OK," I said, "now jump up on my back."

He did, and though I sagged under his weight, I managed to turn around and wade slowly, laboriously, through the thicket and back out to the road.

Needless to say, that ended the romance with the tramway. Even Robbie decided the thrill was gone. And Joan, who'd been somewhat leery about sliding through the sky all along, seemed relieved to be off the hook.

But it didn't end the building. By the next spring Geoffrey had sunk his savings into oak and was building a sailboat. He stored lumber under the couch, in the hall, and at times in the middle of the living room. It took him three years, but he finished it. He sailed in it for a whole summer. And when a winter storm bashed it up against a couple of logs, he hauled it out of the water and worked another year repairing it.

In the meantime, Robbie, who was still leaping off things, this time under the precarious wings of a hang glider, took his turn at the hammer and saw. He built a rack to fit on the car and carry the glider he'd borrowed. It was a ungainly structure, made out of two-by-fours. When it was finished and bolted to the car, the station wagon looked as if it had been delivered in a box and we hadn't taken it out yet.

Joan, however, outdid them all. She sewed. She embroidered. She made cutting boards and candleholders. Then, in her freshman year of high school, she did the ultimate. She made a dollhouse.

It's a glorious building with a porch, an attic, bay windows, and a shingled roof. And ever since the day we hauled it home in the back of the station wagon, she's been painting the ceilings, papering the walls, putting in rugs, staining and upholstering furniture. She's furnished the kitchen. She's created a playroom. She's made bedspreads and polished the stairs.

Unlike Mother's dollhouse, however, this one is well on its way to being elaborate. There's a sewing basket and a pot of daffodils in the bedroom, a meat grinder and a cherry pie in the kitchen, a coatrack, a grandfather clock, a box of stationery, and a rocking horse. All in all it's a place I could easily move into.

And I just might since like Mother, Joan lets me play with her dollhouse. But then why shouldn't she? I've had practice, and I'm very careful, even though I never did have one of my very own.

ε From Dr. Dentons to Calvin Kleins

STRIDE INTO ANY DEPARTMENT STORE IN THE COUN-
try, look at the folks wandering up and down the aisles,
and you'll see two groups of people: those who like to
shop and the rest of us who are there only because our
last pair of clam diggers disintegrated in last week's wash.
It's easy to tell the difference between the two.

Those who like to shop stroll past the lumbering wheels
of pantsuits and coordinated separates. They stop to flip
through an assortment of blouses, pick out one or two,
and are often heard to mumble, "I bet this one will go
well with the mauve jacket I bought last week."

They march without hesitation into dressing rooms and
reappear minutes later to ask, "Do you have this in a
periwinkle blue? This color doesn't seem to do anything
for my eyes." And when they buy a suit, they automatically move on to pick out a blouse, two scarves, a matching purse, shoes, an extra pair of panty hose, just in case,
and they pause in the lingerie department to see if the
new shipment of nylon briefs with a brushed cotton crotch
has come in yet.

Those of us who hate to shop usually stand by the front door for a while in the forlorn hope that someone will announce, "There's a fire on the third floor. Will everyone please evacuate the premises quickly and quietly?" When this doesn't happen, and those trying to edge past us start shoving, or we hear someone mutter, "For God's sake, lady, get out of the way," we take a deep breath and venture down the nearest aisle.

It's usually the one with finer jewelry or cosmetics, and because saleswomen in these departments are perfectly groomed and always look as if they're there under sufferance, we clasp our purses over the missing button on our coats. Then we check our shoes to see if perhaps we've stepped in something. And we proceed.

When we finally find the department we want, and heaven knows we rarely plan to visit more than one, we mince up to the saleswoman and bleat, "Do you have suits?"

Of course, they have suits. We're standing under a sign that says Spring Suits. But those of us who hate to shop live by the credo "They never have what I want." So we hope against hope she'll say, "Sorry, we're all out. Why don't you come back next week?"

This will give us a chance to cluck, "Gee, that's too bad. I was really set on buying a suit today, and I'm all booked up next week. Well...that's the way it goes."

But it never works that way. "We have hundreds of them," the saleswoman announces joyously. "What kind of suit are you looking for?"

"Oh, I don't know," we grumble, "something that fits and will last, I guess."

She flinches ever so slightly. But saleswomen are a hardy lot, and she's not about to let us get her down. So the smile returns, and like John Wayne leading the platoon into battle, she tosses her head and surges forward.

The first suit is usually the same color as the one we bought the year we were married. And since it didn't wear out till our oldest child entered the fourth grade, we shake our heads.

"No, I don't think so."

The second has a skirt that's slightly gathered at the waist. But Jane Pauley recently interviewed a fashion expert who advised women with pudgy torsos to stay away from gathers at the waist. So we demur.

"No, that's not quite right either."

The third is passable.

"How much is it?" we ask meekly.

She shuffles through the tags hanging from the sleeves, checks the label and the care instructions at the neck and digs through the pockets. Finally she comes up with it.

"Sixty-eight ninety-five," she trills.

We gulp. Those of us who hate to shop are never up with the current prices, and all we remember is that our going-away outfits cost $22.50.

"And the skirt's fifty-five dollars."

This is when our breathing gets shallow and we start to hyperventilate.

"You're lucky. It's on sale," she adds, dumping salt into the gaping wound.

Shopping enthusiasts thank her and move on, first to another department, then to other stores. And they compare prices and fabrics and check the workmanship before they come back and say, "I've made a decision. I'll take it." But we who hate to shop don't. Instead, we heave a sigh and say, "Oh, all right, go ahead and ring it up."

This startles the saleswoman. "Wouldn't you like to try it on first?" she asks, appalled that we'd even suggest making a purchase without first seeing that it fit.

We wouldn't, of course. We want nothing more than

to snatch up our packages and flee. But saleswomen intimidate those of us who'd rather be home reading *Dental Surgery—The First Hundred Years.* Since this one's waiting, standing there looking like our fifth grade math teacher, we dare not refuse. We slink off to the dressing rooms.

It should be noted here that dressing rooms are one of the prime reasons we hate to shop. They have an unsavory reputation, and they deserve it. From the louvered barroom doors that give casual passers-by an enticing view of head and bare legs to the fluorescent lighting that sucks out a person's coloring and leaves nothing but freckles, blemishes, and sallow shadows, they are chambers of horrors. And the trauma is increased by the fact that we who hate to shop never come prepared to try on anything.

So while our more enthusiastic sisters in the rooms next to us slide shirtwaists and Ultrasuede over their immaculate laytex and spandex underwear, we stare at an eighteen-hour bra that's in its nineteenth hour and a girdle that's pocked with stretched-out grip marks, the result of too many years of being yanked on and peeled off. While they remember to wear stockings and just the right shoes, we have to imagine how the suit will look without knee-socks and old sneakers.

The dressing room procedure never takes long. If the suit fits, even barely, we buy it. And because we never have any strength left over for picking out accessories, we flash the charge card, sign the receipt, and scurry out of the store before our consciences have a chance to remind us there's a sale on children's sweat shirts in the basement.

That's another thing we hate: sales. The sight of tables laden with odd sizes, last season's newest craze, or a pile of sling-back pumps may quicken the pulse of a dedicated shopper but causes, in the rest of us, something that closely resembles claustrophobia.

While shopping aficionados may spring out of bed in the morning and greet the day with a song because the paper says the Bon Marché is offering a special on car coats, the rest of us flip past the ads and concentrate on Ann Landers's advice to "Pure and Puzzled in Toledo." And though we rejoice with those who got Welsh fisherman's sweaters for thirty percent off, we know the only discount we'll ever get is one we stumble on. So we shake our heads sadly when they plead, "You ought to go down and at least look at what they have." And we wave our arms and scream, "No, no," when they add, "You know, if you buy something and decide you don't like it, you can always take it back."

It's because we know we won't take it back. We never take anything back.

"Oh, I'll fit into it after I've lost a couple of pounds," we tell ourselves when the alternative is another trip downtown, another selection to choose from, and another trip to the dressing room.

"Maybe one of the girls will want it in a couple of years.

"Maybe I can wear the jacket and give the skirt to my cousin."

Of course, the skirt or the blazer or the three-piece dress hangs in the closet till the price tag becomes a collector's item, reminding us of the good old days when "a person could get a good suit for only..." Finally we have to haul it down to the Bargain Boutique, it's sold for a third of what it cost. But we don't mind. Anything's better than going back to the store. And when friends sigh and say, "I don't understand you," we simply shrug. That's because we don't understand them either.

We don't understand why they like to search through two racks of slacks till they find one that's belted in the back. We don't understand why anyone would want to spend a whole January afternoon going from one store to another looking for bathing suits. And I will never understand why anyone would claim to enjoy shopping for school clothes.

But then I'm a throwback. Mother loved hot August days when she, with me in reluctant tow, hit every store in town and traipsed from one department to another till she was satisfied I was ready to go back to school. She didn't mind the fact that I was sweltering as I struggled out of wool skirts and struggled into long-sleeved dresses and coats with their linings zipped in. She looked on the search for the perfect half-slip as a challenge. And she never bolted when our number in the shoe department was eighty-five, there were only two clerks on duty, and they were waiting on thirty-two and thirty-three.

Mother loved to shop. I, as I said, don't. When the children were small and I was in charge of outfitting them for school, I looked forward to the excursion with the same enthusiasm I'd have if I were preparing to lead a group of enraged drug addicts through an exhibit of Steuben crystal.

I began to get uneasy in late July.

"Look at what you've done to your good pants," I'd wail as Geoffrey slithered down out of a tree and wandered into the house. "They're ruined."

"No, they're not," he'd answer as he ripped the rest of his pocket off and picked at the pitch on his knee. "'Cause I'm going to cut them off and make shorts."

"But—"

"Besides, we'll be getting school clothes pretty soon, and then I'll have a new pair of good pants."

"But—"

"You didn't expect me to wear these back to school, did you?"

"No, but—"

"Then what's wrong?"

What was wrong was that the last pair of pants to break out at the knee, shred at the cuff, or give way at the seams meant I could no longer ignore the fact that it was almost that time of year again. And in the next few weeks every time I turned around another sash had pulled loose, another sleeve had torn, and another pair of shoes was flapping like an angry platypus.

When I could ignore the cues no longer, I began the ritual. First came the sorting. I dug through closets, pawed through old trunks, and searched through drawers, looking for anything that might be handed down. Coats and jackets were especially valuable since the sentence "We have to buy new coats for everyone" is synonymous with "Call the bank. We need a loan."

As a rule, not much was available, and no one wanted what was. Oh, Jenny would gladly have taken the dress I'd made for Sylvia when we were in Japan and I had time to sew. It was red plaid, with long sleeves, a Peter Pan collar, a gathered skirt, and a black velveteen vest. It had taken me two weeks to whip it up, and Sylvia hated it. She didn't hate it enough to let Jenny have it, however.

There were also outfits left over from the toddler years, when children grow out of their clothes in three months. These refused to wear out, and like a ball bouncing down the stairs, they went from one child to another until finally even the twins outgrew them and we joyously packed them up and raced them to the nearest Goodwill depository.

After the sorting it was list time.

"Whatcha doing, honey?" Joe always asked brightly when he found me grubbing around checking out everyone's supply of socks and underwear.

"What does it look like?" I snarled. "I'm figuring out who needs what new clothes."

"Oh, good," he exulted. "I was wondering when you were going to get to that."

Joe as a career military officer liked nothing better than to see appointed tasks being done at their appointed time. But he should have had the sense to keep quiet about it. For not only did I resent the fact that it was time to go shopping again, but I also resented the fact that I had to do it. And the realization that Joe would be at home reading the paper or watching a ball game while I staggered through the store with my band of quarreling pint-size consumers infuriated me.

Of course, it was worse later when I shamed him into coming with us and he, who remembered when shoes cost $4 a pair, sucked wind and rattled the change in his pocket every time he caught sight of a price tag.

And eventually, when we divided the sexes and he took the boys, everyone came home grumbling, and no one spoke to him or to each other for days.

But in the beginning I was still the lone shopper, and it was still solely up to me to see that everyone arrived at school on the first day with clean fingernails, a shiny face, and new clothes from inside out.

Once I'd checked to see what would last awhile longer—nothing ever would since all children's clothes are made to self-destruct in August—I wrote out the list. For the most part I used the "one on, one in the drawer, one in the laundry" formula. This applied to shirts, pants, pajamas, and dresses. When T-shirts gained acceptance and were no longer simply the costume of a boy or girl headed for PE, they were included in the shirt quota.

In the single-item category were coats, mittens—invariably they were lost by the time the cold weather set in—hats, bathrobes, boots, and sweaters. Shoes were one for school, one for play until America took to the streets, the highways, and the back roads. When Nikes and A-didas at $50 and $60 a pair began showing up everywhere except at formal weddings and New York debutante parties, I reduced the shoe allotment to one pair.

After I'd finished the list, there was nothing left but the deed itself. So, on the appointed Saturday, I took a deep breath and made sure everyone had on socks that not only matched but were also clean. Then I loaded them all in the car and waved good-bye to a far too cheerful Joe.

During the trip to the store I laid out the ground rules:

"There will be no side trips to the bathroom, the car, the mechanical horse in the parking lot, or the toy department without my permission.

"The boys will go first, the girls second.

"No fooling around in the dressing rooms.

"Everyone has to carry his or her own packages.

"Yes, you can try on all your stuff when we get home.

"No, we're not stopping at the doughnut shop on the way down."

When we got to the store, I looked for a saleswoman who seemed equal to the task. We couldn't link up with someone who'd give out and feign a headache or a coffee break before we got to the cardigans. Then it began.

"Yes, thank you, you may help me. . . . Let's see, I need six of these in size eight, six in size ten, and six in size four. . . . Robbie, come out from behind there. . . . That's perfect, now on to the socks. . . Make his blue, his white, and his striped—I need to be able to tell whose are whose when they come out of the dryer.... Hush, Jenny, I'll get to you in a minute.... You have to what?... Oh, all right, but come right back, and Sylvia, you stay here.... Are these shirts permanent press?... Geoffrey, you forgot your socks."

And so it went. The boys complained because they had to wait for the girls. Geoffrey refused to let the saleswoman bring another shirt into the dressing room because she'd see him in his underwear. Jenny wanted a pair of satin slippers with fuzz on them. Joan wanted to know if she could wear her Snoopy nightgown that night. Sylvia said all her friends had training bras. David begged to be allowed to go out and sit in the car since he was sweating. I lost all feeling in my left hand, and the fingers in my right were atrophied in a permanent clutch position. The saleswoman had developed a tic. And as we all staggered out to the car, it suddenly hit me that a shopping mother must certainly have been the one who first invented martinis.

Once home they had to try on everything—socks, underwear, boots, everything—and model them for Daddy. He oohed and aahed appropriately, and in between he niggled. "Come on, tell me. How much did it all come to?"

But I was exhausted and the prospect of "You spent *how* much? Why, do you know when I was a boy..." was more than I could take. So I declined to answer on the ground that I'd suffered enough and excused myself to go start dinner.

This went on for years. And as the snarling seventies roared in and styles changed, discussions in the dressing room, especially with Sylvia and Jenny, got more heated.

I admit the fault was mine. One look at Bainbridge

High School letting out for the day should have told me that the current uniform was jeans or thirteen-button bell-bottomed trousers, a blouse that looked like my old maternity clothes, four-inch-thick sandals, pierced ears, and long, stringy hair parted down the middle. But Mother objected to the latest "look," and since I was like a rope bridge spanning the gap from her world to theirs and since I'd grown up with "What will people think?" virtually tattooed on my brain, I sided with her.

"Sylvia dear," she'd say in a disapproving tone that automatically canceled out the "dear," "you're such a pretty girl. Why do you have to dress like a slob?"

"I like what I'm wearing," Sylvia would come back with a brazenness I envied. "Besides, no one wears old-fogy clothes anymore."

"Now, now," I, ever the peacemaker, would admonish, "that's enough of that." And because I'm cursed with a tendency to sarcasm, I'd add, "You do look as if you're in your third month, and God knows how you can walk in those shoes."

This encouraged Mother and alienated Sylvia, who until she came downstairs had thought she looked smashing. So jaws tightened, teeth clenched, and a sullen cloud hung over the proceedings.

Eventually I learned that some things matter while others don't. And I learned that if you harp on those that don't, you'll lose out on those that do. Being in school, for instance, matters. Three earrings in one ear don't...not really. Coming in on time matters. Fingernails painted black don't. A fairly even disposition, especially in a family where teen-agers are in the majority, matters. Alice Cooper posters on the bedroom wall don't.

I learned that children aren't like the correct handbag or the perfect scarf. They aren't necessarily supposed to match what you're wearing, nor were they designed to complement your outfit.

I learned that the only answer to "What will people think?" is: "They'll think whatever they please, so there's no use letting real or imagined public opinion determine how you live your life."

And somewhere along the way I learned that shopping for school clothes, like the two o'clock feeding, colic, and diapers, eventually fades into the past.

The first time I was able to hand them the charge cards, set a limit on the total expenditure, and send them out in groups of two and three to augment their wardrobes on their own, I felt like someone who'd just received a call from the governor.

"Do you realize..." I told Joe as I poured myself another cup of coffee and settled down to read the paper, "can you actually grasp how marvelous it is to be sitting here while others decide whether or not the shoe fits, the sleeves bind, the pants ride high, or the press is permanent?"

"I certainly do." He sighed. Then, because to him a day without worry is like a day without sunshine, he added. "I hope to God they don't lose the charge cards."

They didn't, of course, at least not often. They also didn't get everything bought in one day. David did, but then he's like me: He bolts after the first hour. And Robbie got impatient and decided to wear Geoffrey's old corduroy slacks after all. But Geoffrey had to go back twice to find just the right shirts. Jenny had to come home and plead for cash because "the most beautiful coat I've ever seen in my whole life" was on sale in a store where we had no account. And Sylvia and Joan wandered from store to store to store while Sylvia picked out one pair of jeans and Joan bought some knee socks and a sweater.

"You two take after your grandmother," I told them, shuddering at the very thought of spending a full six hours looking for jeans or socks and a sweater.

"Well, at least you didn't have to come with us," Joan reminded me.

"You're right," I said, "and I appreciate it. Now the only improvement would be if I could afford a personal shopper, so I wouldn't have to go with me either."

❧ And the Sound of the School Bus Is Heard in the Land

SO LITTLE WILLY'S HEADING OFF TO KINDERGARTEN, is he? I'll bet you can hardly wait. Finally you're going to be able to paint the bathroom without having to stop and "get this," "reach that," "tie my shoes," and "give me a glass of water." You're going to be able to meet friends for lunch, take in a matinee, register for a class in computer programming, and start playing tennis again. You'll even be able to stay in bed when you have the flu. Right? Wrong.

When little Willy marches off to Millard Fillmore Elementary, you'll probably have just enough time to finish the morning paper and pour yourself another cup of coffee. I certainly wouldn't count on two. For kindergarten, despite what they say, is not the mother liberator it's claimed to be.

For one thing, kindergarten classes never coincide with the schedule followed by the rest of the school. They're an hour later, or second shift, or sometimes in the afternoon. So, while neighborhood children clatter by on their way to the bus stop, or older brothers and sisters race

around the house, looking for their permission slips and
their reports on the Pilgrims' first winter, the budding
student waits, even though he's already washed, combed,
and fully dressed. Unfortunately he doesn't wait patiently. For the first hour or so he does nothing but sit
on the stairs, wailing, "When do I get to go to school?"
every five minutes.

Then, when you finally get through to him that it's
going to be awhile, he goes outside to play. This means
that by the time it actually is his time to go, there are
grass stains on his pants, he's spilled egg salad down his
shirt, and he needs a bath and a whole new set of clothes.

Eventually, however, he's on his way, and as the bus
disappears around the bend, you heave a sigh and say,
"Alone at last." But almost before you can heave another
one, he's back. "Hi, Mom, I'm home," he calls. "Is there
anything to eat?" and "Have you seen my baseball?" and
"Can Mike come over and play?"

Still, kindergarten's big stuff in the world of a five-
year-old. It's admission to the select society of those who
go to school and aren't babies anymore. It's also step one
on the way to being able to add, subtract, and read your
sister's diary.

David took his first step in 1963, when we were in
Japan. Sylvia joined him with half a step of her own—
to nursery school. But after one day she decided to postpone her education for another year. I can't say I blamed
her. Getting all cleaned up to go off and do the same
things you could do at home did seem a bit ridiculous.

But with David it was a different story. Things start to
get serious in kindergarten. At least I assumed they did.
I myself had skipped that phase since in the wilds of the
Philippines Mother was my teacher and she felt it was a
bit redundant. But my contemporaries had regaled me

with tales of gold stars in their workbooks, learning to print the alphabet, and matching the number of cows to the numeral on the opposite page.

So I combed his hair, tucked in his shirt, and sent him off with visions of reading *Mary Poppins* by dinnertime dancing in his head. I needn't have bothered. Things had changed in the twenty-some years since my friends sang about traffic safety and learned there are two lumps in a 3. I realized just how much they'd changed when, two hours later, he raced home, waved a fistful of drawings at me, and announced, "Mrs. Claussen wants you to help me with my skipping...and she said you're wrong. I'm not supposed to know how to write my name."

"How's that again?" I asked a month or so later as perched on one of the Lilliputian chairs in her classroom, I sat through the first of what would be a long line of parent/teacher conferences.

She smiled patiently. She was young, probably no more than a couple of years out of college, and she bristled with youthful sincerity and a complete dedication to all the latest theories in education. "I don't think you've done any permanent harm," she assured me, "and I know you meant well. It's just that nowadays we want our students to be like a clean page in a brand-new book when they enter the first grade."

"A clean page in a brand-new book indeed," I told Joe when I got home. "She makes David sound like someone's five-year diary. I'd like to yank him out of her class and put him in a school where they teach something."

Joe shrugged. "Now, now," he said, "I agree that Mrs. Claussen doesn't sound like the teachers I remember, but as long as we're in Japan, I'm afraid the base kindergarten is the only game in town."

It wasn't, however, and though I let him spend that

year skipping around the classroom, napping, and snacking on graham crackers and milk, by the time the next September rolled around both he and Sylvia were safely enrolled in Sancta Maria, a Roman Catholic school, where the only clean pages were those meant to be filled with the day's lesson.

Sancta Maria was grade school as I'd remembered it, only with an Oriental touch. There were cubbyholes for books and hooks for coats, but there were also special slots by the front door for everyone's shoes. There was a flag in each classroom, but rather than the Stars and Stripes it was the Rising Sun. And though there were holidays, they weren't in honor of Washington and Lincoln, but commemorated the emperor's birthday instead.

The nuns were kind at Sancta Maria. They were also strict and brooked no insolence. If you were told to be quiet, you were quiet. If you had to raise your hand before you could leave the room, you raised your hand. And when Chuck Schibi hid his cheese sandwiches behind the radiator, a note went home to his parents, along with a bagful of seared sandwiches.

Occasionally, however, the language barrier tripped them up. It happened one day when I was talking to David's teacher. She was on recess duty, and I'd come to get some of his assignments since he was home sick. As I was about to leave, a small girl in a bright red coat rushed up and tugged on her sleeve.

"Sister Agnes, Sister Agnes," she panted, "Debbie said shit." I bit my lip and glanced at the tiny nun.

She was smiling the inquisitive smile of someone who's stumbled on something new. "And what is that, my dear?" she asked.

I assume she found out. I didn't stay to see.

There wasn't much emphasis on skipping at Sancta

Maria. They were more concerned with the alphabet and how many sheep Farmer Brown had. The dreaded homework, cut out of the base school curriculum lest it overtax small minds, was a daily task for first graders and something to be finished over the weekend for those in kindergarten. And the children loved it. In fact, it was the first thing they did when they got home. But then neither the nuns nor I had told them homework causes sibling rivalry, social maladjustment, bed-wetting, nervous stomach disorders, pimples, and preadolescent rebellion.

As far as I could see, one year at Sancta Maria was the equivalent of two or three on base. Unfortunately one year was all we got. The graduation ceremonies were hardly over before we were on a plane headed out over the Pacific. And when next the school buses revved their motors, we were back in the world of finger painting, class trips to the zoo, and "see and say" spelling that makes four-syllable words not worth the trouble.

We were also in the land of new math, new English, true and false and multiple choice. New math wasn't much of a problem for me since I'd never fully grasped old math and consequently never was asked to help. Still, it would have been nice if the terms they were using had had at least a slight ring of familiarity. And I could have done without the endless "But let me explain it to you, Mom. It's really simple."

New English was more of a shock. Gone were the old adverbial clauses, prepositional phrases, and dangling participles. In their place, like sanitation engineers in place of garbage men, were officious-sounding labels. Where I knew the word *few* as a noun or an adjective, now it was a *quantifier determiner*. *Sentences* were now *structures* and *functions* made up of *noun phrases* and *verb phrases*. And in my absence someone had invented the vowel *schwa* to make the *i* sound in *bird*, the *e* sound in *berth*, the *o* in *worth*, and the *u* in *murky*. It was more than I could take, and I pleaded the "old dog, new tricks" excuse. I also muttered that this was all a Clean Page Society plot and would result in a generation of functional illiterates.

But no one paid any attention to me, and though new English eventually faded and I was able to cackle, "I told you so," when David came home his senior year in high school and announced, "Miss Gwirtner, my health teacher, did it again. This time she misspelled *menstrual*," I was also proved wrong when new math led to trigonometry and calculus in high school and "Find the equation of the hyperbole when the center is (-3,2), transverse axis parallel to the y-axis, passing through (1,7), the asymptotes are perpendicular to each other" was solved without so much as a single "I'm going to flunk this course for sure."

High school was still a long way off, however, in the mid-sixties. The business at hand was the elementary grades. Each year it seemed Joe and I slipped a new student into the system, and by the time Robbie and Joan marched off to junior high we were experts on the subject.

We knew, for instance, that learning to read and write can be a heady experience. When Jenny mastered *Tip*, she wrote it everywhere. She penned it on scraps of paper, grocery lists, and old envelopes. She etched it on cubes of margarine. She spelled it out on steamy windows. And she scratched it on the garage door.

We knew that all the entrants in the first-grade pet shows win an award. Sometimes it's a blue ribbon for the fluffiest cat. Sometimes it's honorable mention to the biggest dog. Joan got first place for having the best, albeit the only, one-legged canary entered in the competition.

We knew that fourth graders study the voyage of the *Mayflower* and that they bring home at least one picture of the first Thanksgiving complete with Pilgrims, Indians, and a luckless turkey. Sylvia's feast included ice cream for the pumpkin pie.

We knew that elementary school children make presents for their parents at the drop of an orange juice can. By the time ours were all safely in junior high I had enough pencil holders to satisfy even the president of Ticonderoga. They also accompany each present with a card signed with their full names, as in "To Mom and Dad, with love, your son, David Combs."

We knew each class has a party for every special day on the calendar with the possible exception of the day the buzzards return to Hinckley, Ohio. The party always includes refreshments. The refreshments are always furnished by mothers. And Jenny always volunteered me for something dramatic. At least she did until the time I had to make thirty caramel apples and the caramel slid off on the way to school and dripped all over the back seat of the car. Then I rebelled, and by the time Joan was Jenny's age I'd trained them all to volunteer to bring napkins or paper cups—nothing more.

We knew that attendance at parents' night is mandatory and that you must never tell the teacher that Robbie has a crush on her or that Geoffrey beats up on his sisters at home. You're there to admire how neat the desks are. You're to notice that Sylvia has two poems posted while the other children only have one. You're to remember and repeat later any compliments you hear, especially those from the teacher or, wonder of wonders, the principal. But under no circumstances are you to force another parent to admire Jenny's pictures or Joan's spelling paper since they'll mention it to Mary and Patty, and

Jenny and Joan will have enemies for life.

And we knew that while it's fine to have a Snoopy lunch box or a Partridge Family thermos bottle in elementary school, it's strictly brown paper bags when you get into junior high.

But then in junior high everything changes anyway. It's a gradual process. Students bound off to the sixth grade with the usual exuberance and anticipation. Their faces are scrubbed. Their hair's combed. They're loaded down with pee-chees, notebooks, three-hundred pages of college ruled paper, an eraser, a protractor, a ruler, new pens and pencils, and a plastic pencil case. And they can talk of nothing but how exciting it's going to be to have more than one teacher.

Three years later they slouch out of the eighth grade. The boys, in jeans, a ripped T-shirt, and a grimy jacket, look as if they'd been clawed by a Bengal tiger. The girls, in jeans one day and a cocktail dress the next, totter by in stiletto heels or three-inch Wedgies. Their pee-chees and the grocery bag covers on their books look like Chapter 1 in the graffiti handbook with "Woody Wiggins has terminal zits" scrawled next to "Mr. Welper's *BORING*," in old English lettering. Any pens or pencils in their possession—erasers disappear from the face of the earth sometime in the fall of the seventh grade—were either borrowed or found on the bus. And "So who wants to know?" is the standard retort to almost any question.

What happens in between is a mystery. On the surface things seem pretty much the same. True the report on "Manners" is replaced with a report on "The Chain of Life." Now there's also homework—every night and "tons of it" on the weekend. And you have your own locker complete with a combination that's the most closely guarded secret since the development of the atom bomb.

But there's still open house in the fall. It usually co-incides with "Monday Night Football." That is why the fathers who do come get upset when little Marianne is off racing up and down the halls with her friends when he's ready to go. It features the standard clean desk, the regulation "I'm Mr. Blumenthal [chuckle, chuckle], the man responsible for all those questions about the solar system" speech, and the usual coffee and cookies—graciously supplied by homeroom mothers—in the gym.

There are still parent/teacher conferences except now no one congratulates you because Joan has mastered "listening skills." They're now finally concerned with spelling, neatness, and the correct answer to "What is 735 divided by 53?" They're not overly concerned, though, as I discovered when I helped administer quizzes in a remedial math class and was told, "Don't flunk Deborah or she'll lose interest." They are appalled, though, by the shocking fact that Robbie hasn't taken his PE clothes home to be laundered since school started.

And presents still wander home from time to time. By now they originate in art, wood shop, or metal shop. Jenny made a ceramic volcano with a removable top and a hidden city down in the core somewhere. And she gave me a manuscript box for Christmas. David pounded out a metal flour scoop and a barbecue fork and made a tape dispenser for the grocery list. Sylvia cut out a pig-shaped breadboard. Robbie fashioned a salad bowl and a box for paper clips. Joan made a fleet of candleholders, a free-form cutting board, and a meat tenderizer. And Geoffrey built everything from a dictionary stand to a hanging fuchsia basket to a lamp.

Even with all these similarities, though, something happens. The experts call it adolescence. Parents call it "when I took to the cooking sherry." Whatever the term, the junior high years are when your children avoid you in public and dash across the street against the traffic rather than let their friends see you with them. It's when no one talks to you anymore. Teen-agers of every shape and size troop in and out of the house like real estate salesmen on an inspection tour. But they never utter so much as a "humph." Should Peter Wilkes stop and ask after your health or say, "It's nice to see you again, Mrs. Combs," you're so charmed and flattered he's your friend for life. Later, when you hear that he's been arrested for armed robbery, you say, "I don't believe it. He's such a nice young boy."

The junior high years are also when you suddenly remember how you used to say, "One thing's for certain, my children are never going to act like that." And it's when you blame yourself and mutter, "Maybe I shouldn't have insisted Jenny eat her beans when she was six, and maybe I should have let Sylvia paint her room black."

I found it's best not to indulge in too much guilt during the junior high years. After all, there's high school to contend with, and if junior high was *Dr. Jekyll and Mr. Hyde*, high school is "Hitler Signs Up for Fifth Period Study Hall."

The first sign comes with the ground rules for parents of high school students. Parents are not to drop in on their children in high school. If Geoffrey left his lunch at home, he'll bum something to eat from a friend or he'll go without. He does not want you tapping on the classroom door while he's in world history, and if he sees you in the hall between classes, he'll spin around and head the other way.

On the other hand, you may deliver his track shoes, his copy of *The Great Gatsby*, or the algebra assignment he left up in his room as long as you drop it off at the office or else park down by the tennis court and wait till you're contacted.

You may also deliver Sylvia to school or pick her up when she has an appointment with the orthodontist. But under no circumstances are you to pull up to the front entrance. Instead, you're to drive around to the back. You're to stop a hundred yards short of the gym. And once everyone's out of the car or in the car, you're to back around quietly—heaven help you if you kill the engine or grind the gears. Then you're to go.

You may certainly help with homework, except I found that by the time my brood hit high school the curriculum had dropped all the subjects I remembered and in their place had put computer science, trigonometry, and business skills. So I was good for little more than typing book reports. Even creative writing classes, where I claimed to have some expertise, confounded me. Sylvia, for example, showed me a poem by a friend of hers that detailed the sex life of a mallard in free verse.

Parents may attend open house if they wish. But now it's "no big deal" and if you go you go alone since the ban on being seen together in public extends to being seen together by teachers.

On the other side of the coin is the mandatory attendance rule. High school parents must attend any and all choir concerts and theatrical events in which their children are participants. You're to remember everyone who took part in the event so that later, when Joan says, "You know. He's the guy who sang the solo in 'The Windmills of My Mind,'" you'll be able to agree he has gorgeous eyes, and when she wants to know how you liked Ginny's dress, you won't have to ask, "Is she the one who tripped going up the stairs?"

I've been to more concerts than most season ticket

holders. I've seen the whole back row get the giggles
and have to leave. I've sat in the dark while choir members thundered past me at a gallop, shouting, "Joy...
joy...joy to the world." One Christmas season I saw the
choir director squeal with delight as four separate lead
sopranos gave her bouquets of flowers. And I've learned
that since choir concerts never start on time, one should
always take along something to do while waiting: a book
or knitting or, in some cases, the Sunday *New York Times*.

Sports events are also included in the mandatory attendance rule. When David was on the tennis team, I
perched on the side of a hill and watched while he and
his partner destroyed and annoyed the opposition with
their secret weapon—a high, lazy lob.

And for seven straight years, four with Geoffrey and an
overlapping four with Robbie and Joan, I was a member
of the tiny but enthusiastic cheering section at cross-
country events.

We were a unique group and considered ourselves a
step above the regulation parent-spectator. For one thing,
unlike those who trooped to Friday night football games
or watched the play-offs in basketball, we weren't there
to wave at all our friends or impress our enemies with
reflected glory. Nor were we there because the team was
headed for a state championship. The five or six of us,
give or take a little brother or a junior high sister, huddled
together in the stands while the rain whipped out of the
south because we wanted to be there and because, we
told ourselves, "The team needs us."

And in the fall, when a new parent showed up, stared
at the nearly empty stands and said, "Is it all over?" we
welcomed her to our midst and filled her in on the art
of cheering a cross-country team.

"The first rule," we told her, "is never talk directly to

your runner before or after the contest. If you yodel, 'Honey, why don't you put your sweats back on? You'll catch your death of cold,' he'll ignore you and stand out in the rain till his lips turn blue just to prove you have no influence over him."

I spent two years watching Geoffrey trot off into the distance before he finally acknowledged my presence and mumbled brief greetings at me. And though Joan talked to me willingly, voluntarily even, right from the start, Robbie kept his distance most of the time.

"Next," we advised, "memorize the names of everyone on the team so you can yell, 'Way to go, Kirk,' and, 'That's the spirit, Lisa,' instead of, 'Go, team.'

"Watching the event is simple," we informed her. "When everyone finally gathers at the starting line, the gun will go off, or if there's no starting gun, Mr. Wade will yell, 'On your mark, get set, go,' and they'll run by once and disappear over the hill.

"This gives you a chance to go home and check to see if the mail has come. Or you can dash off to the store, or you can stick around and try to keep warm with the rest of us. After fifteen minutes or so the runners will begin to straggle back in. Then you may scream as loud as you like since they're usually so exhausted they don't realize it's you. After that it's over."

For the most part, new members in the cheering section caught on right away. They learned to shout, "Hurry...hurry...he's coming up behind you." They learned not to gasp or run out on the field when their sons or daughters crossed the finish line and staggered around like accident victims. And they gained new respect for the boy or girl who consistently came in fourth or sixth or last but never gave up.

But then high school students have always been known

for their selective stamina. It comes and goes like will-power at a fat farm. When the night is late and a history report's due, they're dizzy, nauseated and suffering from exhaustion. But when the night is equally late and the movie has another hour to go, they've never felt so rested. When there's wood to be brought in or groceries to be unloaded, their legs hurt, their backs ache, and they have to wash their hair or take a bath or find a pair of clean socks. But when someone stops by and suggests getting a basketball game together, they drop everything, bound down the stairs two at a time, and race out to the car. And when they're training for a marathon, they'll run five miles in an ice storm without a word of complaint, but they'll wait to be picked up at the library for an hour on a glorious day rather than walk the mile and a half.

What can you do? The only known cure for high school is college. And coincidentally, Mother, not till your child's in college will you finally be able to have all that free time you were looking forward to when you sent him off to kindergarten. And by then who wants to take up tennis or learn computer programming?

ಈ Go Back to Bed, You're Supposed to Be Sick

I'M GLAD I never knew Florence Nightingale. Then again, maybe Florence should be thankful she never met me. Though I know she's beloved the world over for her unceasing dedication to the sick and the war wounded; though I know she was called the Lady with the Lamp because she believed a nurse should be on duty day and night; and though I know her selfless concern for others eventually affected her own health, I can't help wondering how caring and compassionate she would have been if she'd been ministering to a batch of her own children.

Somehow I have the feeling her name would be missing from the list of the saintly if she'd had to deal with: Monday Flu, also known as the Unfinished Homework Syndrome; with Sermonette Nausea, a cluster of violent symptoms that show up only in the middle of the night; or with Campground Fever, another nocturnal illness that occurs when you're all off somewhere on vacation, shoulder to shoulder in sleeping bags, and the nearest doctor is forty miles away.

I may be wrong, however. Perhaps Florence would

have relished the chance to change four or five beds at two in the morning. Maybe she was even the sort that enjoyed spending endless hours in doctors' waiting rooms. Lord knows there are those who do. I know mothers who'd rather swab off a scraped knee, spray it with disinfectant, and wrap it in a yard or two of gauze than attend a Broadway opening. I've seen mothers freeze in their tracks at the first sound of a sneeze, and I've watched while they paw through the medicine cabinet, searching for aspirin, chest rub, cough drops, and the thermometer, all the while crooning, "Now you take off those clothes, get into your pajamas, and get right into bed, young man. You're not going to school today, that's for sure."

I admire them for their zeal, but I'm not inspired to emulate them. For somewhere along the way I've noticed that mothers who enjoy tending the sick usually have children who enjoy being sick, hence always are sick. And as far as I'm concerned, having someone throw up on your slippers is not the perfect way to start the day.

It's not that I'm callous about serious illnesses. I'm not. I'll sit up for hours with cold cloths and kind words till the fever finally breaks. I'll pace back and forth in the waiting room till the doctor assures us, "Everything's going to be fine." And I'll run up and down stairs with aspirin, ice water, and juice till the crisis passes. But when I nearly break my leg dashing in to answer a piercing, "*Mother, I need you*," only to find that my patient is bored, I get surly.

I noticed this trait in myself early on. It was some time after David was operated on for pyloric stenosis when he was three weeks old. And it was long before Robbie had open heart surgery at the age of nine. It may have been one of the times in the first days of Sylvia's career as a daughter when I was convinced by her whimpers, her sobs, and her incessant howling that she was in great pain, only to find out she simply wanted to come out in the living room and watch "Playhouse 90." Or it may have been one of the times that glancing out the kitchen window, I noticed that David, when he fell down without an audience, was like the infamous trees in the forest. With no one around to witness the event, he rarely made a sound. This, I discovered, is true of all children. At least it's true when they're toddlers.

Once they get older and realize you're on to them, they change their act. One day they trip, roll down a grassy hill, and let go with a bloodcurdling scream that sends you stumbling out of the house, expecting nothing less than to find them pinned under a six-wheeler. The next day they wander into the kitchen, bleeding with every step, and ask casually, "Do you know where the Band-Aids are?"

It happened to me continually. Shortly after Geoffrey had mastered riding a bicycle, he decided to join the "look, Ma, no hands" brigade. And one day after he'd sailed triumphantly past the house, he wobbled, tumbled, and skidded the rest of the way down the hill on his face. But even though he looked as if he'd been in a three-car collision, he merely shrugged, said, "Did you see that?" and limped silently into the house.

Sylvia, on the other hand, plummeted out of a tree one day when she was seven, and though I could find no blood or broken bones, she roared and moaned so I had to rush her to the hospital.

It happened late one afternoon in the spring of 1966. Joe was home from work. I was in the kitchen getting dinner. Sylvia and David were up the street, playing at someone's house. The rest of the crowd was milling about, chanting, "When do we eat?"

Suddenly the front door banged open, and Sylvia straggled in, crying at full bellow.

"What happened?" I gasped as I rushed over, dropped to my knees, and searched for signs of injury. She buried her head in my shoulder and sobbed.

"Sylvia fell out of a tree," David explained.

"Where? When? How did it happen?"

"Up at Marcie's. She slipped."

"How high up was she?" Joe asked as Sylvia transferred from my arms to his and howled anew.

"Not far," David said. "She was on the bottom branch."

"Oh, my back," Sylvia groaned. "My back. It hurts."

We poked and prodded, but she couldn't say exactly where it hurt. It simply hurt.

"Is it a sharp pain?" Joe asked.

"I don't know."

"Does it hurt when I touch here?"

"No."

"How about over here?"

"No."

Finally, since time and a cheeseburger have been known to heal all manner of wounds, I stood up.

"Come on, honey," I said as I led her into the dining room. "Why don't you come sit down? Maybe after a little dinner you'll feel fine again."

I should have known better. She was determined to suffer, and with each bite she winced dramatically or let out a long, tremulous moan. When she showed no signs of letting up, I got worried. Perhaps she really was in pain.

"What do you think?" I asked Joe. "Should we take her out to the hospital?" Of course, by *we* I meant *he* since time spent in a military hospital waiting room is measured in hours, and I hoped to avoid the experience if at all possible.

He was having none of it. Two nights before, he'd been routed out of bed around midnight when Sylvia com-

plained of an excruciating earache. He'd bundled her off
to the emergency room at Andrews Air Force Base, only
to return two and a half hours later with the news that
the doctor could find nothing wrong.

"The doctor said everything was perfectly normal," he'd
informed me through clenched teeth.

Now he was not about to repeat the experience.

"Oh, you can take her if you like," he said, "but I'm
not going. I went last."

"That's cruel," I protested. "This time she may really
be hurt."

He shrugged. "Then take her in," he said. "Just don't
expect me to."

So I vaulted onto my high horse. I reminded Joe that
he could jolly well bathe the others and put them to bed,
and I got our coats and we left.

It was a good twenty-minute drive to Andrews, and
Sylvia obliged me by whimpering softly as I maneuvered
through the early-evening traffic. When we arrived, it
was as I had expected. The emergency waiting room was
jammed with wailing infants, pale and somber airmen,
children lying in their mother's laps, and assorted folks
with crutches.

I sat Sylvia down in a corner and went to check in.

"Yes, may I help you?" a bored corpsman asked after
he was satisfied he'd kept me waiting long enough.

"It's my daughter," I said, pointing to Sylvia, who grimaced on cue. "She fell out of a tree, and she says her
back hurts."

"Oh?" His tone was accusing. "And when did this happen?"

"About an hour or so ago."

"Why didn't you bring her in then?"

"I didn't think she was really hurt."

"And where is this tree?"

"Up the street, at a friend's house."

"May I have the name of the people whose property she was on?"

I cursed children everywhere, and Sylvia in particular, who never know the last name of anyone. "I don't know their name."

"Well, then, can you give me their address?"

"I don't know that either," I stuttered. "We're new in the neighborhood."

"Didn't you see her fall?"

"No, I was home at the time...getting dinner."

"I see." He scribbled something on the form in front of him, and I presumed it had something to do with neglect. "Then how did she get home?"

"Her brother brought her home."

"Oh...and how old is he?"

"He's eight...and a half," I added quickly.

He shook his head and sighed but apparently decided not to call the police just yet. "All right, ma'am," he said. "Take her in the other room there and have her lie down. The doctor will be with her in a few minutes."

By now Sylvia was playing the situation for all it was worth. So I picked her up, lugged her into the other room, and put her down on one of the many examining tables that lined both walls.

"OK, honey," I said, "lie still. The doctor will be here in a bit."

He wasn't, of course. In the meantime, I talked to her. I stroked her head and gently rubbed her back. And while we waited, the room filled up. Mostly it was with parents and children. Some of the little ones were obviously in great pain. Some of the older ones slept. Some simply lay there. Next to us a young couple wrapped their tiny baby in cold wet towels.

"What's the trouble?" I asked.

"She has a fever," the mother told me.

"Can I do anything to help?"

"No, thanks. We simply have to keep changing the towels."

We talked for a while, commiserating with each other and comparing notes on sick children. It's standard waiting room procedure. But apparently Sylvia felt neglected. All at once she tugged on my sleeve. I turned back to her. "Did you come here to get me well," she said petulantly as she hiked up to a sitting position, "or did you come to make friends?"

"Really now, Sylv." I snorted. "You lie down and don't worry about why I came."

"But I'm sick of lying down."

"I'm sorry about that, but you have to, at least till the doctor comes and checks you over."

"I want to go home."

"You can't—not yet. Now do as I say. Lie down and behave yourself."

So she lay down. But the doctor was still a good forty-five minutes away, and by the time he finally got to us she not only was sitting up but was dangling her feet over the edge, swinging them back and forth, and balancing the pillow on her head.

"Well, what have we here?" he asked.

I went through my story again as he tapped, probed, and felt for broken ribs and cracked vertebrae. Finally he straightened up. "Well," he said, "good news. I can't find anything wrong."

"But...she seemed to be in agony," I stammered. "When we first started out, I would have sworn her back was broken at the very least."

He chuckled. "I know," he said. "It happens all the time. But don't worry. I'd rather have you bring her in than risk having something really be wrong."

I thanked him...profusely, for finding nothing wrong and for being kind enough to make me feel like less of a fool than I was. And three hours after we'd left home, we trudged back in the front door, where Joe greeted us with the last laugh and a hearty "I told you so."

Apparently, however, I hadn't learned my lesson because I continued to fall for any number of sad tales. When I cooked up a pot of chili for dinner and Joan paled, excused herself, and trotted into the bathroom to drape herself over the toilet, I believed she was the victim of a sudden attack of the flu. I believed it, that is, until I overheard her tell Robbie how she felt about kidney beans, and I put two and two together and came up with chili.

When Joe and I were called home from a dinner party by a hysterical call from Jenny, who said, "Geoffrey's coming at me with the ax," I was prepared for imminent fatalities. As we raced home, I imagined severed limbs and arteries spurting blood like uncapped oil wells. Of course, when we got home, the ax was by the woodbox, where we'd left it, and all were peacefully asleep.

So later calls were disregarded, and Jenny turned her dramatic talents on her grandmother, who, because parents lose all common sense when they become grandparents, never failed to respond.

I was also the victim of innumerable cases of early-morning nausea, pain, and general discomfort.

"M...o...m, I don't feel good," I'd hear as I stood in the kitchen, slapping rows of bologna sandwiches together for school lunches.

"What's the matter?"

"It's my glands. See? Feel how swollen they are."

As a rule, I never felt anything. But that didn't matter.

If I didn't buy the swollen glands, the symptoms became more general.

"My bones ache."

"My stomach feels yucky."

"I'm dizzy. My throat's sore, and I have a headache."

It was an award winning performance, and at first I gave in. "Oh, all right," I'd say, "go back to bed. But this had better be the real thing, none of this up and down, up and down and building tents in your bed."

"Oh, I won't do that. I promise. I'm really sick."

But by ten o'clock I could hear Jenny washing her hair or Sylvia rearranging her room. By noon Robbie was complaining because the only thing on television was soap operas. And by two in the afternoon Geoffrey wanted to make cookies.

David was smart. He stayed in his room all day and read science fiction or a year's worth of *National Geographics*. And Joan, who was working on a perfect attendance record, had to be almost comatose before she'd stay home. But the rest avoided history tests with the flu, got out of PE with colds, and postponed oral book reports with general malaise.

I tried to outsmart them by requiring they at least have a fever before being allowed to slip back in under the covers. But every now and then I'd send them off to the bus with a casual "If you still feel sick by midmorning, let me know and I'll come get you," only to have the school nurse call me an hour later, saying, "Jenny's here in my office. She fainted in second period. She's thrown up twice. And from the sound of her chest I'd say she may have pneumonia." Then I'd slink up to school, transport her down to the doctor, and chalk another one up in the "Surprise. I'm really sick" column.

Then there were the instances when there was no doubt about the fact that something was wrong. I could see the rash, feel the fever, and tell just by looking in their eyes that this was not an attempt to win an Oscar. Of course, it never happened when I was simply sitting around, looking for a way to fill my days. Heavens, no. The genuine maladies always came when my dance card was already full to overflowing.

At the outset of a two-thousand-mile motor trip, for instance, Sylvia, then only six months old, developed diarrhea. This meant that in addition to keeping David amused, manning the map, pouring Joe coffee, and searching for a gas station, a restaurant, or a suitable motel, I got to spend the next three days on my knees on the front seat, reaching into the back to change diapers every twenty minutes.

In Japan, when we moved from Washington Heights out to Johnson, Jenny came down with raging fever. So while I directed the movers to this room and that, Joe took her up to the new clinic and had words with the corpsman who didn't take kindly to the fact that our records hadn't arrived yet. And the next day, when Joe went back to work, I either carried her around with me as I tried to unpack or else sat with her in the living room and called out, "I think your sweater's in the box in the hall," and "Would someone bring me Jenny's medicine and a glass of orange juice?" and "Come here quick. Geoffrey's crawling up the stairs," to the other two.

Camping usually brought on an illness or two. David as a tiny baby developed a fever and broke out in a rash in a rented trailer on the edge of Lake Texarkana. When no one told us one doesn't take tents and frying pans into the Rockies in June, the wind whistled through the pass, snow piled up against the canvas door, and Sylvia got one of her chronic ear infections and moaned pitifully all through the night.

At the edge of a reservoir outside Denver, Robbie and

Joan lost breakfast, lunch, and dinner into the folds of their sleeping bags. So while Joe stayed behind with the other campers, including three of our neighbor's children, David and I set off into the darkness to drive the twins home.

And in the middle of Missouri, miles from the nearest town, Joan flipped backward off the top of a slide, landed on the cement, and was carried back to the tent by Sylvia. At the time we were fifty miles from any sort of town. It was also a Saturday afternoon, and since she was conscious and seemingly not in pain, we debated about taking her to the doctor.

Finally we decided not to, and after she'd rested quietly for a while, she bounced back. There were other times, though—such as the day she fell into our neighbor's window well or when Robbie and his bike collided with the mail truck—that we sped them off to the closest medical help and brought them home partially encased in plaster of paris.

Still other times we might just as well have rattled gourds or draped the children in garlands of garlic for all the good a doctor did.

When Geoffrey at six months was still cross-eyed, I should have called in a village elder instead of taking him to the dispensary to see Dr. Burleigh. Here was a man who left you scanning the framed diplomas on his wall to see if they were stenciled in crayon. Not that he didn't look the part. He did. He had the regulation starched and pressed white coat. His stethoscope lounged casually in his pocket. And pictures of his wife and children stood like trophies on his desk.

But when I carried Geoffrey in and explained the reason for my visit, he grinned idiotically, turned to the baby in my arms, and said, "Does Mommy think our big blue eyes are a teensy tiny bit crossed? Come, let Doctor hold Mommy's big boy."

A year and a half later Geoffrey went into surgery to correct his condition, and Dr. Yoshida's sole comment was: "Too bad we couldn't have done this earlier."

Thank God for Dr. Yoshida. When we were stationed at Johnson, he was the closest we came to a family pediatrician. He was the one who ordered the tests that checked out Sylvia's hearing problem and discovered colds and allergies were creating a vacuum behind the eardrums and making it hard for her to hear me say, "Have you washed your hands and brushed your teeth?"

Earlier Dr. Burleigh had told me, "All mommies think their little girls don't hear them, but Doctor knows that sometimes little girls just don't pay attention. Isn't that so, Celia?"

Dr. Yoshida was also the one who initiated the "token patient" procedure. When the flu blew through the base like a spring dust storm and I was left with a child in every bed, basins and towels next to every pillow, and the washer and dryer on red alert, when I called to plead for an appointment and alluded to the fact that the dispensary waiting room would soon be littered with four nauseated Combses, he said, "Why don't you just bring one. Obviously they all have the same thing, and I'll simply quadruple the prescription."

So I got David dressed since he was the worst off. And while Fusako-san manned the wet cloths and the flat Coke, he and I trundled up to the dispensary, had a representative temperature taken, went through a symbolic examination, and left with four identical sets of medication.

We repeated the process when they got the measles and the chicken pox together. I bundled up another child.

We presented the miscellaneous symptoms, and I staggered home with boxes and boxes of oatmeal bath solution. And eventually things at the pesthouse cleared up.

But then I knew they would, just as I knew that in time we'd go through another bout of something or other.

I also knew I would never be invited to share in whatever illness we were sampling that season. That's not to say I was immune to all the viruses and diseases we imported or that I never had symptoms. I had symptoms all right. At times chills ran up and down my body like flourishes on a vibraphone. I blazed with fever, and my bones creaked and grated against each other like rusty hinges. But having symptoms and being free to stagger off to bed were two different things entirely.

I was allowed all the symptoms I wanted. But as far as giving in to them was concerned, that was out of the question.

"Who'll take care of the kids?" Joe asked whenever I brought up the idea of my indulging in a horizontal day.

"I thought perhaps you might be able to stay home from work...just this once," I'd venture. It was a radical notion, especially for a military wife. We were supposed to be made of sterner stuff. And we certainly were expected to understand that husbands were officers and gentlemen, not nursemaids. But when you're delirious, you risk it.

"Me?" The shock echoed around the room. "I can't possibly. I have to give a briefing. Besides," he always added, "once you get up and get busy, you'll feel better."

So I got up. I didn't feel better, but I got up. And as I draped myself over the churning dishwasher trying to absorb any available heat, I dreamed of the day when finally I'd be able to crawl back under the covers and simply lie there till life was worth living again.

Eventually it came. One morning when only the twins were still too young to be in school, I woke up, stumbled out of bed, and, when the room began to spin and I started seeing the northern lights flashing and dancing on the bedroom wall, stumbled back in again.

"Sorry," I said when Joe came to rout me out, "not today. I'm sick."

"But—"

"I know. Who'll take care of the kids?" Nausea didn't prevent me from thinking quickly. "I will," I told him. "All you have to do is get the twins dressed and send them in here. They'll be fine, and the others are certainly capable of getting themselves ready for school."

"Well—" he was nonplussed—"all right...if you say so."

I did, and because I was new to the game, I thought, as I snuggled back down and drifted off to sleep, that I'd finally reached nirvana.

Minutes later I woke up.

"Hi, Mom," Robbie said as he crawled over my reclining form. "You sick?" His heel dug into the small of my back as he scooted over to make room for Joan, and I yelped.

"Yes, I'm sick," I muttered. "So you two be good now and play here quietly."

"OK," Joan chirped. "Can we watch TV?"

"Umm."

"Goody." She crawled back over me and rushed to turn the set on. She also trundled into the kitchen to get the last of a box of doughnuts. She stopped off in the living room for some crayons, a pad of paper, and some books. And while Robbie scrambled down to gather up his own amusements, she tossed everything into the middle of my bed and climbed over me once again.

It was a long morning.

Because Joan is thoughtful and caring to a fault, she interspersed cheers for Bert and Ernie and Mar...velous Martha on "Sesame Street," with ministrations. She stroked my forehead and rubbed my back. She read sing-song verses from *The Cat in the Hat*. She fetched water in plastic cups she and Robbie had previously filled with mud and sand. And she brought pillows from every bed in the house and scrunched them under my head till I was almost upright.

Robbie ran his tractor and his dump truck around the bed and parked them in the garage at my back. He rolled Matchbook cars down the lumpy hill of my legs. And he drew pictures.

"Mom...hey, Mom. Guess what this is?"

"I don't know."

"Guess."

"Honey, I can't. I'm sick."

"Just one guess, please."

"Oh, all right. It's an airplane." Airplanes were his passion about then, and even without looking, I figured the odds were good that he'd sketched another helicopter.

"Nope...guess again."

"Oh, Robbie...don't make me guess again."

By noon I could take it no longer. So I struggled out of bed, threw on some clothes, and lumbered into the kitchen to get the twins lunch. And since I was up, I stuffed a load of clothes in the washer, hauled some hamburger out for dinner, and slowly, very slowly, moved from room to room, picking up shoes, stacking books, and retrieving coats, mittens, and an occasional sock.

When Joe got home that night, he was delighted.

"I knew you couldn't stay in bed all day," he said, chortling. "It's just as I've always told you. Getting up and getting busy takes your mind off your troubles and makes you feel better."

"So say you," I snarled. "But you wait. Someday I'm going to spend an entire week in bed, and I'm going to enjoy every minute of it."

He's still waiting, and God knows, so am I.

ᘐ You'll Be As Good As New

THERE'S AN ENORMOUS DIFFERENCE between waking up at 2:00 A.M. to the sound of your son hollering, "Mom...I feel *aw*-ful," and waking up at 2:00 A.M. to the realization that he's scheduled for major surgery at 7:30.

While they both put you on alert, the one snaps your eyes open, drags you to your feet, and sends you stumbling off into the darkness, muttering, "I'm coming. I'm coming," and the other leaves you in bed, staring at the ceiling, watching shadows from the streetlight flicker on the walls and trying not to think: What if?

I didn't know much about life on Ward 3C when I joined the maternal order. As a child, of course, I'd dabbled in all the diseases; chicken pox, mumps, the measles, poison oak every time the wind changed directions. But hospitals weren't the miracle factories they would become, and they weren't in my field of expertise. I didn't have an aunt with gall bladder trouble. No uncle sported a pacemaker. I'd never gone with Mother to visit an ailing neighbor or take flowers to a friend who'd had a hip joint

replaced, a coronary bypass, a varicotomy, or back surgery. And no one I knew had had a nose job or a tummy
tuck.

I had been privy to a tonsillectomy when I was about
five, and I'd had my appendix removed four years later,
but I don't recall much about either episode.

All that stays with me is the memory of lying in my
bed at night with only a sliver of light shining under the
door, wishing with all my might that they'd let Mother
come back and stay with me. They wouldn't, of course.
The propaganda of the day insisted, "Having Mother
around makes brave, little soldiers snivel and whine."
So her comings were prescribed, and her goings were
prompt. I complained, but my complaints were ignored.
Folks had yet to dote on the opinions of children.

Years passed, however, and in the intervening time
apparently the medical profession saw the error of its
ways. Either that or nurses suddenly realized that mothers who know how to read stories, fill water pitchers, and
keep Junior away from the oxygen tanks are rather useful.
While Jonas Salk worked on the polio vaccine, Selman
Waksman fought tuberculosis with his newly discovered
streptomycin, and Daniele Bovet sought relief for allergies, hospitals took a step forward, too, and the doors to
the pediatric ward opened up little by little and let Mom
and Dad in.

So when, on a muggy June morning in 1964, Joe and
I checked eighteen-month-old Geoffrey in for eye surgery at the base hospital in Tachikawa, the nurses offered, even insisted that I stay in his room with him.

"Kids just seem to get along better when their parents
are around," they told us as if it were news. "Besides, it
leaves us free to give more time to those in intensive
care."

So I stayed. Joe and I took Geoffrey over to x-ray for the required pictures. We went with him down to the lab for his blood tests and carried him back.

After Joe had gone home, Geoffrey and I walked up and down the halls, inspecting water fountains, testing all the chairs in the waiting room, and peering out the windows to gasp at cars and trucks and an occasional airplane.

When Geoffrey wouldn't take a nap, I plunked him on my bed, and we read stories about a friendly gorilla, a lisping seal, and a little girl with an expanding red umbrella. We even had dinner together in the dining hall— a great adventure since it included soda crackers in their own separate packages. And when I'd given him a bath, put clean pajamas on him, and made sure he had Eeyore safe in his embrace, he went off to sleep as if he were home in his own bed.

When they brought him back to the room after his surgery the next morning, Joe sat in one of those plastic hospital chairs that sighs whenever you move and held him, breathing secondhand ether fumes, till Geoffrey woke up. I kept him occupied through the afternoon and evening, though he grew impatient with me and made "come on, let's go" noises.

And the next morning Joe returned, we packed Eeyore, bade the nurses and doctors a hasty good-bye and hurried home to Fusako-san and lunch consisting of a peanut butter and jelly sandwich and a fistful of rice crackers.

"Well, thank heaven that's over," I told Joe as he headed back to work. "It wasn't as bad as I thought it would be. But I certainly hope we don't have to go through any more operations."

Silly fool. In less than a year I'd be back at Tachikawa with Sylvia and a tonsillectomy. After that Joan would do an encore of David's pyloric stenosis. Two years later we'd check Robbie into the hospital at Andrews Air Force Base for a hernia operation. And seven years after that he and I would fly to Letterman in San Francisco for his open heart surgery.

By that time I was an old hand at the "mother with child in the hospital" routine. I knew what not to wear: no straight skirts or suits since you may have to sit on the floor in the sunroom and build bridges or play a modified game of catch; no wool jackets since chasing down corridors is hot work; and no silk or shantung since after the dinner tray spills, you may have to wash out your clothes in the bathroom of your dormitory down the street.

I knew there are nurses who treat temperature and blood pressure statistics as if they were classified information, while others will take the time to explain everything, up to and including the hospital laundry system. I knew that some doctors make rounds at a gallop, some stroll through the ward as if they had all day, and others travel only in groups of three or more. And I knew that the janitor is often the most affable person on the ward.

I knew the mother's daily schedule: that the first order of the day is breakfast in the dining hall with the other parents, that if you want a cigarette, you sit out in the corridor or stand by the elevator, that every once in a while the kids on the ward will let you turn the television channel and sneak a look at "Days of Our Lives" during lunch, and that if you hurry, you can make it off the hospital grounds and to a florist or the drugstore and back before naptime is over. But I never learned how to deal with the fact that though my child might be on his way to a complete recovery, another mother's daughter had little chance of living through the summer.

The first clue that Robbie would be needing open heart surgery came in the late fall of 1973. It had been an explosive year for the country. Vietnam's prisoners of war had come home to try pick up lives that had muddled on for six, sometimes eight years without them. Watergate developments had spiced up the nightly news like an extra dash of chili powder in an already blazing sauce. The Mets had almost pulled off a victory in the World Series. Billie Jean King had gloriously trounced Bobby Riggs, while the major minority cheered and sang a chorus or two of "I Am Woman."

"Back to basics" was on its way to becoming a cliché as advocates of granola, whole grain, molasses, and wheat germ sneered at Wonder bread sandwiches and cereals shot from guns. Mung beans and alfalfa were only beginning to sprout. And raw sugar pretended it deserved the price it brought.

On Walton's Mountain John-Boy and Jim-Bob and the rest of the clan were happily wishing each other goodnight. In space the first Skylab crew watched the world go by for twenty-eight days in a row. And down at the corner motorists in line for gasoline had enough time to read *War and Peace* and a couple of chapters of *The Decline and Fall of the Roman Empire* before easing up for their turn at the pump.

At our house things were muddling along as usual. David in his junior year of high school had just discovered computers and consequently left for school in the dark so he'd have his turn at the machine. Sylvia, now a freshman, gave us two representatives in each school and the beginnings of a rebel with a hidden cause. Jenny in the seventh grade chafed at authority and made a ceramic tea set with a pot that poured through mammoth lips. Geoffrey, in the fifth grade, studied volcanoes and drew diagrams of the "creater." Robbie and Joan, mighty third graders, referred to those in kindergarten as "little kids."

Joe, who'd joined his father's wine supply business after he retired from the Air Force, was working long hours, including some nights when he taught assorted groups how to make champagne from a basket of lemons, some limes, and a grapefruit or two. And I, determined to find an acceptable excuse for ignoring the furniture polish and the toilet brush, was writing articles, sending them to every publication but the *Police Gazette*, and finally getting only a majority of them back with a "Thanks but no thanks."

As I remember, it was a dismal November that year. But then November in the Pacific Northwest is always dismal. Rain drips constantly from the eaves. Clouds roll in and pile up on top of one another until noon looks like dusk. Dawn shows up in the middle of the morning. And sometime, shortly after Halloween, the first delivery of colds and the flu arrives on the morning ferry from Seattle.

Robbie met the boat that year. He coughed. He sneezed. He rattled and rasped. One minute his fever climbed and he threw off the covers, and the next thing I knew he was wearing his coat to bed.

We weren't particularly worried. It had been eight and a half years since the doctor had presented us with his list of dire predictions for both Robbie and Joan. We'd lived through the first anxious year. We'd watched. Were their eyes bright and clear? Was the trembling lip a convulsion? Were they reaching, responding, recognizing? Except for the hernia, none of the predictions had come to pass. True, Robbie was a good head shorter than Joan, and he cringed every time someone drew his attention to that fact. But a doctor in Colorado had assured us the heart murmur had disappeared. She also promised him he'd catch up eventually. Besides, his height gave him the world's smallest Little League strike zone.

So when Joe took him down to the navy hospital clinic in Bremerton, we thought it was simply a routine trip to replenish our supply of cough syrup and see if there wasn't something available to help Robbie through this latest bout with November's annual cold. It quickly became anything but routine.

"I'm afraid I have bad news," Joe said when he got home. "Dr. Corrado says the heart murmur's still there."

"But I don't understand. Why did they tell us it had gone?"

"He says he doesn't know, but it's definitely there now."

"What does he think it is?"

"He's not sure, but he suspects there's a hole between the two upper chambers of the heart."

"Suspects? When will he know?"

"After the tests. Dr. Corrado's going to arrange for Robbie to go down to Madigan for a cardiac catherization."

"What's that?"

"As I understand it, it's a procedure where they inject a dye in his veins and then take x-ray movies to see if it spills over from one chamber of the heart to the other. If it does, then they're sure that's the trouble."

"When are they going to do this?"

"Apparently there's no big rush since children's surgery month at Letterman, where they'll send Robbie if he needs an operation, isn't till June."

"Letterman? Where's Letterman?"

"In San Francisco, at the Presidio. Anyway, Dr. Corrado says they'll most likely have Robbie go down to Madigan sometime in February or March."

As it turned out, it was March, and while Joe stayed

home to punch the time clock and take care of the rest of the brood, Robbie and I drove down to Tacoma. After we'd logged a mile or two going from admissions to x-ray to the lab, we checked into the ward.

It wasn't the quiet and peaceful haven for healing one might expect in a hospital. It was awash in small, energetic bodies clad in pastel pajamas. Babies shrieked. Toddlers struggled to climb out of their cribs. Three-year-olds, with thumbs in mouth and security blankets trailing after them, howled for Mama and broke for the door every time someone came on the ward. And nurses ducked as Juan and Bernie sat on the ends of their beds and tossed a bean-bag back and forth across the room.

Fortunately Robbie's stay was brief. He checked in one day, had the catherization the second, and went home on the third. Before we hiked down the long corridor and headed for the car, we stopped in the doctor's office and got the news. There was a hole all right.

The last words I heard as we made our exit were: "Don't worry, Mrs. Combs. We'll make the arrangements for Robert to be admitted to Letterman in June, and we'll get back to you."

I counted up the months on my fingers and began the wait.

It wasn't as long as it seemed, and while Joe and I fidgeted and wished the time away, the world wobbled along and tallied up its usual complement of sunrises and sunsets. The daffodils came out, and the lilacs bloomed. The swallows took up their annual residence under the eaves by the front porch. Around the country spring storms crackled, and a devastating tornado skipped through Cincinnati. In the other Washington the turbulence of Watergate seethed as impeachment hearings got under way in the House Judiciary Committee. Thirty-six million miles beyond the sun Mariner 10 sat on the surface of the planet Mercury and sent picture postcards home to Earth. And in our minds it all paled in comparison to what lay ahead.

I tried to explain to Robbie exactly what was going to happen.

"We'll fly down on a military plane on a Saturday," I told him. "The next day you and I will fool around in San Francisco. We'll go out to Golden Gate Park and the planetarium and see what there is to see. Then, on Monday, you'll check into the hospital."

He grimaced.

"Don't worry," I assured him. "I'll be with you. You'll be there for a week before anything happens. Daddy will drive down the next Saturday. On the next Monday— that's the seventeenth—you'll have your operation. And about a week or ten days later we'll fly home again."

He seemed to understand. He even used his travels to lord it over Joan. "I get to go on a plane...to see the Golden Gate Bridge...to travel clear to California...and you have to stay at home and go to school." She was appropriately envious.

But when the exciting part was over and he and I had made our plane trip and seen the sights and were in the elevator headed up to the children's ward, the bravado vanished. He looked very small, and his eyes implored me not to leave.

"Don't worry, honey," I whispered, bracing myself for another dose of pediatric pandemonium, "I'm right here," and I took his hand as we stepped out onto the fourth floor and headed for the nurses' station.

He took a deep breath and held on tightly. But his grip soon relaxed as no howls of pain or boredom echoed down the halls, no tear-stained toddlers wandered forlornly by, and no frazzled nurses snapped harsh commands at their charges or each other.

The ward was busy but cheerful. The nurses welcomed Robbie warmly. And the accommodations were spacious and airy. There were no beds lined up along a wall. Instead, the patients bedded down in four-child rooms with radios, two television sets, and remote controls for everyone.

Robbie's room, down at the end of the hall and next to the playroom, looked out on the Palace of Fine Arts, Alcatraz, and San Francisco Bay. I could even see the faint outline of the Golden Gate as the morning sun burned the fog away.

Three other boys—Mike, who was in for tests and would go home the next day; Donald, a five-year-old who, like Robbie, was scheduled for heart surgery the following Monday; and Tommy, eight, who was to have a sunken chest built up on Friday—were already in residence. When the nurse ushered us in and assigned Robbie the remaining bed, they gathered around.

"Hi."

"What's your name?"

"You wanna see my truck?"

"I gots new crayons...and comic books...and we made a fire station in the playroom. Wanna see?"

Robbie let go of my hand. But before they could swoop him off, the nurse intervened.

"Hey, wait a minute," she hollered above the din. "He can't play with you just yet. So simmer down."

She turned back to us and handed Robbie his pajamas. "Don't worry," she said. "There'll be lots of time for that later. First I want you to put these on and then come back down to the nurses' station. You and your mom are going on a trip to the third floor." She smoothed his hair gently and pushed his bangs to one side. "Sorry the pajamas don't match," she said, "I'm sure you'll look neat in blue bottoms and a yellow top."

She was right. He looked neat, even when we added the bilious green foam rubber slippers. But he was nervous.

"Why do we have to go to the third floor?" he asked as we got in the elevator.

"They want to take x-rays, do some blood tests, and have you see the doctor in the cardiology clinic."

He winced. "I hate blood tests," he said.

"I know. So do I."

"Will there be lots?"

"I don't know. Why don't we go there first? Then you can get them over with."

"Will they be able to find my vein the first time?" He'd been through this before.

"I'm sure they will."

"Will you ask them how many shots I have to have?"

"I'll ask."

He took my hand again and gripped it. "OK, we can go there first. But don't forget, you're going to ask how many shots I have to have."

"I won't."

And I didn't, but before I could open my mouth, the corpsman in charge of the procedure volunteered the information.

"All right, Robert," he said after he'd checked Robbie's ID bracelet, "I'm going to need four tubes of blood. But don't worry. I'll have to stick you only once. Isn't that clever?"

He worked quickly and surely, and while he worked, he kept up a running conversation. "Now this is going to hurt but only for a second.... You won't feel this at all.... What grade are you in?... Is this the first time you've ever been to San Francisco?"

It was over before we knew it and we were back out in the hall. Robbie looked stunned. "It didn't hurt at all," he said, staring at the Band-Aid on his arm. "And you know what else?"

"What else?"

"That man didn't talk just to you."

"He didn't, did he?"

"Nope, he talked to me." He squared his shoulders. "I like him."

As it turned out, everyone talked to Robbie. The nurse in x-ray told him why they needed pictures. The doctor in cardiology showed him how you can sometimes tell that a person has heart trouble by looking at his fingers. The nurses on the ward explained the whys and wherefores of the ward routine. Even Dr. Hall, Robbie's surgeon, stopped by during lunch to tell him, "Robert, when your dad comes at the end of the week, we're all going to get together. And when we do, I'll tell you exactly what's going to happen during your operation. OK?"

And by the end of the first day the only question left unanswered was, "What time will you be back in the morning, Mom?"

"First thing," I told him. "Right after breakfast."

And then because a kid can't keep track of the plot on "Gunsmoke" if his mother keeps yammering at him, I gave him a kiss and left.

"See you tomorrow," I said as I went out the door.

"See you tomorrow," he echoed. And that was that.

The rest of the week was busy. The days started in the basement of the hospital, in the mess hall, where Donald's mother and Tommy's parents and I met for breakfast. Then it was on to the ward. We helped make beds.

We organized pickup details in the solarium. We fetched juice, read stories, built forts, and ran to the exchange during naptime to get a puzzle or more crayons.

The boys were rarely still. When they weren't cavorting in the solarium or sliding down the hall or building model planes in occupational therapy, they were sitting on their beds watching cartoons or doing their breathing exercises.

Breathing exercises were part of the preparation for surgery.

"You're going to have to cough after your operation," the physical therapist told them. "There'll be junk in your lungs that you'll have to cough up so you won't get pneumonia."

With that she gave them a set of blow bottles, and each boy learned to blow colored water from one bottle through a series of tubes to the other. When they'd mastered the technique, they had contests to see who could blow the longest or the hardest.

We parents cheered. We also amused ourselves. Donald's mother, a native of Samoa, taught the rest of us Samoan dances and jeered at our stiff hips. Tommy's mother knitted beer can hats for all the children on the ward. And in between we sat out by the elevator and had cigarettes.

Sometimes we all went down to the basement to wander through the exchange or check the mailroom for letters from home. Sometimes after lunch we hopped a bus to Ghirardelli Square or walked down to the commissary. Sometimes we simply went back to our rooms in the guest quarters to do some laundry or read.

We were always back by three. And with time out for dinner, we stayed till eight or so in the evening. The days passed: Wednesday, Thursday, and before we knew it, it was Friday and time for Tommy's surgery.

He went down early, right after breakfast. Robbie and Donald watched silently as the gurney came and two corpsmen lifted him up on it and wheeled him down the hall. The boys had known he was going, but until then the reality of it had been easily forgotten. After he left, they were quiet.

In fact, they were uneasy all day long. We tried to reassure them. We told them he'd come through the operation with no trouble. We explained that he was still in the recovery room. But they waited to see for themselves.

Finally, late in the afternoon, he was brought back onto the ward, to a private room across from the nurses' station.

"How's he doing?" I asked Bobbye, his mother.

"Pretty good," she said. "Come on in and say hello."

"Are you sure it's all right?"

"Sure."

So I went in. He was lying partially propped up in bed. There were tubes everywhere. An oxygen mask covered most of his face, and he moaned softly with every breath.

Oh, Lord, I thought. This is what's going to happen to Robbie. For a second I wanted to turn and run. But Bobbye took my hand. "It looks worse than it is," she said. "He's really doing quite well."

Tommy opened his eyes.

"Hi, Tom," I said.

He glanced at me briefly and went back to sleep.

"I'll see you later," I told Bobbye, and I left.

When I came out, Robbie and Donald were waiting.

"He's doing fine," I told them. "He really is."

"Can we see him?"

"Gee, I don't know." I was certain it was against hospital rules to let kids see someone hooked up to all sorts of devices and in obvious pain. "I don't think you're supposed to."

The nurse at the desk looked up from her work. "Sure you can," she said. "But only for a minute. And remember, he's still sleepy from the anesthetic, so he probably won't feel like talking to you."

So in we went. At first Donald and Robbie stared at the tubes and the bandages.

Then Robbie tugged at my sleeve. "What's that mask on his face?" he whispered.

"That's oxygen to help him breathe."

"Does it hurt?"

"No."

Tommy woke up. He didn't smile when he saw them. He didn't say anything. He only looked at them.

They grinned. "Hi, Tommy," Donald said.

"How do you feel?" Robbie added.

Tommy didn't answer. He closed his eyes. But it didn't seem to bother them.

"Well, see ya later." Robbie headed for the door. "Come on, Donald. It's time to eat." And they were off.

The nurse was still there when we came out.

"That's really something," I said as the boys raced back to their room.

"What is?"

"That." I gestured at Tommy's room. "I would have sworn that seeing Tommy fresh out of surgery would have scared those kids something awful. But look at them. This afternoon they were moping around, and now...look at them."

"It's really quite simple," she said. "This afternoon they were imagining all sorts of terrors and seeing it happening to them. Now they know what to expect. So in a way they can relax."

"Amazing." I left her and went to supervise the dinner hour. "Absolutely amazing."

"Say, Mom," Robbie asked as he climbed up on his bed and pulled his tray closer, "will I have tubes and bandages, too?"

I handed him his milk. "I'm not sure," I said. "You'll have tubes, but I don't know about the bandages." I poked the straw into the carton. "I'll ask if you like."

"OK." That was all.

The next day, Saturday, was a big day. Joe was coming. All day we waited. We peered out the solarium window, checking the parking lot for the familiar white station wagon. We jumped at the sound of heavy footsteps coming down the hall. We wandered down to the nurses' station and listened for the elevator. Finally, two minutes after we'd given up hope, he arrived.

There had been car trouble, treks on foot back into Medford, Oregon, and a mechanic who gave up a fishing trip to replace a malfunctioning part. It was quite a tale, and halfway through it, in the middle of the part where no one would pick him up as he trudged along the highway because everyone thought he was the escaped convict reportedly loose in the hills somewhere, he took a deep breath and a voice behind us said, "Excuse me. Could I interrupt for a minute?"

It was Dr. Tunley, the anesthetist, who'd stopped by to explain the procedures he'd be following on Monday.

"Oh, sure," Joe said as he introduced himself. "I was just explaining why I was late." He turned to Robbie. "Honey, why don't you go into the playroom for a while? We'll be there in a minute."

"Oh, that's all right," Dr. Tunley said "Let him stay. After all, it's his operation. He may have questions."

So he stayed, and while the doctor talked, he sat on his bed and fiddled with the tie on his bathrobe. Not until we were through did he look up. But when he did, the doctor reached over and took his hand.

"Robert," he said, "don't you worry. I'll be with you the whole time." Then he stood up. "See you Monday."

After he'd gone, Robbie turned to me, "Does this mean I'll be asleep during the operation?"

"That's right."

"And it won't hurt?"

"It won't hurt. Of course, the shot to make you sleepy will feel like all shots, but you won't feel anything during the operation itself."

"Are you sure?"

"I'm sure."

Satisfied, he jumped down from the bed. "Come on, Dad," he said. "Come see the tower I built this afternoon."

The next day was bleak, but then Sundays in a hospital are always bleak. It was cool outside. The fog poured in over the city, obscuring even the parking lot below, and invisible foghorns grumbled intermittently. Robbie was restless. We all were. We played cards, watched TV, and talked to Tommy, who by now was sitting up in a chair. The nurses' station was quiet. Lights were dim, and only the arrival of an occasional visitor broke the monotony.

In the late afternoon Dr. Hall sent up word that he wanted to talk to us..So we waited. Shortly after six he arrived.

"Let's go in here," he said, indicating the conference room.

So we went in, and when we were seated, he turned to Robbie. "Do you know why you need an operation?" he asked.

Robbie shrugged.

"It's because you have a hole in your heart." He reached

into the pocket of his coat, hauled out a plastic model of a heart, and opened it up. "See," he said, "right here, between the two upper sections."

Robbie moved in closer.

"Now, because of this hole," he continued, "when your heart pumps, some of the blood that should go out to your body, to your head, and to your arms and legs goes into the right side of your heart and then into your lungs."

It was clear so far.

"And if this hole isn't sewn up, this side of your heart will eventually stretch. This means that when you're thirty-five or so, you could suffer a heart failure."

Robbie peered at the model, turned it over in his hands, and snapped it back together.

"Now about the operation itself." Joe shifted in his chair. "I'll make a vertical incision on the chest and through the breastbone, then into the upper part of the heart. During the repair of the hole itself Robert will be on the heart-lung machine. It won't take long. Then I'll sew up the entrance to the heart. I'll wire the breastbone back together, and finally I'll stitch up the initial incision. Do you have any questions?"

Robbie thought for a minute. "How about right after the operation?" he asked. "How will I look?"

"You'll have two drainage tubes in your lower chest and an intravenous tube right up here." He showed him. "For a while in the recovery room there'll be a tube in your nose and down past your vocal cords, so you won't be able to talk. But that will come out soon, and you'll be asleep most of the time anyway."

"How about when it's all over...when I'm home and well again and everything? Will anything else go wrong?"

"Do you mean will you have trouble with your heart?"

"Yes."

"Nope. You'll be good as new."

Robbie grinned. That was what he'd hoped to hear. He jumped up to go.

"Oh, one more thing," the doctor said as we walked out into the hall. "I want Robert to be sure to see the recovery room before tomorrow, so that when he wakes up, he won't be frightened. Check with the nurse on the ward. She should be able to tell you when you can go down there."

"We sure will," Joe said, "and thank you, Doctor. See you tomorrow."

"Right. Good-night." And he was off.

We milled around for a bit, and when the nurse gave us the go-ahead, we went downstairs to visit the recovery room.

It was quiet when we went in. The radio was playing softly, and since there were no patients, the nurse came right over and introduced herself. Then she took us on the tour.

We saw where Robbie's bed would be. We saw the monitoring machines and a modified Ouija board he'd be able to use to spell out words if he wanted to say something. He spelled his name and giggled.

"And another thing," the nurse said to him as we started to go, "when you're in here, your mom and dad will be able to come see you every hour. They'll come in this door, put on one of those"—she indicated a pile of hospital gowns—"and they'll come right around the corner."

He looked up at me and smiled, and as we walked to the elevator, he hiked up his pajamas and took my hand. "I'm glad you can come to see me," he said.

Joe pressed the up button. "Don't worry," he said. "We'll be there."

"We sure will," I repeated later as I gave Robbie his

bath and scrubbed his hair clean. "So all you have to do is get a good night's sleep, and before you know it, it will all be over." I tipped his head back and rinsed out the soap.

He grabbed for a washcloth and covered his eyes. "Mom?" he said, sputtering as a stream of soap ran into his mouth.

"What?"

"Does this mean I'm not going to die?"

I caught my breath. "Oh, honey," I said as I hugged him, soap and all. "Of course it does. You're going to live, and after everything is healed, you'll be back running, climbing trees, and driving Joan crazy."

He snorted. "Good."

I rinsed his hair once more, lifted him out of the tub, and dried him. In honor of the occasion I'd found a pair of clean pajamas that matched. "It's a good omen," I told him. "Now come on, let's go find Daddy, and then it's time for bed."

"OK," he said. "You will come early tomorrow, won't you?"

"We'll come early," I assured him.

And we did. We were there at six-thirty. The ward was still quiet when we arrived. He'd already been given his shot, so he was groggy. We stood by his bed. He seemed calm, and as we chattered on about nothing in particular, I brushed his hair back out of his eyes.

Then I heard the gurney clattering down the hall. Joe went to the door to see, and as he did, Robbie turned to me. "Mom," he said, "would you ask Dad to give me a hug before they come?"

I beckoned Joe, gave him the message, and turned away quickly.

The operation took about three hours. Joe and I waited

it out in the main lobby with endless cups of coffee, cigarettes that smoldered in the ashtray, and disjointed conversations that touched on mulch for weed control in a vegetable garden, the cannons at Fort Point, auto mechanics, sourdough bread, the Tokyo telephone system, overseas postage rates, the NBA and the goings on at home—everything but the operation that was taking place in another part of the hospital.

Finally, at around ten-thirty, Dr. Hall appeared with the news that it was over and everything had gone well. We followed him into recovery. Robbie lay very still. He was hooked up to the machines and tubes. He looked pale, and his blond hair, like straw, stuck out in all directions. Every now and then he frowned briefly as if having a bad dream.

"Hi, honey," I said, taking his hand. "We're here."

He opened his eyes briefly, blinked a time or two, and went back to sleep.

The nurse checked his IV bottle, adjusted it, and glanced at the heart monitor. "He's doing fine," she said with a smile. "But he's still a little sleepy."

Joe kissed him lightly on the forehead. "We'll be back in an hour," he said. Then we moved away, stripped off the gowns, and went out into the hall. Neither of us said anything as we walked back to the lobby. Then Joe took a deep breath. "How about some breakfast?" he said. "Suddenly I'm starved."

"Me too."

Joe and I stayed with Robbie in shifts, day and night, for two days. They weren't easy days for Robbie. It hurt him terribly to have to sit up every hour or two to use the IPPB (intermittent-positive-pressure-breathing) machine and the blow bottles and to cough. It hurt to turn with tubes and needles everywhere. But he didn't complain. And except for the one night when he turned, accidentally unhooked the heart monitor, and sent Joe bellowing out into the hall when the blips went flat, his recovery was swift and uneventful.

When we asked him how he felt, he always said, "Fine." But I'd see him open his eyes wide and wrinkle his nose in the supreme effort it must have taken to do as he was told.

Each day, however, it was better. Each day it was easier. Four days after surgery the tubes came out. And that morning, when we walked into the room we found him sitting up in bed, gently scratching around his stitches with his toothbrush.

"You know, Dad," he said as Joe nonchalantly took the toothbrush away and put it back in the drawer, "I don't see why people say operations are so terrible. Mine wasn't so bad."

Three days later we took him for a brief ride around San Francisco. Ten days after surgery we left the hospital and flew home. After six months he was back riding his bike and building yet another tree house in the fir at the end of the driveway.

And seven years later, in February 1981, I stood at the finish line of the Trail's End Marathon in Seaside, Oregon, and watched him, now tall and strong, reach down somewhere inside himself somewhere for that last bit of energy as he lunged across the finish line.

༄ Look What Followed Me Home

THE TROUBLE WITH those of us raised in the Dick and Jane generation is that we believed all that propaganda about Spot.

You remember Spot, the faithful dog that bounded through the meadow while Dick chirped, "Look, Jane, look. See Spot run. Run, Spot, run."

If we hadn't been so docile and submissive, we might have wondered how Dick's mother felt about Spot. We might even have read between the lines and imagined her saying, "See Spot run, my foot. See Spot shed. See Spot knock over the garbage. See Spot throw up on the rug while Puff drops a dead mouse on my shoe."

If we hadn't been the sort that blindly follows along with the program, we might have questioned the edict that a Spot, a Puff, two budgies, assorted gerbils, and a bowlful of guppies are essential if one is to raise a well-adjusted family of morally responsible children. At least I might have. And if I had, I wouldn't be sitting out here on the back porch at this very moment scraping at the soles of my shoes with a stick.

But no, I believed what they told me: that a home isn't a home without a pet. And when Joe, still a bridegroom, introduced me to Felicia, the stray cat that had chosen his doorstep on which to linger, I blanched inwardly but smiled, and said something inane like "How nice, our own little family."

It's not that I dislike animals. I don't. I grew up with pets. We had cats, one that slept in the bathtub and another that walked up and down the piano keys in the middle of the night. And we had Barney, a collie that went wading but not swimming and that groaned and left the room whenever we praised any of the other dogs on our road. I fully intended that Joe and I would have pets in our life together. But I also hoped we'd have them later...when we weren't living in an apartment about the size of the average place mat and when it wasn't the landlord's draperies and the landlord's couch being used as a scratching post.

Of course, one cat was no trouble. But the one cat had five kittens. And she had them the day Joe, who'd obviously read even more of Dick and Jane than I had, brought home one flea-ridden, soon to be large, soon to be loud, and never to be completely housebroken dog. That's when I had my first vision of Dick's mother saying to Dick's father, "Don't tell me to calm down, Elwin. I've had it. This morning Spot took a nip out of the meter reader. This afternoon he ate a whole box of crayons. And look at the multicolored tracks Dick and Jane just made across the kitchen and over the living room rug."

The visions continued when we left Felicia with our landlord and moved into base housing with the dog, dubbed Vicar so my father wouldn't be upset if we neglected to name our first son Vincent. I had them when we had to tie Vicar to the clothesline and he took all of twenty-three seconds to wind himself around the pole and pin his head to the ground. I had them when we saved for months to buy a beige carpet for the living room and he christened it in seven different places the first day. And I had them when, in a fit of Christmas cheer, I baked a plate of cookies for the mailman.

Vicar was not fond of the mailman, and when I tried to present my humble gift, I had to hold him back with one hand, push the screen door open with my shoulder, and then inch the cookies out to their startled recipient. But the dog got loose and knocked the plate out of my hand. That sent the mailman racing down the block as Vicar scampered after him and I lumbered after Vicar.

Eventually the military life proved too much for Vicar, and we gave him to a man who had a place in the country. That's when Joe and I agreed on the "No more pets till we retire and have a place in the country" rule.

It was a good rule and one we stuck with. We followed it in Japan when the boys next door adopted an enormous beetle, tied a string to the rhinoceroslike tusk in its forehead, and took it for walks. We kept it in Maryland when our neighbor's dog had puppies, when Sylvia's classmate brought her pet rabbit to school, and when my niece, on a visit, described the joys of owning a cageful of hamsters.

Not until the frigid New Year's Eve when Joe was eight months short of retirement and the girls up the street had been ordered to get rid of the cat they'd found did we finally relent.

"All right," we said, "you can keep her, but..." and we echoed the meaningless phrase that has echoed through the ages since Abel first stood plaintively at Adam and Eve's back door, asking to keep the baby dinosaur in his arms. "But," we said, "it's up to you children to take care of her."

"We will," they promised traditionally. "You won't even know she's around."

We called her Midnight in honor of the end of 1969 and the fact that she was all black. And if I'm not mistaken that was the last time any of us thought up a decent name for a pet.

I don't know what happens to us when it comes time to select an appropriate name for an animal we've chosen to feed, curry, and take to the vet for the next fifteen or so years. All our friends and relatives seem to have no trouble being terribly clever. But somehow we manage to miss the mark. While the Persian that adopted the church is christened Magnificat, we end up with Tib, a name that has no meaning and no special significance and is only slightly preferable to Tippy, which is what the animal welfare shelter said she'd been called.

My aunt Sylvia, like me the daughter of an ecclesiastic, calls her dachshund Mercy for "Surely goodness and mercy shall follow me all the days of my life." A friend has terriers named Tic and Toc. I know a lawyer with two pigs called Habeas Porcus and Porcus Delecti. And neighbors abound in sensible Dukes, Sheps, and Luckys. So what do we do? We adopt two puppies of uncertain lineage. Because one promises to be huge, we decide we'll call them David and Goliath. We decide it, that is, until David objects and says he doesn't relish the thought of being roused out of a reverie every time we open up a can of Alpo and announce dinner and until we also discover one of the dogs is female. Then we rummage around with names and titles and end up with Goliath and Bathsheba, Golly and Shebie for short, which, since Bathsheba was once married to David, is like calling them Abraham Lincoln and Mrs. Booth.

At times I think I should have followed in the footsteps

of my other aunt, Mary, and simply called all canine pets Dog, and all felines Cat.

With Midnight, however, we selected the perfect name, and potentially she was a perfect cat. She was small. Her meow, with tinges of Siamese in it, rarely roared malevolently. And she was patient with Robbie, who wanted to carry her upstairs to his room. She was patient with Jenny, who dressed her up because she thought she'd look lovely in a bonnet, and she tolerated Sylvia, who tried to teach her to leap through a Hula-Hoop.

Unfortunately other cats also found her charming, and before I had a chance to realize what was happening, the call had gone out: "There's a gorgeous new kid on the block." The next thing I knew Sylvia was yelling, "Hey, David, Geoffrey, come quick. Midnight's having kittens in the basement."

I must say she was good about having an audience. And with Joe to handle crowd control and answer questions, things went well. Of course, there were several interesting dinner conversations after that, and I had to be on the alert for odd lumps under Robbie's shirt whenever he came up from the basement. But the kittens grew and thrived. And when they were old enough, we put an ad in the paper and gave away all but two.

"I'm only agreeing to keep these two," I told the horde of joyous upturned faces, "because we'll soon be moving home to Bainbridge, where they'll be able to roam around outside. But"—I stopped them in their exuberant flight—"as soon as we get there, we're going to have Midnight spayed. So this is the last of the kittens."

"Fine," they said as children do when they've scored one victory and have not yet begun to fight for the next. "That's fine."

While they promptly started the tradition of odd names

for Combs animals by naming the two Leonard and Judy even though they both were male, I heaved a hesitant sigh of relief because finally I was being a good parent and completing the family picture with pets.

Had I been smart instead of cowed, I would have waited. I would have realized that the trip from Colorado Springs to the island, in a Volkswagen bus, with six children and no Joe (since he had to defend his country for three more months), would not be enhanced by the presence of three cats. But my foresight has never been 20/20.

So the tribe increased by two, and a month or so later I rattled down the highway with the children singing endless verses of every song they ever knew, with the cats leaping from seat to seat, and with the smell of rancid Kitty Litter wafting around the bus like a pungent cloud.

We smuggled them into motels. The children dashed out in their pajamas and chased them around the parking lot when they escaped. While we slept, they bounded from one bed to another, skidded into the bathroom, and slithered under the dressers. And when we finally reached temporary lodging at Mother's and Daddy's, they immediately disgraced themselves and attacked a robin.

The situation didn't improve when we moved into our own house. For one thing, the cats shrieked with delight at the country life and rushed outside to spend their days combing the underbrush for field mice and other assorted rodents. They then dragged them back into the house, tossed them in the air a time or two, and left them draped over the edge of their water dish.

For another thing, I, in all the turmoil, neglected to get Midnight to the vet. So she produced another litter of kittens, and before they were weaned, she disappeared and never returned. This left us with tiny forms blindly crawling around, looking for their mother. It left us feeding them with toy milk bottles until they were finally old enough to give away. And it left me wondering if Dick and Jane's mother had ever resorted to Valium.

But because I never learn from my mistakes, as summer inched into fall and Joe fired his last salute and came home, I forgot the kitten episode and agreed, insisted even, that what we needed now was a couple of dogs. So we brought Golly and Shebie home, increasing the animal population to four if you don't count the wild cat hiding under the house, the raccoon that sat in the fir tree for three days, or the pheasant that stalked across the lawn every now and then. And we all settled down to be the typical American family.

In the year and a half that followed I regretted rescinding the no pet law at least twice a month. I regretted it when Judy disappeared for three days.

I regretted it when Golly and Shebie, who were brother and sister but looked like a fat black setter and an English sheepdog, respectively, produced a blond sway-backed puppy. I regretted it when Hadji—again the name meant nothing and was simply a product of Jenny's or Sylvia's energetic imagination—followed the children up to the bus stop and was hit by a car and killed while they watched and the driver roared off.

And I regretted it when Leonard staggered in the door one day and Sylvia and Jenny went with me as we rushed him to the closest vet in Poulsbo, a town about fifteen miles across the bridge and on the mainland. I thought perhaps I shouldn't have brought them with me, but I needed someone in case he tried to get out of his box. Then, when the doctor said it was a tumor and the best thing to do was to have Leonard put to sleep, I knew I shouldn't have brought them with me. And as we drove home and the girls sat in the back of the bus, sobbing and shouting, "You're a murderer. That's what you are," I vowed I never would again.

Eventually things settled down. We got another cat, Tib. We had Shebie spayed. And things were peaceful again. Well, not exactly peaceful. The girls kept trying to bring home more cats. They presented me with a pregnant one on my birthday. We whisked it back to its owner, and I let them explain they'd been hasty in saying they could keep it. Sylvia also brought home a gray cat and claimed she'd found it on the side of the road. We kept it, even though it had some kind of asthmatic condition and sounded like an obscene phone call from a breather. Eventually it, too, had to be put to sleep. I'd learned my lesson, though. This time I sent Joe off to do the dirty deed.

Still, after a while I got used to having pets. Of course, things got a bit sticky when Golly wandered up the hill to the church and nipped at one of the faithful. There was a certain amount of commotion whenever Tib, the most voracious mouser of them all, climbed up the walnut tree, scampered across the roof, and bounded in through an open window with her latest catch. And I never quite understood why Golly and the Saint Bernard down the road had to celebrate love and the rites of spring right outside the window during dinner. But I learned to shrug whenever anyone hollered, "Look, Mom, look. What are they doing?" And Joe learned to ignore the inevitable "They're having sex, dummy. That's what they're doing."

Then came Christmas and Aunt Sylvia bearing a cage holding Peter, a canary, and the tumult started again. There was the crisis when Tib tired of admiring the bird from afar and leaped off the kitchen counter, knocking over the cage before I could grab it. There was Peter fluttering madly in an attempt to escape and in the process getting his foot caught in the bars. And there was the tool room instantly converted into a bird hospital with the deputy nurses and doctors tiptoeing in and out and administering measured doses of brandy to the recuperating patient.

Fortunately Peter recovered. Of course, his foot fell off and we had to widen the perches. He also looked like a feathered pirate as he hopped around on his stump. But Tib left him alone, and whenever the dishwasher was running, he sang as if he'd just learned how. Accompanying the dishwasher was an eccentricity of his, and I took to running several loads every day just to hear him praise the world of hot spinning water and Calgonite. Months later, however, the machine broke, and before we could get it fixed, Peter died.

We buried him out near the raspberries next to Hadji's grave. Joan, then a devotee of plastic flowers, donated another geranium to mark the spot.

After Peter came Rex and Charlie, two budgies that never learned to talk because I callously said that what with laundry, dusting, cooking, bedmaking, scrubbing the tub, getting groceries, unclogging the sink, and making numerous trips to the ferry, the library, the school, and piano lessons, I didn't have time to spend fifteen minutes a day teaching each of them how to say, "Pretty bird," or, "Hello, lovey." Frankly I was grateful they didn't pick up "Oh, my God, not again" and other uncensored utterances.

One day, however, Robbie accidentally left their cage door open, and they flew out the window, never to be seen again. So I packed away their cage and dishes and toys. I vacuumed up the wide circle of birdseed and feathers from the floor. And I declared the aviary closed.

I also issued a ban against any future snakes, turtles, gerbils, hamsters, chickens, ducks, or creatures of the forest. In the heat of the moment I forgot to mention fish. So one day Robbie came home with a frozen dogfish he'd found by the pond down the hill from our driveway. He insisted it was merely sleeping and begged me to put it in a bucket of water till it woke up. So I did—why I'm not sure. I think I was simply tired of being the bearer of bad news. Besides, I knew he'd lose interest before the thing started to rot. And when he did, I added his contribution to a lower layer of the compost heap.

Once we were back to two dogs and one cat, we all relaxed again. Golly and Shebie chased each other up and down the lawn. They stretched out under the pine tree on summer afternoons. On moonlit nights they thundered around outside the house and answered the sound of their own barking as it echoed back from across the bay. And they protected their terrain from intruders: a neighboring setter, the garbage man, folks wandering through, looking for a path to the water, and occasionally the UPS woman or visiting clergy.

Somewhere Shebie found either a cache of beer or an obliging drunk. She took to wandering home with an empty bottle, an empty can, a discarded six-pack, or, during the holidays, a champagne bottle in her mouth. Golly usually trailed along behind, and every now and then, just to prove he, too, was capable of retrieving, he brought a piece of cardboard or part of a milk carton with him.

They both also lay in wait for Tib. But she was too quick for them and always managed to scuttle up the walnut tree before they could get her. Besides, she ventured out only in the summer. The rest of the time she lounged around on Geoffrey's bed, stretched out in front of the fireplace, curled up on the navy blue coat I forgot to hang up or, when I'd neglected to fold a week's worth of laundry, on top of the dryer.

At night she prowled the house and chased heaven knows what around the attic. When she felt frisky, she raced up and down the temporary banister we'd installed and sharpened her claws on it until she'd reduced it to a splinter factory. And during thunderstorms she sought refuge in an upstairs bedroom.

Not that the noise bothered her. It didn't. She was simply hiding from the dogs, which were sent into a frenzy by the celestial clatter. At the first clap of thunder they hurled themselves at the closest door available. If it refused to burst open, they clawed at the frame till someone rushed to let them in and give them refuge. Unfortunately they felt the same way about firecrackers and the Fourth of July. One year the explosions were too much for Golly, so while Shebie hid upstairs under Jenny's bed, he decided to outrun them.

We searched the island for days, calling, waiting and listening. We saw a hundred dogs that looked like him. We answered a hundred phone calls from people who said they'd seen him in the woods or trudging along the road. But we never found him. And the ache that comes when a pet dies or runs away was back.

Once again, mainly because Shebie seemed so lost and alone, we brought home a puppy. Shebie has yet to thank us. In fact, I have the feeling she looks on Bani (we held to tradition and called her Banisadr not for political reasons but simply because it had a nice ring to it) as the juvenile delinquent she hoped she'd never have. Bani, on the other hand, is a typical Labrador.

For one thing, she's dumb. When we come down the driveway, she dances in front of the car and barely escapes being pinned under the wheels. When I bring home the groceries, she stretches out in front of the back door and invariably gets stepped on or bombed with carrots and cabbages when a bag gives way. And when I took her to the vet for surgery and shots, she went limp and had to be carried in like a giant bag of wet cement.

During the day she nips at Shebie's ears or lavishes unwanted affection on everyone from the mailman to the woman delivering telephone books. She digs up the beer bottles Shebie carefully buried under the rhododendrons. When it's sunny, she wanders around the yard, looking for a place to light, then lies down on the daffodils. When I fill up the large plastic bin we use for a water dish, she immediately drags it down the back stairs and tips it over. She jumps at fuchsia baskets hanging in the willow, attacks pots of nasturtiums up on an old tree stump, and spends hours working off the lid of the garbage can.

At night she rummages around under the house, bashing up against the heating ducts. She stations herself outside our bedroom window and barks warnings to any vicious beasts hiding out in the Scotch broom until Joe is forced to struggle up out of bed, stagger over to the window, and bark out a set of his own warnings. Then she retreats to the front porch, attacks a sleeping Shebie, and thumps around there for a while.

I have a feeling that if she'd belonged to Dick and Jane, we'd all have grown up with a more realistic view of what life with pets is like. And the text instead of "See Spot. See Spot run. Run, Spot, run," would have read, "Down, Spot. No Spot. Back, Spot. Out...out, damn Spot."

८► Advice and Dissent

IT ALL STARTED with Haim Ginott. Until he wandered by and plunked *Between Parent and Child* down on every tricycle-scarred coffee table, until he appeared as the resident guest on every television talk show west of New-foundland's Grand Banks, and until he sprinkled his advice on the pages of every magazine, I thought I had this motherhood thing under control.

I knew, without being told, that letting a toddler touch a hot oven door just once is a more effective deterrent than a week's worth of "No, no"s. I knew better than to holler, "Don't stick your finger in the light socket," at a child who hasn't even considered entertaining himself electrically. And I knew that "I hate you" usually means "I don't want to go to bed" or "What's so terrible about painting the walls with nail polish?" or even "Who says I have to pick up that block I hurled across the room?"

True, when I was nineteen or twenty and still single, I'd vowed that my children, when I had them, would be perfect. They'd never throw tantrums. They'd always be neat and clean, and they'd always finish their dinner…at least they would if they didn't want it for breakfast. But I got over that just as I got over the notion that having a house of one's own to take care of is the ultimate happiness. And once I actually had children of my own, I realized that tantrums get thrown whether you like it or not. I realized that neat and clean are all very well, but they're nothing compared to the thrill of stomping in a mud puddle occasionally or squishing a banana and letting it ooze through your fingers. And I realized that a dinner warmed up for breakfast is never going to make Brussels sprouts palatable. In other words, I soon learned that common sense beats "always" and "never" every time.

So until Haim Ginott came along and complicated things, I greeted the day calmly, confident that for the most part I was up to the task ahead.

I knew that morning becomes almost no one and that a dissertation on spilled milk doesn't put it back in the glass. "Get some paper towels…quickly" is preferable to "How many times have I told you not to reach for the sugar but to ask someone to pass it?" I knew that if David made his bed voluntarily today, he'd be encouraged to repeat the effort tomorrow if I didn't say, "That's fine, but…" and then go on to point out that the spread was hanging at an odd angle and the blankets weren't completely tucked in. And I soon discovered that announcing, "Nancy Dickerson"—her news break came on at seven twenty-five—headed them all out the door and on their way to school faster than "Will you please hurry up?" or "You're going to be late, you know."

As the day progressed, I muddled along fairly effectively. I dished out praise lavishly and said, "Boy, those are neat colors," instead of "What's that?" to Joan's picture of blue circles, squiggly green lines, and a lavender blob in the upper right-hand corner. I kept Geoffrey from belting Jenny when she called him "poopoo face" and told him firmly that, no matter what the provocation, slugging was not allowed. I also told Jenny to knock it off with the name-calling. I let Sylvia help me "mush" the meat loaf and agreed to substitute a salad for those "yucky green peas you always feed us."

I tried to keep my "I'm warning you"s to a minimum. I refrained from snarling, "You just wait till your father hears about this." I didn't faint when Jenny came home for lunch and announced that two of her fellow first graders and a boy in kindergarten had pulled her pants down and "looked at my peepee." I simply sent a note to the teacher and let her take it from there. And I was wonderfully nonchalant when one boy and his mother dropped by to apologize.

I admit I fell once or twice for the "But, Mom, that's not fair" tactic. I was also momentarily buffaloed by "But none of my friends have to…" Still, because I was confident, I soon got over that. I even managed to hold out against Mother's "I don't mean this as criticism, but…"

And when I occasionally caved in, Joe stood firm and said, "Now, now, we're doing the best we know how, and frankly I think we're doing a pretty good job."

Then, sometime in 1968, I stumbled on Haim Ginott. Apparently he'd been around for a while, but I'd been too busy to notice him. I'd also been too busy and too caught up in the world of the very young to pay much attention to the general rebellion being staged by America's teen-agers, college students, and almost everyone else under thirty. I wasn't completely unaware that youth was throwing rocks against the establishment. I'd read the reports on campus rioting. I'd heard all the bizarre details of life in the communes and the art of dropping out in Haight-Ashbury. I'd seen protests, revolts, love-ins, antiwar demonstrations, the maharishi, chanting Hare Krishnas, and Timothy Leary on the evening news. I knew the catch phrases *the plastic society, love children, the vibes are good, let it all hang out,* and *groovy.* And I knew that the older generation was said to have committed the sins of hypocrisy, unfulfillment, loss of idealism, and, above all, rampant materialism.

But as someone barely thirty-three, I didn't feel like the older generation. I didn't feel rebellious either. I'd spent too many years doing as I was told, living up to expectations, and worrying, "What will people think?" to consider rebelling at this late date.

As for my own children, their antagonism was still limited to "Why do I always have to clean my room? I like it messy" and "I don't want to go to bed now. Why do you always make me go to bed so early? My friend Mike gets to stay up all night long if he wants to" and "I hate Sylvia's old dumb coat, and I won't wear it even if I freeze to death." Though the shouting, the foot stomping, and the slammed doors caused my teeth to clench, my jaw to tighten, and often sent me stumbling into my room to lock the door, shake my fist at heaven, and cry, "Why me, God, why me? You promised things would improve after toilet training and the terrible twos," I still naïvely assumed that this was as bad as it would get. And I was confident that like miniskirts, youth's mutiny would pass before my brood entered high school.

Then Haim Ginott whispered, "Silly fool. Nothing's going to get better if you don't shape up as a parent."

"How's that again?" I asked.

"I said shape up," he repeated, "now...while there's still time."

"But I thought we were doing a fairly decent job," I protested. "The children seem happy enough. They're all doing well in school. And as far as I know, none of the neighborhood mothers has declared them off limits as playmates."

"That's all very well," he said, "but tell me, do they argue among themselves?"

"Of course."

"Do they protest when you ask them to pick up their toys?"

"Sometimes."

"Do they get upset when they lose a game?"

"Now and then."

"Did you realize a child can get sexually aroused during a spanking?"

"Lord, no."

"And you actually think you're doing a pretty good job of being a parent?"

"Well…" I stammered, "I did."

"And now?"

"I don't know. I guess I was wrong," I muttered as my confidence quickly slipped sideways a bit.

Haim Ginott chuckled and rattled off a couple of clever anecdotes about other mothers and fathers who had also thought they were succeeding as parents. Then he leaned back and said, "But don't worry. I can teach you how to be a better parent."

"You can?" I blathered, ever so thankful that all was not lost.

"Of course," he said. "It's a little tricky, but you'll get the hang of it soon enough."

He then went on for two hundred and some pages explaining just how Joe and I could clean up our act. By the time I was through reading about "New ways of praise and criticism," "Discipline: permissiveness and limits," "Jealousy," and "Sexual role and social function," I could hardly wait to try out my new skills.

"It's really simple," I told Joe. "When Jenny says, 'Daddy, Geoffrey won't let me read *The Mean Man*,' for instance, we've always tried to reason with both of them, haven't we?"

"Huh?" Joe wasn't as convinced as I that I'd discovered the secret of parental perfection. "What'd you say?"

I went through it again.

"Yeah," he said, "I guess we have tried to settle things peacefully."

"Well," I said, "according to Haim Ginott, we don't even have to do that. All we have to do is repeat to Geoffrey what Jenny has said, then repeat to Jenny what Geoffrey says, and so on till they both get bored and forget what they were arguing about."

"Sounds weird to me."

"I know, but what can we lose? He says we've been doing it wrong all this time anyway."

So we gave it a try, and sure enough, we bored them out of their tennis shoes. At least we did for a while. Then they got surly, and every time I opened my mouth to say, "David, Sylvia says you threw your smelly socks at her," he'd turn on his heel and groan, "Oh, Mom, come on, not that dumb trick again."

I let that go for a while and went to work on another of my shortcomings: my tendency when things get raucous to holler, "You kids are driving me crazy...absolutely crazy. Do you always have to fight over every little thing? Tell me, do you?"

"What we're supposed to do," I told Joe, "is simply state how we feel. And while we're at it"—I snickered at the cleverness of it all—"Dr. Ginott says we might as well improve our children's vocabulary by using big words."

Joe shrugged and shook his head. "All right," he said, "I guess we can give it a try."

So when Sylvia bellowed just for the hell of it and I was so startled I knocked over my coffee cup, I refrained from bellowing back, "You idiot. Don't you ever do that to me again." Instead, I turned on her and roared, "I am livid. I am seething with indignation. It infuriates me to be jolted like that."

"I, too, am incensed," Joe added, getting into the swing of it. "Needless screaming frays my nerves and makes me bellicose."

Sylvia's mouth dropped open. "Huh?" she said.

I managed a few more four-syllable adjectives.

"What does that mean?"

"It means you drive me crazy when you scream like that," I snarled.

"Oh." She skipped off.

"Good try," Joe said. "I don't think it did any good, but at least you gave it a shot."

"Well, I'm not giving up," I snapped. "Haim Ginott says none of us knows how to talk to our children. He says that we preach and criticize too much, that we don't try to understand children's inner feelings, and that we undermine their self-respect."

"Oh, I don't know that I agree with that," Joe countered. "I think we're fairly sensitive to their feelings."

"Well, Haim Ginott says we're not. And he promises peace and tranquillity if we only follow his rules and learn how to talk to our children. I'm going to do as he says."

Joe shook his head. "Be my guest," he said.

And I tried.

When Sylvia wanted to stay up till eleven watching "Mission Impossible," I refrained from the old "Sorry. Tomorrow's a school day, and you should have been in bed an hour ago as it is." This time I chose my words carefully and said, "You'd like to stay up late, wouldn't you?"

"You bet," she said, sensing a crack in the old armor.

"You like watching the clever way they solve their cases, don't you?"

"I sure do." She stretched out on the end of our bed and propped her head on her hand.

"And it's upsetting to have to go to bed when something you enjoy is on television," I continued, wondering if I sounded as stilted as I felt but willing to carry on if it meant there'd be no tears and no "But, M...o...m." Haim Ginott had assured me that right about now Sylvia, overwhelmed at my understanding attitude, would see her duty and volunteer to go right to bed.

Haim, however, had never met Sylvia, and half an hour later, when I'd exhausted every sympathetic phrase I knew, she was still at the foot of my bed and still watching a small dog with an electronic beeper on his collar work his way through the air-conditioning system of a foreign embassy. About then is when I reverted to form and announced, "To bed...now." And because she'd assumed I'd finally gone soft and decided to let her stay up, she was horrified at the thought of being forced to her room right in the middle of the best part.

So we had a delayed broadcast of the tears and the "But, M...o...m." Later that night, just before I went to sleep, I started the ritual of promising myself that tomorrow I'd do better. I'd try harder. I'd be more understanding. And I'd be the sort of parent Haim Ginott approved of.

Nevertheless, I usually managed to fall short. So when he climbed back down the best-seller list, I toddled after the next guru who claimed to have discovered the secret of successful parenthood, and the next and the next. While I was at it, I sifted through the other prescriptions for success, happiness, and eternal youth put forth by all the neo and self-acclaimed "experts."

I draped a towel over my head and hunched over a vaporizer twice a day because I'd read an article in the paper that said I'd end up looking like W. H. Auden if I didn't close my pores and give my face moisture while there was still time. I gave away my striped dress because a fashion consultant in a magazine reminded me that the chunky of this world have no business wandering around looking like a walking flag of Uruguay. I made bunny rabbit salads out of pear halves and mounds of cottage cheese and put pimiento smiles on tuna fish sandwiches because a home economist on a TV show said it was up to me to make lunch a festive occasion.

One author described how to be my own and presumably everyone else's best friend. Another said I could stop smoking if I drank lots of water with baking soda in it and left my cigarettes out in the mailbox. A psychiatrist's wife told me how to make the house look presentable in thirty minutes. A fellow housewife chastised me for not making everyone go outside to comb his or her hair. A clergyman turned counselor mumbled something about taking charge of my emotional life. I read at least six articles telling me I should fight constructively and stop reminding Joe of the time he refused to eat my red flannel hash. And three of them suggested Joe and I light up our lives and have sex in the yard.

I stocked up on diet books and articles the way a homeroom mother stocks up on Styrofoam cups and Hawaiian

Punch. And I tried them all. I ate steak, grapefruit, and hard boiled eggs. I ate celery sticks, cottage cheese, and peach halves. I munched on diet graham crackers, washed them down with a chaser of water, and waited for them to swell in my stomach and block out all thoughts of potato chips. With Mother nipping at my heels, I tried high-protein diets, low-protein diets, the Stillman diet, the Atkins diet, the Scarsdale diet, and a few others named after no one in particular.

While I was at it, I exercised. I exercised with a set of Wallace reducing records that had belonged to my grandmother. They came complete with photographs of Wallace, in a shapeless tank suit and Oxfords, practicing what he preached. I whiled away the predawn hours rolling around on the living room floor in response to *Miss Craig's 21 Day Shape-up Program.* I paused in midmorning to bend and stretch with Jack LaLanne. At long stoplights I grimaced, yawned, and stretched my sagging facial muscles. And I bought a pair of running shoes and stumbled along the island roads till as I slumped against a mailbox, my life flashed before my eyes.

Then, for all my shortcomings that had yet to be corrected in print, I listened to friends and relatives. They never failed me. "Surely you're not going to wear a winter white hat after Easter?" and "Don't you know that if you'd go over your kitchen floor with a wet mop once a day, it wouldn't get to this state?" and "You do realize there are dog obedience schools, don't you?" and "Let me show you the right way to make a hospital corner" and "You mean you don't supervise your children's flossing?" "Oh, come now, any fool can raise a Christmas cactus" and "I always wrap my cookie sheets in aluminum foil. It keeps them shiny and bright" and "I hate to say this, but rust simply isn't your color" and "What's that horrible smell?"

and "Well, maybe permanent press is fine for you, but my John likes to have me touch up his shirts with an iron."

All the while I continued to pore over books, to read articles and to watch television programs featuring Haim Ginott's successors. The more I read and watched, the less competent I felt. But I needn't have worried. The hordes of counselor-turned-author had stumbled on a new gold mine: classes, seminars, workshops, and encounters.

Joe and I signed up for the Wednesday night sessions. They were informal. We all took off our shoes. We all sat on the floor. We all had coffee. And we all heard once again that we were making a mess of this business of being parents.

It was Haim Ginott with ruffles and flourishes:

"The reason you're blowing it is that you haven't mastered the skills of effective parenting."

"You don't know how to listen to your children."

"You don't know how to talk to your children."

"You need to develop problem-solving techniques."

"Follow the instructions, and miraculously all will be sunshine and roses forever more."

We all nodded. "Wow," we said.

Then we listened to an assortment of horror stories about parents who rant and rave when Judy spits at her sister, George refuses to mow the lawn, and Melissa wants to paint her room black. "Boy, that's us," we agreed. "That's just what happens at our house."

"But there's hope," we were told.

"Really?"

"You bet. Pay attention and we'll show you how you, too, can have a 'Brady Bunch' family." ("Father Knows Best," as the prototype of familial excellence, had long since been replaced by "The Brady Bunch": one father, one mother, three sons, three daughters, and most important of all, one tireless cook, housekeeper, laundress, baby-sitter, and good friend.)

So we paid attention. We listened. We discussed. We confessed our parental sins. We drew partners. We acted out imaginary situations, and we learned to say things like "Why don't we role play this and see where it goes?"

Then we all went home to try it out in Peoria.

We listened passively:

"Hm."

"I see."

"You don't say. Flunked your algebra test, did you?"

We listened actively:

"I sense you're angry and frustrated."

"It sounds as if you decided you had no other course of action."

"It seems to me you feel better now that you've slugged your sister in the stomach."

And we made nonaccusatory statements:

"Brothers aren't for kicking. Footballs are for kicking."

"Kitchens aren't for roller skating. Sidewalks are for roller skating."

"Beds aren't for jumping on. Beds are for sleeping in."

And the children responded:

"Why are you talking so funny?"

"I thought you weren't supposed to end a sentence with a preposition."

"Is this another one of those 'how to be a good parent' things?"

Then one day Joan ran into the kitchen in tears. "Geoffrey's a puke," she said, sobbing. "He threw the basketball at me and knocked my glasses off and broke them...and...he said it was my fault 'cause I should have ducked."

I took a breath. Let's see, I thought, now's the time to say, "I can see you're angry at your brother." But the words wouldn't come. All right, I thought, then I'll get Geoffrey in here and tell him, "Glasses are not for breaking, and basketballs aren't for throwing at your sister." But I choked on that, too.

"Well?" Joan said as I stood there with my mouth open and nothing coming out. "Well?" she repeated.

I looked down at her standing there with her broken glasses in her hand and tears still wobbling down her cheeks. Then I looked outside at Geoffrey, who was casually practicing hook shots. And deep down inside a small voice I hadn't heard in a long time whispered, "Come on, Ann. You know what to do. Forget all that robot talk, and trust your instincts for once."

So I bent down, picked up Joan, and hugged her. "There, there," I murmured. "Don't cry. It's going to be all right." Then I went to the back door. "Geoffrey," I called, "come here."

He wandered over. "She was in the way," he said. "I didn't mean to break her glasses, but she was in the way."

"That very well may be the case," I said with new-found confidence. "But the fact of the matter is you broke them, and it's up to you to have them fixed. Now go upstairs and get your piggy bank. You and I are going to Dr. Hanley's."

As luck would have it, the glasses were easily fixed and the cost was nominal. But when we got home, I gathered up Haim Ginott and the rest of the clan. I put them all together in a corner on the top shelf in the library as a monument to gullibility.

And then because tapering off is hard, I went out and bought *Teaching Yourself to Tap Dance.*

३● I'll Do It, I'll Do It . . . As Soon As I Finish This

IN THE BEGINNING was the hired girl, the girl who lived in the back room and earned her keep by helping out around the house.

She was an institution. Everyone, it seems, had one. Mother's stories of growing up in an Oregon mill town always included the mention of a Mildred or a Lillian, the hired girl. And Daddy's childhood at the rectory featured tales of intricate practical jokes played on Maud, the hired girl.

The hired girl was the poor man's upstairs maid. But though she lacked an official title, had to make do without the amenities of starched apron and ruffled cap, and was led to believe she was just one of the family, she was denied none of the responsibilities of her more lofty sisters. According to an old notebook that my grandmother prepared for some unnamed hired girl, her days were full and her nights were short.

Daily duties included, among other things, "dusting,"

"carpets swept with sweeper," "help with big meals," "kitchen linoleum and border washed with clear water and wiped dry," and "walks and porches swept." Mondays added "laundry," "tidy basement," and "clean bathrooms." Tuesdays were reserved for ironing and waxing the kitchen floor. On Wednesdays it was back to the bathrooms with silver polishing and a little window washing thrown in for variety. Thursdays called for a thorough cleaning of the living room and dining room. In case the hired girl was hazy about the particulars of "a thorough cleaning," an explanation followed. "This means a moving of furniture so every inch of border is wiped up and means a going over of every inch of rugs with sweeper. This *keeps* rugs clean and free from moths. *Dust thoroughly first.*"

Fridays, Saturdays, and Sundays took care of all the other rooms and the front and back porches and ran the bathrooms by once again. They also allowed for additional dusting, filling the wood basket, the regular dishwashing, sweeping, curtain dusting—"but don't wrinkle them"—washing the car when necessary, and "anything undone-up-to-date."

On the final page my grandmother added, "You may be asked to do something not in this plan. Do it with a smile. He who never does anything he isn't paid for never gets paid for anything he doesn't do. So see that you do your work cheerfully and regularly...without being reminded."

By the end of World War II, however, the hired girl had joined the ranks of spats, bugle beads, and the cloche. She was a relic of days past, and her replacement was the cleaning lady, a once- or twice-a-week phenomenon that came only to those who could afford her.

Unlike her predecessor, the cleaning lady was neither

meek nor subservient. She was also not the sort who took kindly to having her list of duties sprinkled with homilies about the cheerful laborer. She came to work around nine. There was none of this "up at seven and build the fires." She set her own schedule. She worked at her own pace. She didn't do windows, and she left at three. "I'm not about to miss my bus for anyone."

In between her visits "Mom" ran a dustcloth over the buffet, the coffee table, and the piano. She did the laundry, wielded the Electrolux, and mopped the orange juice spills off the kitchen floor. Because she had neither the time nor the stamina to stack the firewood or wash the car or sweep the pine needles off the front walk, she enlisted the reluctant help of her children. And while she was at it, she made the dinner dishes their responsibility.

My brother, Geoff, and I took this responsibility lightly. We argued for a while over whose turn it was to wash. The one assigned to dry quoted the latest theories on the transmission of germs by dishtowel and claimed, "Auntie Sylvia said the nurses in the TB sanitarium told her never to dry dishes. She said you're supposed to pour boiling water over them and leave them alone."

Mother didn't hold with this dictum, mainly because it meant she ended up putting the dishes away. She also objected when we snapped each other with dishtowels. And she protested vehemently when we cupped our hands, submerged them in the dishwater, and shot sudsy geysers into the air and at each other. In fact, much of the time she elected to do the job herself.

"It's easier than watching you two fool around, taking an hour and a half to do twenty minutes' work," she said. "Besides," she continued, "when I do it, at least I know it's being done well."

I felt no such compulsive stirrings when I became a mother. Of course, my standards were considerably lower than Mother's (my family was larger, a fact she failed to take into account), and they fluctuated in direct proportion to the amount of work I myself was avoiding. I also was consumed with the notion that regular responsibilities at home make for fine, upstanding children. So quality was less important to me than the fact that they were learning to make a contribution to the family life.

I admit that at first I was a bit overzealous in my attempt to make sure that all play and no work didn't make John a spoiled brat. Trying to teach Sylvia and David to make their beds when they were only three and four, for instance, was jumping the gun a bit. But I had the best of intentions. I thought I was encouraging them to develop good habits. And I assumed that because of my conscientious, albeit early, training they'd march through their adolescence with, at the very least, a made bed to their credit.

Of course, at the time I didn't realize that good habits, no matter when they're started, are broken more easily than Dresden teacups. And in the years that followed, unmade beds lay around the house like summer houseguests.

But that didn't deter me. In 1965, when they wrenched me away from Fusako-san, a spotless kitchen floor, clothes ironed the same day they were washed, and an oven that didn't burst into flames every time we turned it on, when they plunked me down in the middle of suburban Maryland with six children under the age of seven, I decided the time had come to divide the labor.

David, of course, drew the short straw. Being the oldest and more reliable than usual, he always did. He was awarded the job of washing the pots and pans. The dishwasher, eccentric as it was, took care of the dishes. But that didn't increase his appreciation of pots coated with greasy spaghetti sauce or make him happier about patches of burned goulash in the bottom of the pressure cooker.

He also resisted Joe's constant advice. Partially it was because any child worth his salt resists all parental advice. But I must admit Joe's military training does tend to make him less than tolerant of any way other than *the* way to do things.

"All right, son," he'd say after he'd stared at David's struggle with a stubborn frying pan for a minute or two. "I'll go over it once more. You fill the sink with hot, sudsy water, like this..."

"That's what I did, Dad."

"No, you didn't. This water's barely warm."

"It isn't. It's scalding. You just don't feel it."

I had to agree there. Joe's hands are impervious to heat. He can haul casseroles out of the oven without benefit of potholders. He can pull a baked potato out of a campfire and not scream for something to soothe the burns. And he regularly dips his fingers into a pot of boiling water to nab himself an ear of corn. He also refuses to believe his condition is unique.

So the arguments over how to wash the pots continued. They continued through David's sentence at the sink and boiled over whenever Joe found noodles still sticking to the colander or whenever a slippery frying pan slid out of Joe's hand and clattered to the floor. They resurfaced several years later, when Sylvia inherited the job and elected to forgo the sinkful of hot water in favor of a soapy sponge and lots of rinsing. And they boiled anew when Jenny opted for handfuls of Brillo pads, which she then left scattered on the drainboard to rust.

They rang out when Geoffrey insisted everything—

pots, pans, bowls, casseroles, bread pans, even cutting boards—needed to soak for a minimum of twenty-four hours. They exploded when Joan managed to wash the pots three nights in a row without ever once disturbing the carrot peelings lounging in the bottom of the sink. And they raged continually during Robbie's hitch, which we affectionately called ptomaine time.

The complaints weren't all from Joe's corner either.

"Aw, gee, Dad," the cry would ring out, "do I have to?"

"That's not fair."

"How come I always get the casserole dishes?"

Despite the din and clamor, the grumblings and objections, and the plaintive "None of my friends have to spend all their free time in slave labor," we continued to ladle out the chores.

Sylvia set and cleared the table until such time as Jenny's coordination reached the point where a trip into the kitchen with two salad plates and half a glass of milk didn't ressemble an "I Love Lucy" rerun. Then Sylvia moved up to loading and unloading the dishwasher, and I joined in the fracas with "Rinse...you have to rinse the dishes, or else the food bakes on."

When Geoffrey reached the age of responsibility, he was handed the vacuum cleaner and told to remove all traces of dinner from the dining room carpet. Joe, of course, showed him the proper way to do it. He upended all the chairs and put them on the table. He ran the vacuum back and forth, this way and that. Then he put the chairs back down, wound up the cord, and rolled the cleaner back into the closet.

Geoffrey did it his own way. He left the chairs where they were. He attacked them from behind, running the head of the vacuum cleaner under their rungs in short, violent jabs. Then he worked his way around the table till the cord reached as far as it could. And when it pulled out of the socket, he dragged the vacuum back to the closet and threw the cord in after it.

Things got sticky when Robbie and Joan were old enough to participate, for by then the dinner hour was pretty much covered. But they had to do their share, so we divided the chores even further, and we ended up with Robbie's setting the table—when I could find him, that is—and Joan's clearing it when she didn't swear she had so much homework she was going to have to stay up all night as it was. Jenny put the leftovers away unless, of course, she could get away with sneaking half a cup of peas, a glob of tuna casserole, and the last of the salad to the dogs.

Sylvia remained where she was, loading the dishwasher. When Joe marched through the kitchen and said, "Why don't you wipe off the counters and the stove, too?" she complained that she had the worst job in the whole world. David challenged her to trade with him and said he'd been doing pots since he was old enough to reach the sink. And Geoffrey insisted that our move to Bainbridge and a shag rug in the dining room had made his job three times harder than it had been.

It was like attending an eternal "vote to strike" meeting. If I'd been more energetic or less stubborn, I would have thrown in the towel and said, "Forget it. I'll do the whole damn thing myself."

But by then the world was echoing with cries of "irresponsible youth" and "parental indifference" and shouting, "Modern children expect a handout." So I stuck to my guns and countered all grievances with "Sorry, but that's the way life is." And I prayed I'd be able to hold onto my sanity until they all grew up and moved out on their own.

If I'd been smart, I'd have come up with some alternative. But I wasn't smart. Luckily David and Sylvia were.

"How about if we combine the jobs till there are only five?" they said one day when discontent hung like a low cloud cover over everything. "Then each of us can do one job for two weeks and move on."

"What about the sixth person?" I asked. "What'll he do?"

They grinned. "He'll get a vacation."

"Gee, I don't know." The thought of one child's doing nothing for two whole weeks went against my Puritan grain. But looked at from their point of view, it did have a certain tantalizing appeal. "Would this mean you'd all do your jobs willingly?"

"Sure."

"And you wouldn't cry 'unfair'?"

"Nope."

"Or leave Daddy and me filling in whenever you had something else you had to do?"

"Oh, no, we wouldn't do that. We wouldn't have to," Sylvia explained. "Because now we'd be able to trade job for job. If I wanted Joan to do the pots for me, I could tell her I would do them for her when it was her turn."

"I see." It sounded like a good idea to me, and I looked over at Joe to see his reaction. "What do you think?"

He shrugged. "Why not?" he said. "Anything to get it all done and get rid of the nightly ruckus."

So the new system went into effect, and life turned peaceful for a change. Well, maybe not exactly peaceful. There were a few flare-ups when no one would trade with Jenny so she could go to a rock concert with Mary and SheriAnn. Sylvia was forced to promise three nights of pots for one loading when she wanted to go to the movies. When Joan was headed off to a slumber party during her stint at clearing the table, she whisked the plates away so fast Geoffrey had to follow his hamburger into the kitchen and finish it there. And every time the flu struck, midterm exams overwhelmed, headaches suddenly appeared, thumbs were sprained, arms lay safely in plaster casts, or any of a hundred other contingencies prevented the children from the swift completion of their appointed tasks, Joe and I reluctantly stepped in. As he scrubbed away at the broiler pan and I searched for something to put the leftover gravy in, we consoled ourselves with "At least this is an improvement over the way it used to be."

The spirit of goodwill and cooperation, however, was limited to the dinner hour. The rest of the time it was "Aw, gee, Mom..."

"Aw, gee, Mom, why do I have to clean my room today? It's not so bad, and I was going to wash my hair and sit out in the sun. If I have to clean my room, I'll never get a tan."

"Aw, gee, Mom, I helped carry in the groceries last time. You never make David bring them in. Why can't he do it this time?"

"Aw, gee, Mom, I have a stomach ache. Can't someone else get you the scissors? They're clear upstairs in the bathroom."

If I hollered, "I have to go to the ferry to get Daddy. Will someone turn off the oven, take out the bread, grease the top with some margarine, and put it on a cooling rack when the buzzer rings?" the echo replied, "I'm going to take a bath" and "I have to call Chuck" and "I've got my radio on so I can't hear the buzzer" and "I don't know how."

If three coats were slung over the couch, a pair of track shoes huddled under a chair, a stack of books and papers lay strewn on the coffee table, a skateboard waited expectantly in the doorway, and I was able to nab Jenny on her way upstairs and ask her to take an armload of junk with her, she wandered into the living room, carefully picked out one notebook and a pencil, and sniffed, "The rest of this stuff isn't mine."

Even "Would you pass me the salt?" was greeted with "It's closer to Geoffrey."

So once every day or two I bellowed out a sermon on how families are supposed to work together. And I heard muttered rumblings about "Mom's on her 'Father Knows Best' kick again" and not so muttered rumblings about mythical friends who "don't have to make their beds," who "get paid three dollars an hour when they so much as brush the dog," and who "get to go to Hawaii for spring vacation if they maintain a B average."

I tried to ignore all such complaints. I reminded myself that right makes might and wished to hell I knew for sure exactly what was right. I consoled myself with wild imaginings of how they'd learn. When they had children of their own and found handprints on the ceiling, spongy bars of soap in the bottom of the tub, and saw the dog brought in to snuffle up a spilled box of cornflakes, they'd understand why parents grit their teeth and swear a lot. And when nothing soothed my shattered nerves, I vowed to divide my senile years into equal parts so each child would get a chance to pick up and clean up after me.

Of course, every now and then Joe and I would come home from a day in town and find the kitchen spotless, the wood chopped and stacked, all the laundry washed and folded. When we'd recovered from the shock and listened to a joyous recitation of who did what and how and why, I'd whisper, "See, honey, they aren't self-centered and lazy. They're thoughtful, industrious children, and we shouldn't be so hard on them."

Joe usually shrugged and remained silent. Of course, he wasn't as gullible as I. He knew one swallow didn't make a summer. And experience had taught him that this sort of performance from six children was either a form of bribery or an atonement for sins yet to be admitted. And if perchance there were no ulterior motives, he knew that like a hole in one, this sort of occurrence was not likely to be repeated in the near future.

I accused him of being heartless and unappreciative, but he knew whereof he spoke. He'd spent more than one weekend presiding over assorted work parties, and the experience had not left him with a warm feeling all over.

Of course, Joe remembered how it had been when he was the boy with the hoe...or the rake...or the hedge clippers. No one had ever asked him if he would mind weeding the flower bed—if he had time, that is. If the flower bed was awash in clover and dandelions, it was his job to remove them, and he'd better get at it, so he'd have time to mow the lawn, sweep the patio, and hose down the walk before lunch.

He also remembered his early days in the Air Force, when whole platoons had marched when he told them to march, stopped when he ordered them to stop, and policed the grounds the rest of the time. So when he barked, "Today we're going to rake leaves" or "prune the fruit trees" or "load shingles onto the truck and take them to the dump," he didn't appreciate:

"Not me. I just washed my hair."

"I'm waiting for a phone call."

"I think I have appendicitis."

"I have to take my bike down to the gas station and have the inner tube fixed."

And the old favorite "Why do *we* always have to do *all*

of the work?" was guaranteed to tighten his jaws and send him stumbling off to beat his head against the side of the house.

Even when he did manage to herd one or all outside to stack wood or pick blackberries or rake the gravel on the driveway, most of his energies were spent bellowing orders: "Come on now. You can carry more than one piece of wood at a time.... Get back in there. You missed a huge patch of berries—over there on your right.... Stop trying to break the hoe. It won't work." It took two double martinis and a good night's sleep to recover from supervising only three hours of communal labor.

Assigning one task to one child was even harder. So he did it from a distance and through a reluctant interpreter—me.

"Say, Annie," he'd say when he called home to see if the mail had come or if the garbage man had taken the hunks of plasterboard we left out for him, "will you ask David if he'll straighten up the workshop, clean the paint-brushes, and sort out that can of nails?"

"Just a minute." I'd put my hand over the receiver and holler up the stairs, "Hey, David, Daddy wants to know if you'll clean out the workshop today."

"Me?"

"Yes, you."

"Why me?"

"I don't know. He just told me to ask you if you'd do it."

"But Robbie's the one who messed it up. Why can't he do it?"

He had a point there, and because I'd been raised to be a good little intermediary and had yet to experience the heady joy that comes with handing over the phone and saying, "Here, you tell him," I'd go ahead and deliver the message. "Joe?" I'd say. "David says Robbie made the mess, so he thinks Robbie should have to clean it up."

"Well, tell him I want *him* to do it."

"Daddy wants you to do it."

"But I was going to go rowing. Can't I do it tomorrow?"

"He'd planned to go rowing. Can he do it tomorrow?"

"No, dammit, I want it done today. I'm sick of having everything put off and put off and put off. If those children would just do what I ask when I ask it, we wouldn't have any trouble. You tell him that when I was a boy . . ."

"Daddy wants it done today."

The trialogue went on and on till finally Joe'd hang up on me, David would stomp off to the workshop which he'd slam and bang into a semblance of order, and I'd be left wishing I'd had the presence of mind when asked, "Do you, Ann, take this man," etc., to say, "No, now that I think of it, I don't."

It was even worse when the lawn was the subject of controversy. Of course, I should have expected it. Our lawn is only slightly smaller than North Dakota, and even on days when Joe phoned every other hour to check up on how David or Geoffrey or Robbie was doing, none of them ever managed to get more than a third of it completed at one time.

Joe knew why. At least he said he did. "It's because they dawdle. They fool around. They come inside every ten minutes to get a glass of water or go to the bathroom. And they simply don't stick to the job at hand."

The boys had a different story. "It's that stupid lawn mower. It keeps conking out on me" and "The grass is too wet" and "It's too hot [or cold] to be mowing the lawn today" and "I hate mowing lawns."

Finally Joe had had enough. "I'll show them," he said

early one Sunday morning. "I'll prove that the job isn't as hard as they say it is and that it can be done in one day." With that he gulped down the last of his coffee and marched outside.

Seven and a half hours later he stumbled back in. The lawn was glorious. Every blade of grass was cropped. All the clover and dandelions and moss blended to form a veritable carpet of green. All it lacked was a croquet set or perhaps a pair of strolling peacocks. Joe, on the other hand, was a wreck. His face and arms were bright red, and I could almost feel the heat radiating from them. His shirt was wringing wet. His white Keds were a motley shade of green. And I wondered if the ring around his head where his hat had been was permanent.

"There," he said as he sank into a chair, "I did it. I mowed the entire lawn in one day. Oh, my God, I actually mowed it in one day."

After that he was more understanding. In fact, he even took an occasional turn at the Toro. And when summer jobs gave the boys a legitimate excuse for begging off lawn duty, he took over completely. He did a little every night after dinner. And when I gave him a transistor radio complete with earphones so he could listen to the ball game while he marched up and down the estate, we had to drag him in at dark.

He was lucky. Modern science has yet to come up with anything distracting enough to make housecleaning palatable. And though every now and then, when they're desperate for money I'm able to hire one of the girls to dust and vacuum and remove the various sets of track shoes from the couch for me, it's not like the good old days I've heard about.

Not only do my "hired girls" refuse to "dust the curtains thoroughly" or "sweep the kitchen, nook, and back porch with a brush," they also snort at my grandmother's "He who never does anything he isn't paid for never gets paid for anything he doesn't do."

ૢ Up in the Morning, Out on the Route

THERE ARE TWO SIDES TO EVERY COIN, two versions to every story, and if I despaired because it seemed that the children's attitude toward hard work was doomed to leave them languishing in the unemployment lines till the end of time, I should have remembered there are also two ways of approaching every job.

There's the listless sigh that tells the world it's simply too much to ask you to take your laundry upstairs and put it away. And there's the snappy "You bet" that says, "Of course, I'm not too tired to help unload a truckful of folding chairs."

What makes the difference is money.

A child will do almost anything for money. He'll clean out a neighbor's garage. He'll clear an acre's worth of Scotch broom for his civics teacher. He'll also mow his grandmother's lawn—if Mom will drive him over to Grandmother's, that is. She'll iron pillowcases, handkerchiefs, and anything else that's flat. She'll polish silver, arrange mints, and slice lemons for Mrs. Tanella's summer garden party. And for a year or two, till she gets tired

214

of babies who won't stop crying and parents who never make it home till three in the morning, she'll baby-sit.

If, however, he's still too little to have a paper route and even Grandmother won't hire her to wash windows, a child will come up with a money-making scheme of his own, and our children were no exception.

When Sylvia was eight, she sold pinwheels. She made them herself. She also made a large sign that assured potential buyers, "You Can Do It in the Wind. You Can Do It on a Hill. You Can Do It Anywhere." Then she parked herself out on the front lawn, where the average car sped by at 30 mph, and she waited for customers.

Unfortunately they never materialized. I guess they didn't want to do it in the wind and on a hill. Maybe they'd already done it "anywhere" and decided they'd rather not repeat the experience. Who knows? After an hour or so she came inside and tried to sell me the whole lot, cheap.

Jenny embarked on a different venture. She grew seeds. I think they were candytufts. I know they came free with a large bag of Fritos. As I remember, she put three seeds each in the dozen or so plastic bedding containers she'd found under the house when we moved in.

It took them weeks to sprout. In fact, judging from the variety of leaves that finally uncurled, I'd say the candytufts died early on and sent up a couple of weeds in their stead. It didn't matter. When they were two or three inches tall, she loaded them all into the wheelbarrow and trundled them up to the main road. She sold several. Some kind soul who probably said, "Oh, look at that poor little girl sitting there all by herself trying to sell plants," bought them. I hope she's enjoying her dandelions or clover or Queen Anne's lace. I know Jenny certainly appreciated the business.

I also know that Robbie, on seeing the fifty cents or so she'd earned, envisioned paving streets of his own with silver. And the next thing I knew he was headed out the driveway, hoping to sell a gross of shells and rocks he'd colored with his crayons. His hopes would have been dashed if Mother hadn't volunteered to be his one, his only, and his more than generous customer. But I have a feeling he knew she'd come through. She always did. Unlike me, her daughter, she didn't believe in letting the little nipper find out for himself that the demand for hand-colored rocks and shells is negligible and that life can be hard.

To her it was enough that he thought he needed some money. And when he had a dollar bill safely clutched in his hand, she even took him up to the store and let him race back and forth from one thing to another, chirping, "I think I'll get this...or maybe this...no, I think this is what I want."

I didn't much approve. In my role as the always-trying-to-be-perfect mother I wanted my children to earn what they got and learn something from the earning. After all, I'd had to. When at thirteen—the mid-forties equivalent of today's eight—I'd decided I simply had to have a Mickey Mouse watch, I spent all summer working to earn the $4 or $5 it cost.

It wasn't easy. No one wanted pinwheels or potted weeds or colored rocks in those days. And my grandmother wasn't quite so philanthropic. So I had to come up with a marketable product to sell, and the only one around was wild blackberries.

"So what?" my children say with a sneer when I try to force this particular story of my youth on them. "The island's covered with blackberry bushes."

"True," I tell them, "it's covered with Himalayan and

evergreen blackberry bushes. But no one wanted those, not when they could pick them themselves. The only ones people would buy were the wild ones. And they were hard to find.

"I knew of two patches. Neither was right out by the side of the road. To get to the first one, I had to wade through a field of nettles, then scramble up a hill and hack my way through the woods for a while till finally, in a clearing next to an old muddy pond, there they were, a whole circle of bushes laden with tiny, seedless, and unbelievably sweet blackberries. This was the easy patch.

"The other one was back in an area that had been logged some years before. And though it may have been larger than the first, it was also more precarious, for the only way to get at the berries was to climb up on some old rotten logs and teeter along. Eventually I got to be pretty good at it, but every now and then I'd miss a step and sink up to my armpits in leaves, runners, and thorns. I'd scrape and scratch my legs till they looked as if I'd been attacked, and invariably I'd spill all the berries I'd picked so far."

"So how much did you get for these stupid berries?" Robbie asks.

"Seventy-five cents a gallon."

"Jeez. You wouldn't catch me going through all that for only seventy-five cents a gallon."

"It was either that or nothing."

"Boy, I'd take nothing, or else I'd charge by the hour."

"That's because you're spoiled." Sylvia counters with the disdain common to most older sisters who've watched the iron hand of discipline unclench a bit with younger siblings. "When I picked raspberries the summer I was thirteen, they only paid me forty cents a flat."

"So what?"

"So it was hard work."

It was, too. The fields were hot and dusty. The picking, while not as backbreaking as it was if you were crawling up and down rows of strawberry plants, was slow. And once you'd started the day, there was no turning back—not, that is, unless you wanted to walk the three long miles home. For when I dropped her off at eight in the morning, we agreed on a pickup time, and not till then did I reappear.

She earned $69 that year, though, and most of it went to help pay for her school clothes. I'm sure she would much rather have blown it on records or jewelry and perfume. She would rather have been at the beach getting a tan or swimming in the frozen waters of Puget Sound, too. But our total clothing bill in August usually ran close to $600, and we needed whatever she could contribute.

Besides, I'd always turned my earnings in to the general fund. When at fourteen I spent the summer taking care of four children five days a week, I used my salary to pay for all my books and supplies at boarding school.

Later the money I made working as a bank messenger during the summers went for expenses at Smith. And any extra cash came not as a result of a pitiful letter home but from odds jobs as a waitress, a dishwasher, a babysitter for faculty children, and, in my junior and senior years, the sales representative for the *New York Times*.

Joe, too, had earned his way. He'd driven a truck. He'd washed dishes and waited tables. And he'd spent nights in an old folks' home, taking care of old Willie, a former engineer who had to be lifted up and spun around the roundhouse before he'd settle down and go to sleep.

So despite the maxim of the early 1970s which stated that children, the fragile creatures that they are, should spend their summers sleeping in, taking tennis lessons, learning to sail, lying in the sun, and generally messing around, our children worked.

David washed dishes at a local restaurant. He started at three in the afternoon. At midnight or one the phone jolted me out of a sound sleep, and I threw on a bathrobe, staggered out to the car, and went to pick him up. Luckily the roads were usually deserted and I was too groggy to speed or run a stop sign or back into a telephone pole. So the local police never had the dubious pleasure of arresting someone clad only in a blue nightgown, an orange bathrobe, and tennis shoes.

When college loomed and there was tuition to pay and bills for board and room to remit, he got a job as a computer programmer. This meant coming home Friday, working through that night and the next, only to go back Sunday afternoon to his homework.

Jenny worked days. One year it was at a cheesecake factory where the temperature shimmered in the nineties and the conveyor belt was never still. One year she made soup and sandwiches, waited on the lunch crowd, and helped spread the gospel of yogurt and alfalfa sprouts.

Sylvia served a stint as a nurse's aide at a convalescent center. It wasn't far away, and since I was rapidly becoming allergic to midnight retrievals, I managed to bully her into riding her bike to and from work. Of course, this backfired the night the dogs followed her and I had to go get them.

We chased through the darkness, whistling and calling. We stumbled over rocks and ran into bushes as we herded them back to the car. And as I drove home, they leaped over the seats and steamed up the windows until I could barely see to drive.

Geoffrey had a varied employment record. He manned

a pedicab, driving tourists around the Seattle waterfront. He washed dishes for two years and worked in a cafeteria a third year. He baked chocolate cakes and sold them to the lunchroom where Jenny worked. He also painted houses, mowed lawns, and helped a man reroof his rental cottage.

Joan earned her keep at a dessert bar on the same waterfront Geoffrey had shown to the tourists from Kansas and the plains of Alberta. She scooped out double strawberry cones. She dipped bananas in chocolate sauces. She fought with the soft ice cream machine. And every night I ran her apron through the wash till by the end of summer the logo on the bib had faded to a shadow.

That's not all I did every night, however. I also made trips to the ferry to bring the weary laborers home. Naturally no two ever came on the same boat. But then they never left on the same boat in the morning either.

"Let's see," I'd say to Joan as Monday dawned, "what's your schedule today?"

She'd think a minute. Then she'd check the calendar. "Today and tomorrow I take the eleven-ten ferry and come home on the eight-ten."

I'd turn to Geoffrey "How about you?"

"Huh? Oh, I have to go in on the eight-thirty boat."

"When will you be home?"

"I don't know. There's a square dance convention at the Seattle Center, and if things go the way they did yesterday, I'll be lucky if I make the twelve something boat tonight."

"I have to go to work at three," Robbie would chime in.

"But I thought today was your day off." For three days a week he was the cleanup man at a diner on the island.

"It is, but I traded with Steve so I could go hang gliding on Saturday."

I'd take a deep breath. "All right," I'd say, "let me see if I have it straight. Daddy and Jenny took the seven-ten and she'll be home on the three and he'll come as usual on the five-fifteen. Geoffrey, you have to go at eight-thirty. Joan you're taking the eleven-ten. But you'll be home by twenty minutes to nine and who knows when you'll be home, Geoffrey? Is that right?"

"Right," Joan would chirp. "At least for today and to-morrow. Then I go on the three to close shift for two days."

About then I began to wonder exactly who was learning to be responsible and whose character was being built. I also wondered if I'd have time to get my hair cut be-tween taking Robbie to work and picking up Jenny. I wondered if I should go to the store and get the package of chicken thighs for dinner when I took Joan to the boat or whether I should wait until after I got Jenny. And I wondered if I'd be able to outsmart Joe and get him to pick up Geoffrey in the black and silent hours of the night.

The odds were not in my favor. Not that he refused to rise out of his warm bed to retrieve one of his own. He didn't.

"Sure, I'll pick him up," he'd say around eleven when he was just sliding in under the covers. "I'll be glad to get him."

"Then why are you going to sleep?" I'd snarl.

"I'm not. I'm only dozing."

The dozing was soon accompanied by soft snoring, which then deepened to whiffles and flourishes. By the time the boat was due nothing short of a cannon could have moved him out of bed. I, on the other hand, was usually wide-awake, mainly because the oath of moth-erhood insists on Mom staring at the ceiling till all her children are safely home and tucked in for the night. I also knew that the phone, always on my side of the bed, would wake me up anyway. So off I'd go, this time in a yellow nightgown and a blue bathrobe.

Respite came when they all got their driver's licenses and I was able to find at least one child who wasn't too tired, out on a date, watching a late movie "I've waited three years to see," incapacitated by sunburn, a headache, muscle strain, or "just an icky feeling," and was sympathetic to the fact I had to get up in the morning at six o'clock.

Respite came too late, though. I could have used someone else at the wheel when Robbie was in his paper route phase.

I think he was eleven when he first galloped home and informed me that wonder of wonders, he'd landed a job as a *Seattle Times* carrier. I'm not sure. I tend to try to forget the specifics of unpleasant events like labor pains, oral surgery, and paper routes. All I remember is that he seemed awfully little to be pedaling around, delivering papers and collecting on past-due accounts.

"I can do it," he insisted. "I know I can. Besides, I need the money."

In the interest of appearing enthusiastic, and because I was under the impression that paper routes are the all-American experience for boys and girls, I agreed. I even sprang for a saddlebag bike basket, and I stood out in the cold, cheering while he loaded it up with a stack of our old newspapers and then practiced by riding up and down the driveway. Then he was on his own.

During the week he had no trouble. The *Times* was an afternoon paper, so right after school he whipped through his route pedaling up driveways, dashing across lawns, climbing the stairs to second-floor apartments. I left him to it.

Mother didn't. She skulked around, offering to drive him through his paces because "It's so cold" or "It's raining" or "He looked so little lugging all those heavy papers around." She showed up at the gas station where he picked up the papers. And she intercepted him at the library as he scooted past on his way to the housing development.

I objected strenuously. "But, Mother," I snarled, "how's he going to learn that it takes hard work and diligence to earn all the money he thinks is out there? If you're always there to protect him from the weather, how's he going to find out that he has to follow through and do his job no matter what the conditions?"

She shrugged. "I was only trying to help."

"Maybe so, but I wish you wouldn't. You've spoiled him enough as it is."

It was like talking to a tree.

"I have not," she said in a huff, and she continued to show up with a nice warm car whenever the wind was whipping papers up and down the street, whenever there were dogs gathered on his route, whenever the rain was torrential, and, for the most part, whenever she felt like it.

She vanished, however, when he was sick. Then it was my turn.

At first I took him with me. I bundled him up in a blanket and carried him out to the car. And while he alternately shivered and perspired, I followed his directions.

"Turn right here and go clear around to the back."

"Put the Scheuers' paper in their mailbox. Someone stole their tube."

"There's a rock on the Hudnuts' porch. Mrs. Hudnut wants you to put the paper under that."

"Back up, you missed one."

Once I'd learned the route, I left him home in bed and traveled the course on my own. I even got to be pretty good at it. And although I was usually battling snowstorms or gale force winds—because Robbie never seemed to get sick when the skies were clear and still— I never came home to find I'd forgotten the fellow in 3C of the Olympian apartments or that I'd let Mrs. Hudnut's sports section blow away.

But then why should I have? I had a refresher course every other Sunday morning. That's when a saddlebag bike basket simply wasn't enough. The Sunday paper rivaled the Manhattan telephone directory in weight, and with the ten or twenty extra customers that day, Robbie would have been pedaling papers clear into the afternoon if we hadn't helped him.

Joe and I traded off. One week he got up at five-fifteen and staggered out into the blackness to help deliver the news of the world to Bainbridge Island, and the next week it was my turn.

We started at Roy's gas station unless, of course, there'd been a mixup and the papers were still sitting on the dock in Seattle. Then we waited down at the terminal till the *Spokane* or the *Walla Walla* pulled into the slip, and we loaded the bundles into the car there.

Then we took off. The first stop was an apartment house: "two on the second floor, three on the first, and don't forget Mr. Roth, who's already up and waiting." After that there were two houses on the right and one on the left, and because most of the police were still home in bed, I wove from one side of the road to the other and back again.

At the convalescent center Robbie grabbed five papers and disappeared, while I, who'd spent the previous afternoon in line at the gas station and did not relish the thought of spending Monday the same way, killed the engine and waited. Then it was off again, down the street, up a back road, left at the corner, be sure to band Mrs. Gaines's paper, remember how upset she was when it blew all over the parking lot. Now around the cul-de-sac and backtrack to the Baggetts', turn around in the middle of the road, and head out again.

I gave up the turn around in the middle of the road the morning I backed into a ditch and a sleepy home-owner went to fetch the police to pull me out again.

By the time we finished it was close to dawn. And every now and then, if Joe was awake when we got home, the three of us sneaked off and treated ourselves to breakfast in the still-somnolent town.

Eventually the charms of the workaday world palled, and Robbie turned his route over to another anxious millionaire in the making. I remember the first Sunday both Joe and I were able to sleep in.

"Do you think he learned responsibility from his paper route?" I asked as I lay wallowing in the luxury of being in a warm bed with no place I had to go. "Do you think he has a better sense of the value of money and what it takes to earn it?"

Joe thought for a minute. "I doubt it," he said. "But don't worry. It was worth it anyway."

"It was?"

"Of course it was. It taught us responsibility, the value of money, and it gave us a better sense of what it takes to earn it."

ॐ 'Twixt Twelve and Twenty

I NEVER BELIEVED those who warned me about teen-agers. When neighbors, friends, relatives, and complete strangers shook their heads and said, "If you think it's tough now, just wait till your kids are teen-agers," I nodded sympathetically and said to myself, "Who are they kidding? Teen-agers may be a bit temperamental at times. I know they're famous for being perennially hungry and they always want to use the car. I even know that teen-age girls are rumored to spend whole weeks in the bathroom, but what's so terrible about that?

"At least teen-agers tie their own shoes and button their own shirts. They put themselves to bed. They don't go through half a dozen diapers on a rainy Thursday when the dryer's broken. You don't have to hiss, 'I said stop blowing bubbles in your milk, and I mean it,' at them in restaurants. Teen-agers don't try to drink Mr. Clean or flush crayons down the toilet. They don't get lost in department stores. And they don't come home and announce they've invited the entire first grade class to their birthday party.

226

"They don't throw tantrums in grocery stores. They don't ask the boss's wife if she has a baby in there under that big tummy of hers. They don't get into the nail polish and paint the walls with streaks of Passionate Persimmon. And they don't get gum in their hair or fill their pockets with rocks, old jellybeans, and recently shed snakeskins.

"In fact," I told myself, "I can hardly wait till all six of the children are safely into their double-digit years."

What a dreamer. I should have known that the only reason the grass looked greener was that it was still clear over there on the other side of the fence. If I'd been smart, I'd have given the 1960s a long, hard look. I'd have envisioned what the natural progression of things would do to the 1970s, and I'd have taken to drink then and there.

But as a military dependent accustomed to packing up every three or four years and leaving our troubles at the last duty station, the last neighborhood, or the last school, I witnessed what was happening to the world, drew in a shallow and tentative breath, and whispered foolishly to myself, "Maybe it will all go away."

And when it was obvious that the terrors haunting those of us from the "Yes, sir" and "No, sir" and "Please may I be excused" generation were not about to disappear, I consoled myself with the thought that it'll never happen to us.

After all, I reasoned naïvely, Joe and I had done a fairly good job as parents. We were firm without being dictatorial. The children didn't have to stand at attention or wait for Joe to bounce a quarter off their beds before they had permission to leave for school. But then they weren't allowed to wander around the streets at night or to bring home the stop sign that just happened to be lying by the side of the road either. We didn't condone their helping themselves to each other's belongings or their classmates' answers. And we discouraged disrespect and talking back.

I didn't faint at the sight of a ripped coat or flee to my room sobbing when an irate Jenny screamed, "You're the most horrible mother in the whole world." Joe didn't resort to physical violence when he overheard Sylvia and Jenny discussing the specifics of the male anatomy. And he didn't rage over an occasional vulgar epithet. But neither would he stand for lying about who had carved up his bed slat. He refused to tolerate cheating, even at parcheesi. And when Robbie and Joan, barely four, toddled off to the local grocery store and helped themselves to some candy and a pack of balloons, I marched them back to return their booty and apologize. I also delivered my standard "Thou shalt not steal" lecture.

As far as I could see, we'd been companionable parents, too. Joe had played ball and flown kites for hours on end. I'd read *Green Eggs and Ham*, *The Giving Tree*, *The Perfect Pancake*, and *Now We Are Six* till I knew them all by heart. Joe had trundled through every zoo we came across. I'd supervised chocolate chip cookie bake-offs. And we'd both spent almost every vacation sitting in a wet tent in the mountains, at the beach, by the reservoir, or under a shedding chestnut tree.

So it stood to reason that while children from broken homes who were starved for attention might cut classes and sneak out behind the shop to have a cigarette, while I expected daughters of tyrannical parents to be caught pocketing tubes of lipstick in Woolworth's, while it seemed natural that sons of alcoholic mothers might run away from home, and while it was almost traditional that those who'd grown up in ghetto neighborhoods and had lived with poverty and fear all their lives would disrupt a class in modern American literature, our children, whose greatest worry to date involved little more than whose turn was it to lick the beaters, would march through their teen years in a fairly respectable lock step.

And so it began. David hit thirteen in 1971. As expected, he snarled a bit. He bristled at the strain of being the oldest a little more often than he had before. He spent long hours by himself in his room. And when I challenged his health teacher's pronunciation of *larynx*—Mr. Roth referred to it as the "larnyx"—he fought back with uncommon vehemence.

But his basic sweetness still showed through. His fascination with math, computers, and general learning kept him from open rebellion. My only trip to the principal in his behalf was to rage at the fact that a group of "stoners" were threatening him. (Apparently they resented anyone who was enthusiastic about school and studies.)

Sylvia and Jenny were more turbulent about their adolescence. Where David had objected to having me hug him when he left with the math club for a conference in Arkansas, Sylvia and Jenny crossed the street rather than have their friends see us together. On the ferry into Seattle they sat at the other end of the boat and approached me only when they wanted a dime or a quarter for the candy machine.

When Sylvia entered her teens, everyone over the age of twenty became the enemy. Aimless wandering in Winslow, Bainbridge Island's only incorporated city, became the standard after-school entertainment. And a surly "I'm sure" was the automatic reply to any and all parental statements.

In school, teachers were "nerds," cut classes were "no big...," and most free time was spent smoking in the girls' bathroom.

Jenny hit thirteen two years later. But by then Joe and

I were somewhat smarter. We also remembered Sancta Maria and the power of positive discipline. So the fall she entered her freshman year Jenny found herself safely enrolled in Holy Names Academy in Seattle.

True, the commute on the ferry was long. The homework was sometimes overwhelming. But it curbed her rebellion somewhat. Not entirely, of course. She still went through phases.

During the vegetarian phase she came to the dinner table and delivered long, graphic lectures on the evils of eating the flesh of dead animals. When she embraced transcendental meditation, she sat cross-legged in her room and hummed a lot. She also fell in love with a young man who, for the then price of two years in college, went to California to learn to levitate. When he came home at Christmas and I asked her if the low cloud cover meant he'd have to make an instrument landing, she was not amused.

I know I shouldn't have gone for the cheap shot, but I probably thought she'd see the humor in my remark. She didn't. Teen-agers rarely do. Eventually parents learn to save their droll observances for adult conversations.

At the time, however, I was still naïve. I thought that when I said, "You can have your ears pierced when you're sixteen and not before," that would be that. I had yet to reckon with the power of peer pressure and the fact that "everyone else" was doing it. So until I learned that you save your "No"s, your "Never"s and your "I absolutely forbid it"s for the truly important issues and until I replaced the "What will people think?" creed of the 1940s and 1950s with the "Does it actually matter?" reality of the 1970s, I saw a lot of amateur ear-piercing jobs.

I also saw a lot of things that in my naïveté I took at face value. The plants growing in the bathroom, for instance. Jenny's room was full of ferns, ivy, and steamy terrariums. I as a child had filled a flower box with pine tree seedlings. So when Sylvia decided to grow plants in the bathroom, I assumed she too had had an attack of green thumb. I even commiserated with her when they all died—until I read a "know your marijuana" article, that is.

I believed that the incense she burned was just a harmless fad. I believed the long hours of work at the convalescent center were a devotion to duty rather than a chemically induced sleeplessness. And I believed her when she told me, "Mrs. Zlotoff's class is boring. That's why I hate it. Besides, I'm not the only one who got an F. Practically everyone flunked the last test."

Because I still thought of drugs as something only college kids fooled around with, I believed the denials: "What do you mean I'm acting strange? That's the dumbest thing I ever heard." When Joe and I despaired, I explained away the insolence, the fits of temper, and the transformation of our bright, witty, responsible, fun-loving daughter by saying, "I guess this is the modern version of a teen-ager. Funny, I don't remember being this cantankerous."

Then, right around Christmastime in 1973, when Sylvia was fourteen, my naïveté and blind trust bade me a sudden farewell.

It was a Saturday night. Joe and I had been to an open house in Seattle, and when we came home, around ten-thirty or so, there was a note Jenny had left on the kitchen counter, saying, "Sylvia called. She's spending the night at Jenice's." There was nothing unusual about that. Spending the night is one of the fringe benefits of being a teen-ager. But I needed her home early the next morning. So I called to tell her I'd pick her up at nine.

She wasn't there, nor was she expected. In fact, according to Jenice's mother, both girls were at our house. I mumbled something about having misunderstood and hung up. As I did, a gnawing apprehension took up residence inside me.

"You don't suppose she's at a kegger, do you?" I asked Joe.

I'd heard about keggers. Sylvia herself had told me that Melinda, also fourteen, went to them all the time.

"And at the last one," Sylvia had said, "she got so drunk she threw up all over John Strayka, and he had to carry her out to the car and take her home."

I shuddered. "Yuck," I said. "What did her parents do when they found out?"

"Oh, they didn't find out. But even if they had, I don't think they would have cared."

"Don't be silly. Of course they would have cared."

"Not really."

"Well, I won't argue with you, but I'll tell you one thing: Daddy and I care. And if you're as smart as I think you are, you won't ever test us to see how much."

She'd laughed. "Oh, don't worry, Mom. I'm not into keggers and all that stuff."

I'd believed her, but now I wondered. Had she told me the truth, or was I just too stupid to recognize a good lie when I heard it? I scrounged around in my purse, looking for a cigarette. "What do we do now?" I asked.

"I don't know," Joe answered. "I guess I'll just have to go look for her and bring her home."

"But where will you start?"

"Damned if I know."

But he started anyway. He got in the car, drove off, and I stayed home and waited.

I must say I'm not good at waiting. I wander around

the house, listening for sounds of someone coming up the driveway. I turn on the television and try to lose myself in the plot of the late movie. That night it was Audrey Hepburn and Peter O'Toole in *How to Steal a Million*. I consider calling a friend for comfort and consolation. But it was late, and I was afraid that Lee, the friend I would have called, would be asleep. I drink coffee and smoke till I can't tell whether I'm shaking because of the caffeine and nicotine or whether it's because I'm afraid. I alternate between terror and anger. I remember how it was when I was fourteen, when an exciting Saturday night was a double date at the local movie theater and home by ten. I imagine six different versions of the worst. I plan six different ways I'll handle the whole thing when it's over. And I jump every time the phone rings.

The phone rang often that night. Joe checked in from Melinda's house.

"No," he said, "they haven't seen Sylvia. In fact, they're not exactly sure where Melinda is either."

He checked in from the police station.

"They're not that impressed with one daughter who isn't where she said she'd be. Besides, they say they can't spare anyone to follow me around the island all night."

He checked in from the various parties he interrupted.

"Honey, no one here is going to tell me anything. They couldn't if they wanted to, which they don't. These kids are high on more than just a little beer."

Finally, after Audrey Hepburn and Peter O'Toole had outfoxed the gendarmes for the last time, Joe checked in again.

"I've found her," he said wearily.

"Where?"

"Well, I'm not sure. I'm over here at the Bollingers',

and their son, Mark, who just got home, says he knows where she is."

"Is she all right? Is...is she sober?"

"Honey"—his voice was strained—"I don't know. I haven't seen her. Mark's gone to get her."

"When will he get back?"

"I don't know that either. It shouldn't be long, though. Don't worry, we'll be home in a little while."

"OK." I hung up, flooded with relief but still apprehensive about what would happen next.

While I waited, I rehearsed what I'd say. It varied from "Oh, thank God you're safe" to "Why did you lie?" to "Do you realize how worried we've been?" to "Young lady, you're on restriction for a month at the very least."

Finally I heard the car come up the driveway. Then the back door burst open, and Sylvia marched in with Joe close behind.

"Well?" I said as she brushed past me and headed for the stairs.

"Well, what?" There was rage in her voice, and if I'd expected an apology, I was out of luck.

"Do you have any explanation for your actions tonight?"

She looked me straight in the eye, and the hatred I saw was frightening. "No," she said. "No, I don't. And even if I did, you wouldn't believe me."

"Oh, sweetheart, of course I would."

I reached out to touch her arm; but she pulled away, and behind her Joe shook his head, telling me, "Leave it alone for a while."

"All right," I said. "Have it your own way. Now get on upstairs to bed. We'll talk tomorrow."

She went, and while I checked the back door and Joe turned off the lights, we heard her slam her door shut and bang around the room.

"It'll be better in the morning," Joe said as he squeezed my hand. "Really it will."

He's right, I thought as I crawled into bed and pulled the blankets up over my shoulders, tempers will have cooled, and we'll be able to discuss this rationally. I'll explain that a person simply can't go around hurting herself and others this way. And, I thought as sleep finally inched over me, I'll be able to tell her how much we love her.

I'd hold many of these "In the morning I'll be able to..." conversations with myself in the years that followed, for things did not improve. "It's just that we love you and are concerned" was answered with "Get off my back." "Can't we talk about it?" elicited "Leave me alone. You wouldn't understand." And "Do you realize what you're doing to yourself?" brought "Why do you care? It's my life, you know."

I did manage to talk her into getting professional help by promising that Joe and I would go along with whatever Mrs. Ruston, a social worker I'd located through local agencies, suggested. But it didn't change the situation much. For one thing, Mrs. Ruston decided ours was a family problem, meaning we all had to meet with her once a week. And this did not sit well with the family.

David objected to being dragged out at dawn to gather in a cold room behind the Congregational church. Geoffrey balked at being asked to express his opinion about life at home. And Robbie asked, "Why do I have to come? I didn't do anything." Except for Joan, who was tolerant and acquiescent, and for Sylvia and Jenny, who giggled, spun their chairs around, and held whispered conversations with each other, everyone hated Tuesday mornings.

As time went on, Joe and I tried to tell ourselves there was some improvement. But there wasn't. The arguments went on. Curfews were broken. The school reported unexplained absences. And in May 1974 Sylvia and Melinda, now best of friends again, decided, just for the fun of it, to run away and hitchhike to California.

They came back after a few days, on a bus for which we'd wired them tickets. But by then I'd learned how it feels, after school is out and everyone else is home, to stare out the window and hope to see a familiar form striding across the lawn. I knew the sensation of leaping for the phone and praying I'd hear, "Hi, Mom. I had to stay after school to work on an assignment. Can you come pick me up?" And I'd spent more than my share of time watching daylight fade into another long and sleepless night.

I learned how to answer the phone and hear, "Mrs. Combs, this is the store detective. We've picked up your daughter for shoplifting." I learned that from Jenny, too, when she also decided that sneaking something out of a store sounded like fun.

I grew to expect locked bedroom doors and a flurry of activity whenever I knocked. And I learned not to assume that Sylvia's or Jenny's friends would do anything more than grunt as they shuffled through the door and fled past me on their way upstairs.

But I also learned how to put things out of my mind because troubles get boring after a while, even to the one whose troubles they are. When Lee and I talked, she commiserated for a while. Then we turned the conversation to the latest episode of Mary Tyler Moore and discussed the genius behind the line "Funny you don't look Canadian." We chortled over the latest news about Watergate. We compared housekeeping hatreds, and she regaled me with the story of a woman whose home was apparently immaculate but whose cat trotted through the living room during a luncheon one day with dust balls dragging from its tail. And we marveled at the logistics of the local man who was having simultaneous affairs with four different married women.

Even Joe and I developed a macabre sense of humor.

"Here comes Eddie Haskell," he'd say, referring to Debbie Erman, who, like Wally's two-faced friend in the old "Leave It to Beaver" series, was all smiles and "My, but that's a good-looking blouse, Mrs. Combs" to me and "I see the old bat's still hanging around in the kitchen" to Sylvia.

"Well, at least she speaks to us," I'd tell him.

"Yeah. I guess we should be thankful."

And we tried to be optimistic. When a whole day passed without a shouting match, when I didn't find myself inadvertently clenching my fists or gritting my teeth, and when Joe didn't come home to another "You'll never believe what happened today," we crossed our fingers and said, "Maybe the phase is passing. Maybe the worst is over."

It wasn't. In the spring of 1975 Sylvia's mood changed from sullen and glum to exhilarated and fiery. She was going to do everything: clean her room, publish a book of poetry, get a tan, write letters to all her friends in Colorado, wash her hair, go to college, join the Air Force, do all next week's homework in one afternoon. But like a honeybee in a field of snapdragons, she flitted from one thing to another and stayed with each only long enough to get started and lose interest.

Where before she'd sulked in her room or walked out on an argument, now she exploded in rage. And I found my rage and frustration rising to match hers. I also found that more and more often when I lay in bed, staring at the ceiling and promising myself that tomorrow would be better, that the questions, Why us?, Why Sylvia?, and Where did we go wrong? rattled around in my head like loose bolts in an empty oil drum: Had we been too strict or too lenient, demanded too much or asked too little? Had I forced too much responsibility on her when she was six, and I needed help with the twins? Had I let her down when I wouldn't make her a Halloween costume in the fourth grade? Why had I insisted on continually criticizing the clothes she wore in her freshman year? I knew better than to undermine her self-confidence that way.

For hours I'd toss and turn, searching for answers that never came and wishing the obvious yet nonspecific guilt would go away. Joe did too, and sometimes we'd lie there in the dark, holding each other, wordlessly trying to give and take all the comfort we possibly could. But it was never enough. And in our naïveté we never suspected that drugs—uppers, downers, speed, and who knows what else—were at the root of her bizarre behavior.

"Your daughter needs help," John Bolasni, a doctor stationed at the Bremerton naval hospital, told me one bright May morning when all the world was sunshine, there was a breeze off the bay, the dogwoods were in full bloom, and it seemed impossible that anything ugly or painful could exist. "She needs to see someone better equipped than I to deal with this."

So we got help. We took her to Adam Roberts, a psychologist who seemed to think he could help. But it was too late. At that point she'd been on speed for ten days straight and, like an airplane in a nose dive, had gone too far to pull herself out of it. The explosion came two days later, when Joe, unable to get in touch with Mr. Roberts, took her back to the Bremerton hospital. This time I stayed home. Lee came down to keep me company.

We drank coffee, smoked too many cigarettes, avoided the subject at hand, and waited to hear from Joe.

It would be a while. When they got there, Dr. Bolasni called them in right away. "I see things aren't any better," he said after he'd talked to Sylvia for a few minutes, and then sent her into another room with his nurse.

"We're at our wit's end." Joe sighed. "I don't think she's slept at all in over twenty-four hours. She sees things that aren't there, talks to imaginary people. She isn't still for more than a few minutes at a time. And we simply don't know what to do."

"Obviously she has to be hospitalized."

"Are you sure?"

"It's for her own good."

"Well, can you admit her?"

"I wish I could, but we simply don't have the facilities here."

"So what do we do then?"

"Let me call Duane Hayter. He's a local psychiatrist affiliated with a private hospital in Seattle. I'm sure he'll be able to do something."

While he located Dr. Hayter, Joe called me from a pay phone in the waiting room. I could hear a child whining in the background and the sound of Sylvia's voice talking to him in short, staccato sentences.

"Just a minute," he told her, "I'm talking to your mother. I'll be with you in a minute."

Then the tone of his voice changed. "Annie?" he said. "I'm still here, and I don't know when I'll be home."

"What's going on?"

"Well, Dr. Bolasni's trying to get in touch with a local shrink, a Dr. Hayter. And from what I gather, Dr. Hayter will probably put her in a hospital in Seattle."

"Seattle?"

"Yeah...there's nothing here."

"But how will she get there?"

"I don't know. But I'm sure we'll work that out. Listen, I have to go. I'll call you as soon as I know anything more."

"OK...I love you."

"Me too. G'bye."

I hung up. "They're trying to get hold of a doctor who can get Sylvia to a hospital," I told Lee.

"Poor thing." She sipped her coffee. "Why do the kids these days seem so determined to destroy themselves?"

"Damned if I know." I sat down and poured myself another cup. "Do you want some more?"

"No...thanks. I've got to get home. Everyone will be home from school pretty soon, and Maria has a dentist appointment."

"OK."

"Are you going to be all right?"

"Oh, sure. The kids will be home soon, too. Besides, I've still got three loads of laundry to do. And...oh, Lord ...I forgot to take the roast out of the freezer."

"I don't wonder. This has not been what you'd call your average day." As she left, she squeezed my arm. "Let me know what happens when Joe calls," she said.

"I will."

But Joe didn't call. The phone rang some time after Lee left, but it was Dr. Bolasni.

"Oh, Mrs. Combs," he said, "I feel just terrible."

"What happened?"

"Well, when your husband took your daughter over to Dr. Hayter's office, I forgot to tell him I'd arrange to have a navy ambulance take them into town. And when I remembered and called over there, they'd already left."

"Oh, dear," I said. "I wonder what he did. Do you

suppose he took the ferry from Bremerton?"

"I imagine so. It's the closest."

But he hadn't. No sooner had I hung up the phone than I heard the car come up the driveway. I ran outside. Sylvia, in the front seat, glared at me and made a face. Joe motioned for me to come around to his side of the car.

"Listen, honey," he said, "would you go in and get David?"

"Why? What do you want him for?"

"I need him to come with me. I just don't dare go any farther by myself. I was sure she was going to leap out of the car in the middle of rush-hour traffic back there. And I'd just feel better if David came along to keep her occupied."

So I ran into the house and got David.

"Do I have to go?" he asked, pleading.

"Daddy needs you. He's afraid Sylvia might try to jump out of the car."

"Maybe she should," he snapped.

"Oh, come on, you don't mean that."

"I don't know if I do or not. But I do know I'm sick of having everything revolve around Sylvia."

"I know," I said. "Now go on. Daddy wants to make the next boat."

So they left. They caught the ferry into Seattle and drove across town to the hospital. And after she'd been admitted, and Joe had watched as the nurses and order-lies led her away, they came home. It was David's seventeenth birthday.

By the time he celebrated his twenty-first birthday he'd almost forgotten about the trip out to the hospital. Not because that was the end of our turmoil with Sylvia. It wasn't. When she came home from the hospital, she was docile and subdued. But after a week or so the defiance and resentment returned. She chafed at restrictions. "Oh, come on now. No one comes home by eleven o'clock anymore." "I'll do the pots and pans when I'm good and ready. Don't hassle me" and "Geez, it's not like I'm asking for big bucks. I only want to borrow five dollars."

She sneered at "Mommy and Poppy and all my good little brothers and sisters." And every now and then, when the days were long and the nights were warm, she took to the road once more.

At first we went after her. Joe flew to California when instead of going to school, she decided to hitchhike to San Jose to see Melinda, who was now on her own. When he got there, he stormed through the house that served as a minicommune. He stepped over rows of mattresses slapped down on the floor like belongings left over from a fire. He gagged on the acrid smell of urine that hung in the hot, airless rooms. He saw a young girl, fully clothed, sitting in a bathtub, smiling idiotically as she dabbed at the tiles with a dry sponge. And because no one was coherent enough to tell him where Sylvia and Melinda had gone, he came home empty-handed.

After that we sent tickets: bus tickets, plane tickets, train tickets. We'd long since learned you don't wire money to a runaway. Joe met planes and had stewardesses tell him Sylvia had tried to get off in Portland. He put her on the ferry and then went back to work. I, on the Bainbridge side, chatted casually with friends or acquaintances who were also down at the dock waiting to meet someone. And when the boat slid into the slip and Sylvia wasn't among those getting off, I made some offhand remark to cover once again my chagrin and discomfiture. Then I excused myself and hurried onto the ferry to retrieve her before the deck hands pulled back the gangplank. And I took her home.

Though we never mentioned it out loud, Joe and I both crossed our fingers and tried to prepare for the call we feared would come someday, the call that would tell us, "We found your daughter's body..."

The breathers, the times when she was home and safe, were no less chaotic, however. Like an actress upstaging the rest of the cast, she hogged the family spotlight. The other players resented it, and in their resentment they did what they could.

When the dinner hour dissolved into a shouting match, David simply left the table and retreated to his room. When Sylvia raced out to the car to join us on an uneventful trip to pick up a few things at the store, Geoffrey went back in the house, saying, "Never mind, Mom. I'll get my notebooks later." Robbie ignored her. At times Jenny joined her, whispering and giggling behind locked bedroom doors. At other times she bolstered me and assured me, "Don't worry, Mom. It'll be all right. Really it will." Only Joan offered unqualified love to all parties.

"I can't order the kids to like their sister or even to be civil to her," I told Lee one day when Geoffrey had come to me saying Sylvia had taken money out of his drawer and had already spent it. "If she's going to help herself to their things, if she's going to be disruptive and make life miserable for everyone, they're bound to hate her. She might as well learn that right away."

"And what about you?" Lee asked. "Do you hate her?"

"Yes...sometimes. But that doesn't mean I'm going to give up on her. Something has to make her see she can't go through life doing whatever she damn well pleases. And I intend to find out what that something is."

"But you can't check up on everything she does."

"I can sure try, though. And if she thinks she can get away with stuff because Mom's too embarrassed to do anything about it, she's wrong. I'm well past the stage where appearances count for anything. My friends understand what's going on, and that's all that matters."

Lee laughed. "You mean you've forgiven Sandy Muller for coming up to you on the ferry and telling you she always keeps an eye on Sylvia whenever she's in her store so Sylvia won't get away with stealing anything?"

"Not hardly." I chuckled. "For her I wish terminal fat and a month's worth of gum surgery."

Lee nodded. "Yeah," she said, "that sounds appropriate." Then she shook her head. "I don't know why we're laughing."

"I do," I told her. "It beats agonizing. But don't worry. There's hope. I've found another psychiatrist, and at least Sylvia's agreed to see him."

It hadn't been easy. Dr. Hayter, out of boredom or frustration or both, had declared her fine. He'd said her flirtation with drugs, however constant or sporadic it had been—there was no way to tell, and she hadn't offered the information—was over. And he'd assured me that whatever caused it, and whatever damage it had done to her and the rest of us, would work themselves out eventually.

He was wrong, though. The sullenness was still there. There were still explosions of temper. Joe and I were still the enemy. And I still found conversations about any but the most trivial subjects impossible. So on the glowing recommendation of a friend of a friend I made an appointment with another psychiatrist, Eric Strachan.

It was an act of desperation. I had to do something, and though I hoped for the best, I pretty much expected more of the same: fifty-minute hours, during which we'd all wade leisurely through the stream of consciousness, only to come out on the other side saying, "How's that again?"

I was pleasantly surprised. Eric Strachan, though he looked the part of a psychiatrist (he was tall and bearded and appeared unflappable), didn't speak in Freudian parables, and he didn't peer over the tops of his glasses or tap his fingertips together in an aloof blessing to the poor in spirit. Instead, he was blunt: "That's bullshit." He was irreverent, "So as the great mother figure you think you have to solve everyone's problems, do you?" He cared: "Call me if you need me...anytime." And his suggestions made sense: "If some local gossip simpers up to you and says, 'Tell me. How's your daughter Sylvia these days?' simply answer, 'Fine, why do you ask?'"

We saw him once a week. So did Sylvia.

But it wasn't like taking two aspirin for a headache or putting a splint on a broken finger. The patient insisted she liked her migraine and would set her own bones. And since no amount of worry and concern helps someone who won't help herself, we simply tried to live through each day and to fight off the familiar panic whenever we spotted signs of impending flight.

Then, when she was gone again, we steeled ourselves for the inevitable collect phone calls. She called from a diner in California to giggle and tell me, "Don't worry. I'm fine. I got a ride clear from Grants Pass in Oregon." She called from a gas station in Chicago to whisper, "Mom, someone's following me. Will you call the Chicago police?" When Joe and I were at the church attending a reception to honor Daddy's long years as a priest, Robbie ran up the road to call out to me, "Mom, Sylvia's on the phone. She's calling from a police station in Ohio." He snorted. "They arrested her for hitchhiking on the freeway, and she locked all the doors in the squad car."

The calls came on the average of once every two weeks. I accepted them when the guilt and the worry were riding high and refused to pay the charges when the only emotions left were anger and exhaustion.

On her eighteenth birthday I wrote her a letter.

Dear Sylvia,

Well, you're gone. You're on your own and living the life you've chosen, and the rest of us are trying to put things back together and forget the pain of these last four years. For some it's easier than others. Tears come easily, and regrets are hard to throw away. But just once more, on the occasion of your birthday, I want to remember my little girl, who came roaring into the world on a hot August morning eighteen years ago.

I'm sitting at my desk in my study, and all around me are memories. On one wall is a picture of a baby with spaghetti dripping over her head. You were like that, smashing your dinner with your fist till it shot out spraying everything in the room. You bellowed and sang and laughed and cried and escaped from your bath to gallop nude through the neighborhood. You kangarooed your crib around the room and threw wet diapers at David and generally rolled in life.

On my left is a picture of you peering out from under an umbrella. That was when we were in Tokyo, when you and David learned to ride bikes, and you thought a Japanese toilet was a foot bath, and Jenny tiptoed around in black leotards, and you had a green rabbit cake on your birthday. You liked to listen to stories about Muffin—remember, he was the little dog with the cinder in his eye. And you liked to go to Mrs. Robbins's house for breakfast. One day you told her, "Daddy sleeps in his underwear."

When we moved to Johnson, we had the cryptomeria trees out in the back and the neat hill for bicycling and the swimming pool, and Daddy used to swim around like a submerged whale and give rides on his back. We still have movies of that and movies of you going off to nursery school—waiting all by yourself at the bus stop.

There are hundreds of other memories. I can still hear you sobbing over *The Little Match Girl*. I remember how you suffered when the dog followed you to school and you had to stand out in the blizzard till I came to get him and how terrified you were when the principal called you to his office the day Robbie and Joan wandered off and showed up at school. I was proud of you when you tried to like the dreaded Miss Parks and delighted when you got Mrs. Sullivan as your fifth grade teacher. It'll be hard to tell her you've gone.

Do you remember the camping trips? The fireflies? When Joan fell and you brought her home? When you swam across the lake with me?

And do you remember when we moved to Bainbridge? I can still see you sitting up on the rock at the church waiting for Daddy and me to bring the puppies, Golly and Shebie, home. But I'm getting close to the time when the pain began, and so, as the song says, "When it's too painful to remember, I'll simply choose to forget."

I wish the Sylvia I remember were here now. It's a glorious day. The August sun is hot, and I can hear the Scotch broom seeds popping out in the field. The dogs are lying out under a tree, and the cat's stretched out in the grass being dive-bombed by a couple of over-protective swallows. The garden has been lovely this year. We even have sweet peas.

Geoffrey, Robbie, and Joan are over at Auntie

Sylvia's, swimming. David worked all night and is sleeping, and Jenny's waiting for her date. I think they're going sailing. I'm about to go in and make applesauce, and Daddy just finished harvesting some potatoes. It's peaceful today, kind of lazy and slow, and a cool breeze is blowing through the kitchen. My little girl would like it. You'd be out getting a tan, or running through the sprinkler, or reading a book.

But you're not here. You're gone, and now two thousand miles away you're going to celebrate your eighteenth birthday. I won't give you any advice, sweetheart. It's much too late for that. Except to say: Be happy, try to brighten your corner of the world, and try not to hurt anyone knowingly. And when you make your peace with life, come back and gather up the gentle, generous, loving parts that are yours, too. They'll be here.

All my love,
Mother

She didn't get the letter. By the time it reached the address I had she was gone again.

Life went on. Alarm clocks rang in the morning. Coffee perked. There were the usual fights over who ate the last banana and the usual searches for permission slips and math books. Joe rushed to make the seven-ten ferry. The children went off to school. I sorted the laundry, ran the dishes through their cycle, and called Lee to see if she'd read the piece in the paper about Idi Amin deciding to become a famous race car driver.

In the afternoon one by one, at his or her appointed time, everyone came home. Geoffrey announced his latest time on the cross-country course. Jenny said she'd sold another box of chocolate bars to an insurance company in Winslow and was a shoo-in to win the candy sale. Robbie claimed a boy in his class could swallow his tongue. Joan followed me around the kitchen, telling me the complete plot of *Anne of Green Gables*.

As dinnertime approached, I scrubbed potatoes, peeled carrots, and put the meat loaf in the oven, then went down to pick up Joe at the boat. When he got home, he sifted through the mail, then poured us a glass of wine. The news came on. The oven timer buzzed, and I called out, "Time to eat."

In the evening someone turned on "Eight Is Enough" or "Chico and the Man." In the dining room Joan worked on a book report. I quizzed Jenny on her grammar: "OK, which is the adverbial clause in 'Before I went to the store, I cashed a check'?" David, now in college, phoned home from the dorm to say he was in the Ping-Pong finals and that he had a computer science exam in the morning. Someone yelled at Robbie to turn off the shower and save some hot water for the rest of us. Joe fiddled with the radio, checking to see how the Sonics were doing in Detroit. Geoffrey went to bed.

As the weeks went by, we went to the store. We went to parents' night at school. We took in Jenny's piano recitals. We repainted the bathroom, washed the kitchen curtains, fixed the leak in the roof, and made thirty quarts of applesauce. We kept dentist appointments. Joe renewed our subscription to *Time*. I sent away for a Swedish back massager. And we both tried another new diet. We laughed. We argued. Joan and Robbie taught me all the verses to *The Cat Came Back*. In short, we were the average family picking up the pieces. But under it all, like the snatch of a song that buzzes at the back of your mind and won't go away, was Sylvia.

Mother didn't want to talk about her. She couldn't understand. "Why won't she behave herself?" Daddy, from a position once removed, assured me he was praying for her safety. Joe's parents insisted that, "No one in our family ever acted like this." Auntie Sylvia, one of the few of the generation once removed to offer aid and comfort, cheered any signs of progress and commiserated when the news turned glum.

Only our friends actually understood. Only those whose sons were cutting classes or being suspended from school and whose daughters refused to wear bras or to say anything more cheerful than a snide "big deal" in answer to any and all statements, felt the same bewilderment. Only those whose days were turbulent and whose nights were sleepless would admit they sometimes found themselves whispering, "I don't think I can take it anymore." Only those of us caught between the two generations understood the burning resentment against both those who preached, "What will people think?" and those who snarled, "Who gives a shit?"

Finally, when one of her brief, unannounced, and fierce trips home threw everything into a turmoil again, I resigned myself to the fact that there was nothing more Joe or I could do. Whether or not we'd failed, whether or not we'd "left undone those things which we ought to have done," whether or not we were responsible for what had happened, this obviously was how it was. All the guilt in the world wouldn't change it. All the threats and pleas wouldn't alter her chosen course. And we had lives to live, too.

So after a particularly intense outburst I took her by the arm and, with all the strength I could muster, forced her out to the car.

"That's it," I said. "I've had enough."

She looked at me with loathing. "What do you mean you've had enough?"

I turned the car around and headed down the driveway. "Just that," I said. "I've had enough: enough of your running away, enough of bailing you out and sending you a ticket so you can come home. I'm tired of talking to policemen and social workers. I've had it with screaming fights here at home. And most of all, I won't stand by and watch you destroy your life anymore."

"It is my life, you know," she said with a sneer.

"Precisely," I said as I drove through Winslow. "It's your life, and I'm bowing out of it. You're on your own."

"Where are we going?"

"To the ferry." I handed her a ticket. "Here."

"What's this for?"

"It's for you. Take it. Go back to the life you seem intent on leading, and leave the rest of us be."

She tore it out of my hand. "I will," she said. "I'll do just that."

I bit my lip. This was it. But as I pulled up in front of the terminal and stopped, I reached over and took her hand. "One more thing," I said, "and I want you to remember this: If at some point you decide you want to pull things together and live by society's rules, I'm here, and I'll do what I can to help you."

She snatched her hand away. "That'll be the day," she said as she jumped out of the car and slammed the door behind her. "That'll really be the day," she yelled, and she disappeared into the building.

All the way home I shook uncontrollably, but I'd meant every word of it, and like someone who's just come home from a funeral, I felt an odd sense of relief.

After that the phone calls and the sudden appearances at the back door stopped. Months went by.

Then slowly, ever so slowly, the demons in her died. Gradually she left the drugs behind, and the adolescent chemistry that had roiled inside her for so many years quieted down.

When I next heard from her, there was a change. I sensed it immediately, and I was right. She was sleeping again. She was reading again: books, magazines, anything she could find. And she was laughing again, the free-and-easy laugh that bubbles up and explodes with genuine amusement.

Her mouth, so long a tight, pursed O, was finally relaxing. Her eyes, wide and gorgeous, with lashes I would kill for, gradually brightened and lost their glazed look. And her voice no longer attacked or droned inaudibly. It sparkled, shifted, murmured, and rang out with the clarity of conviction.

In time she studied, took tests, and received the equivalent of a high school diploma. Weeks passed, and she was back at work, earning her way and paying her debts. More time, and she moved into her own apartment.

Summer came, and she didn't flee. We didn't spend autumn sitting in a airport lounge, waiting for her to stomp off a plane. Christmas was the hectic, tumultuous, exhausting holiday it's supposed to be. And the tension of waiting for the explosion went out of spring.

Now our conversations on the phone are about recipes, tax deductions, her new cat, the price of jeans, and where she and her date are going tonight. Her visits home no longer bring on a chorus of "Don't expect me to stick around" from her brothers and sisters. She's won them over. Jenny calls her. Robbie stops by to see her at work. Joan and Geoffrey stay over at her apartment. David, now on his own and living in California, writes to her and looks forward to her answers. On his trips home they go out and have a drink together or stay up all night talking. She and Joe meet every now and then for lunch.

And I? I hold my breath as one by one the rest wander through their teens. I trust, knowing that by now, at this age, there's little else I can do. I try not to judge or to force the compulsions of the 1940s and the 1950s on those whose good old days lie in the 1970s.

And whenever I hear a young mother sigh over yet another untied shoelace or another load of diapers, I smile the smile of a veteran who's earned the right and say, "If you think you've got it tough now, just wait till they get to be teen-agers."

ನ Oh, My Stars

"As long as we're here," I always say to Joe when I manage to drag him into a department store, "we might as well look around and see what they've come up with lately to make life a little easier."

So it was with our Tuesday morning appointments with Dr. Strachan.

"As long as we're here figuring what to do about Sylvia," I said one day when most of the crises had passed and we were finally headed up out of the depths, "why don't we see if we can iron out some problems of our own?"

"What do you mean, problems of our own? I think we get along pretty well considering how things have been going the last few years."

"Oh, I agree. It's just that with marriages breaking up all around us and with divorce the new national pastime, I thought we might invest in a little preventive maintenance."

He muttered something to himself. Joe's reaction to all my various plans for improving his, my, and/or the family's life, health, and character is always negative at first.

254

As usual, I blathered on. "What I mean," I stammered, "what I'm trying to say is...that...well...for instance, I know I could certainly use an unbiased opinion on whether or not I'm, as you contend, unreasonable about your fanatic love of sports."

"My what?"

"Your...your...shall we say, sick devotion to football, basketball, and baseball." ,

It was an old argument, one that had raged off and on ever since the days I sat in our first apartment and wailed, "You don't love me. If you did, you'd talk to me instead of sitting there watching a bunch of hulks in tight pants and shoulder pads knock each other down."

In the ensuing years I'd learned to adapt somewhat. I'd picked up enough of the basics of football so I voluntarily watched the Seattle Seahawks and cheered the Washington Huskies on to the Rose Bowl. I'd developed a definite fondness for the Sonics. And I'd at least kept track of the Mariners as they rattled around in the basement of the American League.

But as for taking the radio on the ferry so that I wouldn't miss so much as an infield fly, as for "Monday Night Football" with Howard Cosell intoning, "This man, as Dandy Don, with his matchless spontaneity of articulation, told you earlier, can really run. With all the jocularity about draft choices, they've managed to acquire a pretty tough cookie," and as for lying in bed with a plug in my ear and the radio balanced on my stomach so I'd be able to catch the Sonics game with the Lakers, I wasn't up to it, and I didn't appreciate the fact that Joe was either.

"Are you going to start that again?" he snarled.

"No...it's just that I think you should be able to compromise a bit, and I think that—"

"You talk about compromise. How about your constant demand that I talk to you all the time? I certainly wouldn't mind if you toned that down a bit."

So we continued to show up at Eric Strachan's office every Tuesday at seven-thirty in the morning. We sat in the waiting room reading last week's *People* magazine. We sipped coffee. We smiled at the patients of other doctors in the building and tried to look terribly well adjusted while we took note of their chewed fingernails, their nervous fidgeting, and their chain-smoking.

When Eric called us in, we made light-hearted references to the fact that he had double doors and accepted his explanation that they kept out office noises, though I still had the feeling they were there to keep patients from bolting. I headed for the "neurotic's chair." It was the one next to the desk. Joe perched on the "paranoid seat" next to the lamp table. Eric skated his high-backed black leather I-am-the-doctor's chair around on the plastic island that served as a carpet protector, and together we tackled the good, the bad, and the aggravating.

Naturally we discussed guilt, the force that may not move mountains but certainly shuffles people around at a great rate.

It was an appropriate subject, for as a rule, I feel guilty about almost everything. I feel guilty when the steamed carrots are crunchy or I haven't folded the laundry and Joe's underwear drawer is empty. I get a twinge when my second cousin twice removed says it's her birthday and I know I haven't sent her a card. I get uneasy when they're calling for volunteers and my hand isn't in the air. I stew about forgetting to vote for the park district initiative.

I feel guilty because I'm sick of going to parents' night at the high school and because I sent a package of napkins

instead of two dozen freshly baked brownies to the sophomore class picnic. I worry when it's December 20 and
I haven't started writing my Christmas cards yet and when
the tree's still up and shedding on inauguration day. I
fuss over the fact I haven't cleaned the oven since the
last wild blackberry pie and fret when I go off my diet
for a bowl of cold spaghetti that's been in the back of the
refrigerator since a week ago Wednesday.

Of course, I embrace blame like a long lost friend and
accept the responsibility for everything from no gas in
the car to a sickly philodendron or the fact that the dogs
turned over the garbage can and there are now coffee
grounds and chicken bones in the nasturtium bed.

So we discussed my guilt. We discussed procrastina-
tion, of which guilt is an end product. We established
the fact that it's a waste of emotional energy to feel responsible for situations beyond our control. We examined
and identified the people whose sole joy in life is making
others feel guilty. And after each session I headed home
with a list of things to do to conquer guilt. Sometimes I
followed through. Sometimes I didn't. When I didn't, I
felt guilty. But in time I made progress.

Joe made progress, too.

When he'd retired from the Air Force, his practical
skills were limited to the care and feeding of peace while
keeping an eye out for war. But there's not much call on
the open market for photo-radar intelligence men. So
with a wife and six children clamoring for food, clothes,
and a place to put the basketball hoop, he took the one
job available, as the manager of his father's home wine
supply store.

It was hardly an executive position. There were no long
lunches, no afternoons on the golf course, and no three-
day weekends. Joe opened the store. He swept out the

front, fed the cat, and dusted off the cider press. On some Saturdays he ran the ancient bottle washer in the back and loaded gallon jugs onto the truck. On others he sacked sugar and packaged wine yeast. And during the great canning jar crisis of 1973 he helped keep the hordes in line and carted case after case of quart jars out to waiting cars in the parking lot.

But aside from a discount price on carboys and saccharometers, the fringe benefits were few. Scarcer still were holidays and raises in pay. If Christmas fell on a Sunday, Monday was business as usual. If the cost of living rose six percent, the word was: "Mail orders are off, and things may be tight for a while." And then there was the age-old conflict between father and son, with the one saying, "Why isn't he more interested in the business? After all, it will all be his someday," and the other replying, "How come at age forty-nine I'm still being treated like a sixteen-year-old kid?" And it resulted in the standard SOB (Sons of Bosses) Syndrome.

So we talked about it in Eric Strachan's office. I grumbled and described the times Joe had vowed as he left the house in the morning that today was definitely the day he would quit. Joe agonized and explained how it feels to face the prospect of being out of work with seven people depending on you for support. Eric separated the pertinent from the impertinent. He outlined the choices, listed the best and the worst. And on March 31, 1978, two weeks before his fiftieth birthday and two weeks after giving notice, Joe walked out the door an unemployed but happy man.

He stayed that way for three months while he leisurely, almost casually, looked for something else to do. And till he found it, till he became a collector for the credit card division of a Seattle bank, we trundled into Eric's office as usual, this time to exult in the feeling of freedom and accomplishment.

But a psychiatrist's office is no place for prolonged sessions of "Isn't life marvelous?" The apostles of Freud and Jung get nervous when hands go unwrung and psyches don't need probing. So we got back to Joe's preoccupation with the boys of summer…and winter…and spring…and fall. We got back to my efforts to extricate myself from the middle of family arguments between Joe, who wanted the gravel raked, and Geoffrey, who insisted, "I always have to do everything?"; between Jenny, who'd borrowed Joan's wall hangings, and Joan, who wanted them back; and between David, who couldn't find his tennis balls, and Robbie, who in a fit of boredom had used them for a variation of golf the day before.

We got back to ironing out differences. And when it seemed the iron was heating up, Eric leaned back in his chair, ran his hand over his beard, and asked, "So how's your sex life?"

I knew the question would come up sooner or later. I'd heard the theory that as sex goes, so goes the marriage. But for someone who at thirteen had draped a dishtowel over her head to hide the embarrassment when her mother tried to tell her the facts of life, for someone who at sixteen still thought of Kathleen Norris and the adventures of Mary Worth as the epitome of passion, and for someone whose British upbringing insisted, "Do it if you must, my dear, but for heaven's sake maintain your dignity, and don't disgrace the family," I hadn't looked forward to delving into the subject of Joe, Ann, and love in the afternoon.

I admit I was behind the times. Everyone else seemed to be perfectly at ease with his or her sex life as the main topic of conversation. Talk show hosts nodded wisely and urged their guests to be more specific about steps 3 and 4 in "How to Prolong an Orgasm." Tom, Dick, and Gloria smiled for the cameras and described their communal marriage while Gloria intoned, "We've been very open with the children, and they understand that Mommy loves both Tom and Daddy." And a clinical psychologist came on to discuss his latest book, *Sex and the Octogenarian.*

But then these folks were in the front lines of the sexual revolution. I was still in the rear guard, saving tin foil and remembering Pearl Harbor. Not that I fainted at the thought of people living together without benefit of clergy. I didn't. There's much to be said for the practice, though personally I'd feel a bit uneasy settling down in a house where the back door is always open.

I didn't storm the principal's office and demand he cut out sex education courses. As far as I was concerned, it was a good idea, long overdue. I didn't rant and rave about teen-age girls' having access to the Pill since reality told me the days of "No, no, kind sir, I never kiss on the first date" were long past and practicality added, "It's better to be safe than pushing a stroller at graduation." Besides, I thought, age sixteen or seventeen is a bit late for the first lessons in basic self-restraint.

I didn't gasp at the sight of *Playboy* or burn copies of *Everything You Always Wanted to Know About Sex, but Were Afraid to Ask.* I did suggest to Jenny, when she was barely eleven, that she postpone the reading of David Reuben's manual until she was a little older. And she agreed with me. She even admitted it was boring, and said, "Besides, I already know what a 'puhniss' is."

But I did blanch slightly when I came across a children's picture book that featured a two-page spread showing how well Mommy and Daddy can get along when they have the opportunity. I sneered at obligatory sex scenes stuffed into novels like random page markers.

I trembled at the thought of being invited to a party where exchanging house keys replaced charades as the evening's entertainment. After the first "Oh, my God. Look at what they're doing?" I lost all prurient interest in both soft- and hard-core films. And I squirmed at the prospect of having to discuss Joe's and my sex life.

Still, there it was, the topic of the hour. So I stammered. I stuttered. I stared at the ceiling and memorized the diplomas on the far wall. Joe seemed to be perfectly at ease, and except for a nervous chuckle every now and then, he and Eric could have been discussing high-pressure systems off the Gulf of Alaska for all anyone could tell.

This went on for weeks, mostly because I became adept at changing the subject. But Eric persisted. Finally he shook his head and said, "What you two need is to loosen up a bit. Forget that you were taught to believe sex is dirty and nice girls don't French-kiss. You're two married adults now. No one's going to tell on you, and besides, you'll find that if you loosen up your sex life, other aspects of your relationship will loosen up, too."

"And how do you recommend we go about this?" I asked as I fiddled with the clasp on my purse.

"Well, you can't do it alone."

"Ho-ho."

"No, I mean it. You have to talk to each other. You have to tell each other how you feel. And you have to try new things."

I reached for my coffee and took a long gulp.

"In fact," he continued, "I'd suggest you get a couple of copies of *Playboy* or some such magazine and look through them together. And I think you ought to buy a copy of Alex Comfort's *The Joy of Sex*, and read that, too."

"That's a good idea," Joe said in a manner that suggested he'd get to it right away. "That's exactly what we'll do."

What he meant, however, was that's exactly what Ann will do. For somehow he kept forgetting to stop at the drugstore, and the bookstore was always closed when he got home from work. Of course, he was much too busy on Saturdays. He had to mow the lawn "because if I let it get away from me, I'll have to go over it twice just to get it under control again." He had to take his chain saw up to be sharpened: "There's a tree down on the property next to us, and since no one's done anything about it, it would be nice to get some free firewood for a change." And he had to pick blackberries. "You do want me to make wine this year, don't you?" So the task of finding an issue of *Playboy* and picking up a copy of *The Joy of Sex* fell to me.

Playboy, fortunately, was no trouble. David had a couple of issues hidden away in the back of his closet, and Robbie had one stashed in his dresser drawer under his T-shirts. I dug them out and looked them over one day when everyone was in school.

It had been awhile since I'd last seen Miss February or read Hugh Hefner's ramblings—about fifteen years, in fact. Joe had let his subscription run out shortly after David took to inviting some of his first-grade classmates over to admire Miss April's more obvious attributes. And now as the pages fell open to a pictorial review of "The Year in Sex," I realized that Hugh had not been marking time in our absence.

"Oh, dear...oh, my stars." I gasped as I turned the pages. "How things have changed."

And they had. For one thing, coy was certainly passé. So was hiding one's light under a veil of chiffon or behind a strip of satin. The let-it-all-hang-out generation appeared to be doing just that. Mitsy was draped uncomfortably over a split-rail fence. Rhonda was trolling athletically for salmon. And Michelle, I gathered, had just sat down on a slab of cold cement.

The captions under the pictures hastened to add that "Mitsy loves sashimi, Yorkshire pudding, and Hans Christian Andersen fairy tales." They assured me that "Rhonda makes all her own clothes, grows begonias, and has two cats named Fluff and Muff." And they informed me that "Michelle's heroes are Clarence Darrow and Leonardo da Vinci."

"I don't know," I told Joe that evening as I drove him home from the ferry. "Loosening up is one thing, but from what I saw the trend nowadays is to fall apart at the seams."

"Well, what about that book Eric recommended? Did you get that yet?"

I hadn't. I'd made a few attempts. But a 1952 graduate of the Annie Wright Seminary for Girls simply doesn't stride into a bookstore and say, "Let's see, I'd like a copy of *Tristram Shandy, The Farmer's Almanac, Grandma Rose's Book of Sinfully Delicious Snacks, Nibbles, Noshes, and Other Delights*, and oh, yes...*The Joy of Sex*."

She doesn't dare. For though it's been twenty-some years since she last hid *The Kinsey Report* in the back of her closet and though she's sure nine- and ten-year-olds are now reading the infamous *You and Your Body* which used to come through the mails in a plain brown wrapper, she still hears Mrs. Crump's voice ringing out to ask, "What's that book you have there?"

So though I'd wandered into the bookstore in Winslow a time or two, I'd also wandered right back out. Now, however, it had been at least six weeks since Eric first mentioned the subject, and I could put it off no longer.

I went the next afternoon, around three, when I figured everyone else on Bainbridge would be at work, at home with the children, or at the grocery store, checking out the sale on chuck roasts. I was wrong. The place was packed. A woman at the front was thumbing through the best sellers. A couple who'd parked their bikes out on the sidewalk were looking at the selection of books on wilderness hikes and nature trails. An ascetic young girl with a single braid that hung to her waist stood with her head cocked to one side as she looked over the titles in the occult and mystical experience section. Two children sat on the floor in the back and flipped through a copy of *Charlotte's Web*. And on the second level I could hear someone rummaging through the paperbacks.

Julie, the owner, was counting the change a small boy had given her to pay for *Runaway Ralph*. She looked up, smiled, said, "Hi, Ann. How are you doing?" and went back to her customer.

I edged past the woman in front and tried to look as if I were hunting for the perfect book to give as a birthday present. Every now and then I took a volume down, read the flyleaf, and put it back. I even squatted down and studied the books on the bottom shelf.

Finally the woman next to me picked up a copy of *The Vicar of Christ*. She sighed. "Well, I guess I'll get this," she said to herself, and she went over to the cash register to pay for it and to have Julie wrap it.

Good, I thought, one down and four or five more to go. Of course, it wasn't that simple, for no sooner had one person left than two more would come in. After a while I moved over a section to where there were three shelves of home improvement books.

"Great," I muttered to myself, "while I'm waiting, I'll figure out what to do about our kitchen."

I did. I also figured out what to do about the bedroom, the bathroom, and the upstairs hall. I learned how to make a three-tiered deck and how to make individual barbecue grills out of clay pots. And I learned how to paper a wall with bed sheets.

"Is there anything special you're looking for?" Julie asked between customers.

I shook my head. "I'm waiting till everyone's gone," I whispered.

She looked at me quizzically, and since she's a good friend, I was about to explain further; but someone came up to ask about a typing manual, and I moved on to cookbooks.

After that I checked out the latest in dictionaries. I looked to see if the newest Evelyn Anthony novel had come out in paperback yet. I picked out another copy of Ray Bradbury's *Dandelion Wine* to replace the one I'd lent to someone who never returned it. And I thumbed through a book of George Booth's cartoons.

Finally, between the comings and goings, there was a brief pause when the store was free of customers.

"Quick," I told Julie. "I have to buy a copy of *The Joy of Sex.*"

"*The Joy of Sex?*" she hooted. "That's why you've been lurking around here like an undercover agent...because you want to buy *The Joy of Sex?*" She chuckled. "Boy, you're something else."

"Well, you can laugh all you want," I said, defending myself, "but it's not easy for a staid old Puritan like me to swing...even intermaritally, or is it intra...or is there even such a word?"

"Come on," she said as she reached up to the top shelf and pulled out a copy of the book. "Do want it gift-wrapped?"

"No, that's all right."

"How about a bag?"

"Lord, yes, do you think I'm going to carry it, just like this, into the house, where who knows how many children are milling around in the kitchen?"

So she put it in a bag, and I hurried home. Fortunately no one was there, at least no one was downstairs, when I got there. But I took no chances. I went into my room, glanced through it briefly, and gasped a time or two, especially at the Japanese prints, which weren't the "Mist over Distant Mountains," the "Samurai Warrior," or the "Carp Under a Lily Pad" I was used to. Then I looked for a safe place to put it so the children wouldn't find it.

First I tried one of my drawers. I stuffed it under a stack of sweaters.

"No, that won't work," I muttered as I took it out again. "Someone's always wanting to borrow one of my sweaters."

I slid it under the mattress on Joe's side of the bed.

"No, that's no good either. If they hide things under their mattresses, it's the first place they'd look.

"How about behind the books in the bookshelf?"

I stood on the window seat and wedged it down behind *Birds of North America* and *The White House, a Pictorial History.* Then I jumped down, stepped back, and looked.

"Nope. I can see it plain as day."

I tried to think of a place in the closet where it would be safe. There was my little suitcase, but with my luck I'd probably forget about it and one of the children would borrow the suitcase to take on an overnight. I couldn't put it up on the shelf or under my shoes in the back of the closet.

"I know," I said to myself in what was now becoming an extensive conversation, "I'll find a place in my study."

I heard the sound of feet shuffling upstairs, and I hurried into the study.

"I can lock it up in my file cabinet," I said.

But that was no good. I'd done that before with Christmas presents, and everyone in the house knew all my hiding places for the key. Besides, if they found the file locked, they'd ask questions, and I wasn't up to elaborate lies. Someone thundered down the stairs, and I could hear the refrigerator opening and closing.

"Hey, Mom...Mom. Are you home?"

"Just a minute," I called as I desperately searched for a safe place.

"Whatcha doing in there?"

"Oh, nothing...nothing. Stay there. I'm coming."

Finally I shoved it into a drawer under some of my old college notebooks. At least that's what I think I did. Who knows?

The following Tuesday when Eric said, "Well, did you read *The Joy of Sex*, or are you still thinking up reasons as to why you haven't bought it," I told him, "No, I got it all right."

He was surprised. "Congratulations," he said. "And did you both read it?"

"No, not yet."

"Why not?"

"Well...let me put it this way. I went into the store, and I bought it. I brought it home. I even looked at it for a couple of minutes. But then I heard the children coming, so I hid it...and now I can't remember where it is."

☎ Isn't It Time You Brought Home a Slice of the Bacon?

WHEN I WENT OFF TO COLLEGE and decided to major in English with an accent on creative writing, no one told me there's not much call in the business world for someone who can recite Dylan Thomas's "Do Not Go Gentle into That Good Night." When I congratulated myself on knowing the difference between *who* and *whom*, no one whispered, "That's lovely, dear, but it's not really a marketable skill." And when I signed up for a course in East Indian literature, no one suggested I might also do well to learn how to type.

But then no one expected that those of us who were leaping on our bicycles and pedaling across campus to an eight o'clock myth, metaphor and symbol class in the mid-1950s would be out looking for work twenty years later.

True, we knew we might have to hold down a job for a year or two after college while we waited for Mr. Right to come along. We might even have to work during the early years of marriage. But once the children arrived, we were told, we need never concern ourselves with time clocks, brown bag lunches, overtime, and merit raises again.

So, though I spent a year turning my limited talents to a secretarial job at the Wichita Falls Symphony Orchestra when Joe and I were first married, I joined the sheltered ranks of the gainfully unemployed when David was born. And there I stayed for the next nineteen years.

I did venture out briefly in 1969, when the price of milk, peanut butter, Super Sugar Crisp, and ten pounds of hamburger a week combined with school shoes, coats, mittens, and thirty-six sets of underwear to make Joe's paycheck look like a Band-Aid on a gaping wound. But the only position open to someone like me who couldn't work full time, who had to stay home with the children during the day, who had no office skills, and who hadn't held a job in eleven years was as a telephone canvasser.

And after three nights of having to go through the phone book so I could ring up folks and drag them away from television or the dishes or a tubful of waterlogged children to say, "Hi there. Did you know that the Arthur Murray Dance Studio has moved from its old location to Fourth and Lamar? Well, it has," I turned in my script and quit.

Luckily Joe and I decided, shortly thereafter, that when he retired, instead of staying where we were, we'd move back to Bainbridge. So I canceled what was left of my plans for employment. And I went back to being the infamous "just a housewife."

I was "just a housewife" with aspirations, however. For now that Robbie and Joan were in kindergarten, now that the danger of having an affectionate toddler pour corn-flakes and chocolate milk into my typewriter had passed, and now that we had a house big enough to let me move myself out of the traffic pattern, I decided to resume my long-interrupted plans to try my hand at writing.

I'd wanted to write for as long as I could remember. As a child I'd scribbled poems and left them on Daddy's desk with a program note that stated, "Daddy, I wrote the first half of this last night in bed, and I finished it this morning in the bathroom." In school I'd gone in for fanciful stories with a preponderance of elves, fairies, and trips from here to there by moonbeam.

My correspondence, mostly limited to thank-you letters I was forced to write if I wanted to go out and play, was brief and to the point. My first letter to my grandparents after nearly three years in an internment camp said, "I long to get home to you and roast potatoes."

In college, of course, I was led to believe that if I hadn't published a three-act play at the age of four, I probably was not meant to be a writer. My stories, melodramatic and full of pathos, usually came back with the notation "You have a flair for humor." And for every B+ I got two Cs because "Your punctuation is abominable."

For some reason this didn't discourage me completely. But then I'm the sort that thrives on dissuasion. It's a result of having an older brother who spent most of my formative years telling me, "You can't do that. You're too little, and besides, you're just a dumb girl." So when, after being a dutiful wife and mother for some eleven years, I read a writers' manual that stated, "Happily married women with children should forget writing since they obviously haven't suffered enough," when the author further advised against writing humor since one man's giggle is another man's yawn, and when it all began to sound like admonitions I'd heard before, I snarled, "The hell you say," and got out my little portable typewriter and rolled in a blank piece of paper.

The resulting "Ode to a Neglected Dustcloth" was published in the February 1969 issue of *Redbook*. But that was while we were still in Colorado Springs. And that was before I learned that one sale does not a Dorothy Parker having lunch at the Algonquin make.

By the time we moved to Bainbridge I'd accumulated my first eight or ten rejection slips. By then I could recite, "Thank you for submitting this material for our consideration. Unfortunately it does not fit into our editorial needs...." And by then Joe and I had acquired a full-time hobby in the form of an old house that needed three solid years of work.

So my attempts to put typewriter key to paper were somewhat thwarted. They were interrupted by Joe's injunctions to "tote that plasterboard; lift that two-by-four." And they were frustrated by the fact that my rejection slips had started arriving in matched sets.

But I learned to squeeze in a paragraph or two during the lull between the morning dishes and the first trip to the lumberyard or during the pause between framing the bedroom wall and nailing on the plasterboard. I also learned to limit my periods of dejection to the brief moments when I draped myself over the mailbox and toyed with the idea of burning my thesaurus and converting my typewriter into a table lamp. And eventually persistence began to pay off.

First a piece I'd dashed off in three weeks and sent out after only six revisions and three retypings sold to a Sunday supplement in Tacoma. Then one of the Seattle papers agreed to publish something I'd written.

"How about that?" I chortled as I opened up the envelope and waved a check for $35 in Joe's face. "I'm on my way to fame and fortune."

Joe ignored me as he thumbed through the rest of the mail and came up with an advertisement from Emil's tree service, a flyer announcing a sale on nectarines, and a fistful of bills. "Fame and fortune, eh?" he said. "Well, you'll have to do better than an occasional thirty-five dollars if you expect to make a dent in these.

"In fact," he continued, far too pragmatically for my taste, "I think it's about time you considered the idea of getting a job."

"A what?"

"A job. You know, work...for which you are paid a salary."

"But, Joe," I protested, "I'm just beginning to sell some of the stuff I write."

"I know," he said, "and I think it's great, but with prices the way they are—I mean, good Lord, you can't get a decent pair of shoes for less than twenty dollars these days and our grocery bill has almost doubled in the last five years." He paused. "What I'm trying to say is we need more money coming in, and I'm afraid what you earn writing simply isn't enough."

He was right, of course. I knew that. But I also knew I wasn't about to give up doing something I'd always wanted to do, not when I was finally beginning to succeed at it. Besides twenty years of marriage and raising children had not honed my secretarial skills. I still belonged to the search-and-destroy school of typing, and I still was totally ignorant as far as shorthand was concerned.

As for other training, I had none. I didn't teach. It was all I could do to get Robbie to stop saying, "Me and him are going to go swimming." I wasn't a nurse. My bedside manner when one of the children rushed past two bathrooms and then threw up in my shoe was less than Hippocratic. And though I'd worked in a bank during the summers in college, there wasn't much call for a thirty-eight-year-old messenger.

So I ranted and I raved. I inflated accounts of my worth as a mother and homemaker. I cited imaginary statistics that linked divorce and juvenile delinquency to Mom's absence from the kitchen. I exaggerated the cost of the wardrobe I'd need if I went back to work. For the time being Joe dropped the subject.

While it lay dormant, I gathered ammunition. I wrote. I rewrote. And I revised revisions. I sent manuscripts out, and when they came back, I sent them out again. And little by little the "Unfortunately your piece does not fit our editorial needs at this time" changed to "Tentative publication date is..."

"See," I told Joe every time I sold a piece, "I'm getting there. It shouldn't be long now."

But Joe's a worrier. When paying the bills became an exercise in having to ignore Peter to pay Paul, Joe worried. He worried when the phone rang and it was someone asking when we intended to bring our account up-to-date. He worried when the lady in linens and bedding said, "I'm sorry, sir, but I'm afraid you've already gone over the limit."

And when Joe worried, the question of my possible employment came up again. "I don't see what else we can do," he said. At the time he was still working for his father, and though he'd been promised a Christmas bonus, its size hinged on a number of variables, none of which was predictable.

"But—"

"We've cut our expenses to the bone as it is."

"I know, but—"

"So you're just going to have to find a job. That's all there is to it."

Eric agreed. I knew he would. He thrived on sending me out to do battle, especially when the mere thought terrified me, and the mere thought of looking for work certainly terrified me. "You can do it," he said.

"But I can't. I'm too old. No one hires anyone my age these days."

"Of course they do."

"But I can't do anything."

"Sure you can. You can wait on tables if you have to."

"You've never seen me wait on tables. Believe me, I'm not adept at it. Besides, I have something in the works."

"Like what?"

"Well, you know I belong to a writers' workshop..."

"So?"

"So a couple of weeks ago Jean, the woman who runs the workshop, asked me what it was I wanted to do with my writing, and I told her I wanted to write a column."

He started to interrupt.

"Wait," I told him. "There's more. When I told her what I wanted to do, she figured out a plan. She said, 'Find someone on one of the papers that you can get to read your work. Then send him or her a column every week till he or she gets a court order telling you to stop.'" I paused triumphantly. "And that's what I'm doing. I'm sending a column a week to the *P-I* [The Seattle Post-Intelligencer]."

"So?"

"So that's why I can't look for a job."

"Why not?"

"Because if I get a job and then suddenly the paper hires me, what do I do?"

"Simple. You quit the job."

"But that's not how you're supposed to do things."

"Says who?"

"I don't know. That's just the way I was raised. If you start something, you finish it."

"That's all very well if you're talking about building a

house or graduating from college. But in this case it doesn't apply. So here's what I want you to do..."

His plan was brief. In the week that followed I was to go out and interview for at least one job.

"But where do I start?" I asked as I felt my stomach flip over a time or two.

"Start anywhere. Start at the *P-I*."

"But I told you—"

"I know what you told me. But there's no law against your going to personnel and filling out an application form, too, is there?"

Joe was beside himself with delight. "Of course, there isn't, honey." He beamed. "There's no law at all. In fact, you could probably do it this afternoon, as long as you're already in Seattle."

I gave him a steely look. "Don't push," I snarled. "I'll get to it in my own time."

Unfortunately my own time passed far too quickly. The next thing I knew it was Monday, and I had one day left before I had to report in. So after changing my clothes three times, after trying to do something with my hair, and after cursing myself for not having stayed on the diet I had started three months before, I forced myself to get in the car, drive onto the ferry, and head into town.

I got out to the *P-I* shortly after two in the afternoon. After circling the block a time or two, I finally found a parking place and pulled in.

"OK," I muttered to myself as I blotted my lipstick and ran a comb through my hair one more time. "This is it. Get out of the car. Go across the street there. Walk right in. Ask for the personnel office. And go to it."

I got out of the car and dug through my purse for some change. There was barely enough for half an hour's worth of parking, and since the panic that had been lurking right under my ribs for a week was now working its way up to my throat and down to my knees, I considered postponing the ordeal and coming back when I had another quarter or two. But the voice of conscience and duty that was bred into me before I was ten vetoed the idea. So I put in what change I had and headed across the street.

When I walked into the building, the lobby was deserted.

"Now what do I do?" I mumbled.

Then I spied a woman way over to the left behind a counter.

"Excuse me," I said. "Could you tell me where I can find the personnel office?"

She looked up, and I half expected her to say, "It's *would*, lady, not *could*. 'Would you tell me where I can find the personnel office?' If you expect to get a job here, you'd better learn the difference."

I also thought I detected a look of "Good Lord, surely you don't think they're going to hire someone of your vintage, do you?" on her face. I know she probably wasn't thinking anything of the sort, but on that particular day I'd brought my paranoia along with me for company.

"It's on the third floor," she said. "Take the elevator. Turn left when you get out and go down the hall. It's not hard to find."

I thanked her and went over to the elevator. By now two men were standing there waiting for it, too. As we all got in, my paranoia informed me they were either editors or surly, world-weary reporters. "And they're asking themselves, 'Who in the hell is this old bat, and what's she doing here?'" it added.

I stared at the panel above the door and watched as the numbers lit up. When the door opened at three, I got out, turned to the right, then remembered I was supposed to go left. I spun around in my tracks and almost collided with my elevator mates.

"That's it," my paranoia sneered. "Show 'em you're clumsy, too."

"Oh, excuse me. I'm terribly sorry," I babbled, and before they could say anything, I hurried on down the hall.

There was only one girl in the personnel office, and to my relief she didn't burst into gales of hysterics when I announced that I was looking for work. In fact, she was quite affable.

"Let's see," she said, "we don't have any positions open at the moment, but if you'd like to fill out this form, we'll certainly keep you in mind."

She handed me an application form, and I searched through my purse, looking for a pen.

"You can fill it out later if you like," she said. "And then you can mail it in or bring it back, whichever is more convenient."

"That's all right," I told her. "I might as well do it now." And I retreated to a chair in the corner and sat down.

The form was standard: last name; first name; middle initial. I followed instructions and printed clearly. I put down my address, my date of birth, my sex, and remembered the friend of my uncle's who, under "Sex," had put "once a week." I listed my health as "Good" and resisted the impulse, under "Marital Status," to comment, "I didn't know that being married gave one any status."

Then I came to the part about previous employment. Oh, Lord, I thought, I don't think I'll mention my brief stint as a shill for the Arthur Murray Dance Studios. This left "Secretary for the Wichita Falls Symphony Orchestra" as my most recent work experience.

"Boy, that should give them a laugh," my paranoia chortled as I noted that my salary in 1958 had been a whopping $50 a week.

How about the job before that, when I was a bank messenger I thought. It's been so long ago I can't even remember what I made. Oh, well, I doubt they'll bother to read this far.

And with a flourish I scribbled in the required names of three references. Then I handed back the form, said my thank-yous, and was gone.

"Well," I told Eric the next morning, "I did it, and I hope you know it wasn't easy."

"I didn't expect it would be," he said. "But it won't be as bad the next time."

"The next time?"

"Of course. You didn't think you were through, did you?"

"I hoped I was."

"Don't be silly. This week I want you to check in with an employment agency."

"Yeah," Joe echoed, "that's what you should do next."

"Oh, shut up."

But I did as I was told. The following afternoon I signed up with the one agency on the island.

"And I must admit," I told Joe that night, "this time it wasn't so bad. In fact, Barbara, the woman who runs the agency, was quite encouraging."

It was true. The ordeal had been relatively painless, and Barbara had assured me she'd have no difficulty finding me a job. "In fact," she told me, "you'll probably have your pick of several." My troubles didn't start till she sent me out on interviews. The first one sounded like the ideal job.

"It's for a weekly newspaper," she told me. "It's close

enough to the ferry, so you won't have to take a car in. You can get there by bus."

"What exactly do they want?"

"I'm not sure," she said since employment agencies are secretive about the actual job and tell you only the name of the company under duress. "Just be there at two-thirty and ask for Tim."

So I arrived at two-thirty. How I made it I don't know. The address was for a warehouse someone had plunked down on a triangular lot where one street ended and two others began and I got lost twice. Then, when I finally found the place, I couldn't locate the office and had to pick my way along dingy aisles that threaded through stacks of boxes and rolls of paper and head for the voices I heard at the other end of the building.

It didn't help when I paused briefly by a pile of papers and realized this "weekly newspaper" was *The Vox Box*, a publication for swinging singles.

"Oh, great," I said to myself, "They're going to want me the way *Hustler* wants Norman Vincent Peale."

But I'd come this far, so I kept going, and finally, almost by accident, I stumbled into a brightly lit office.

"Yes? May I help you?" The woman behind the desk— Velma Tilley, according to her nameplate—stood up. She was short and sturdy and looked as if she might once have managed a roller derby champion.

"I have an appointment with Tim," I said. "My name is Ann Combs."

She scowled. "Tim went home...a couple of hours ago," she said.

"He did?"

"Yeah. What did you want to see him about?"

"I was told he had a job opening."

"Huh?" She shuffled through the papers on her desk,

then shrugged. "There's nothing here." Then she stood up. "Hey, Leroy," she bellowed to an unseen soul who was off at the other end of the warehouse somewhere. "Do you know anything about a job Tim was going to interview this lady for?"

Leroy's answer was muffled, and she hollered again. This time he wandered back to the office.

"We don't have any jobs," he said as if I'd made the whole thing up because it was a slow Thursday and I was bored.

"But Barbara Garretson, the woman from the Winslow Employment Agency, talked to Tim, and he said he wanted me here at two-thirty."

Leroy and Velma exchanged knowing looks. "Sorry," she said, "Tim didn't say anything when he left, and as far as I know, there aren't any jobs available."

So I wended my way back out of the warehouse, more relieved than disappointed, and I went home to finish up the column I'd been working on when Barbara called. It was column no.7, and though I'd heard from a friend of a friend that the *P-I* liked a couple of my offerings, I wished it'd hurry up and let me know so I wouldn't have to go through this sort of thing much longer.

But writers learn to wait. Either that or they do what God intended for them in the first place. And since I had the feeling God was taken with the notion that I actually enjoyed scrubbing bathtubs and sorting through socks, I elected to wait.

In the meantime, Barbara came up with another "perfect job." This one was in the office of the Seattle Repertory Theater, but it required no secretarial skills. And since lightning eventually has to strike someone, somewhere, it struck me, and I got the job...well almost.

"The final approval, of course, is up to the director,"

Mike, the office manager, told me. "But don't worry. To-morrow, after you have your interview with him, I'll show you what you're going to be doing."

So I appeared the next morning with Joe's "hoorays" and "halloos" still ringing in my ears. Mike looked less enthusiastic than he had the day before. "We have a little problem here," he said, using the same tone the exterminator uses when he's about to tell you that carpenter ants have eaten away the foundation of your house. "The director decided last night that he wants someone who can type up some of the office correspondence, too."

I made a face, and he shrugged sympathetically. "Any-way," he continued, "he wants you to take a typing test."

Now there are several things in this life I'd rather not do. One is walk to the North Pole. Another is take a typing test. But it was too late to back out. So I let myself be led into a cubicle. I accepted the text I was to copy. I sat down and rolled a blank sheet of paper into the machine. And I started to type.

```
Herman  Mwlville  met  Nathaniel  Hawthorne
thruogh  a  mutual  friend  in  Aigust  of  1850.  Both
authors  had  resd  and  appreciated  each  other's
work/
```

I ripped the page out and started again.

```
Herman  Melville  met  Nathaniel  Hawthorne
through  a  mytual  friend  in  August  of  1850.  Bith
authors  had  read  and  appreciated  each  other's
wprk.
```

"Damn," I muttered as I crumbled up the second piece of paper and tossed it into the wastebasket. "I'll be here forever if I have to do this whole paragraph right." I glanced around to see if there was any Ko-Rec-Type or any white-out. There wasn't, but it wouldn't have done me any good if there had been since everyone knows secretaries aren't hired for their ability to correct mistakes.

Finally, after what I was sure had been at least an hour and a half, I took my last sheet of paper and rolled it into place. "I might as well just do it and get it over with," I said. "I've lost the job anyway."

So I did it. I banged and tapped my way through Melville's friendship with Hawthorne as if I were making the announcement to the world for the first time. And when I was through, I didn't look it over. I didn't consider trying it one more time. I didn't even bother to wonder if perhaps I ought to do two paragraphs. I simply ripped it out of the machine. I left it on the secretary's desk, and I escaped before I had to bluff my way through a shorthand test.

"I'm sorry," I told Joe that night when I picked him up at the boat. "I really thought I had it. But don't worry. I talked to Marv at the *P-I* today, and he showed some of my columns to the book editor and he said they weren't bad."

Joe mumbled something unintelligible, and because I knew how discouraged he was I promised I'd check in with Barbara in the morning. Then I changed the subject.

I saw Barbara in the morning. I also saw her a week later and twice the week after that. And in between trips to her office and trips to an architect's office, a stationer's office, a florist, and a children's shoe store I pounded out my one column a week.

Then one day, while I was snatching my "interview" outfit out of the dryer before it wrinkled, the phone rang.

"Hello, Ann?" a man's voice said. "This is Jack Doughty from the *P-I*. How'd you like to write a column for us once a week?"

I resisted the impulse to bellow *"Wahoo,"* and tried to sound as if I were doing nothing more exciting than accepting an invitation to lunch.

"Why, I'd love to," I said as I waved my free hand, leaped in the air, and clicked my heels.

He then explained when I'd start, what I'd earn, and who my editor would be, and I drank it all in. When he finally hung up, I let out a war whoop, whirled around the kitchen a time or two, and dialed the phone.

"Hello, Joe?" I said. "I just called to tell you I refuse to go to any more of these stinking interviews."

"Huh?"

"That's right. My groveling days are over. Because I, kind sir, am now a columnist."

"You what? You are? You got it?" His voice echoed my delirium.

"I got it," I said, "and from now on, honey, I too will be bringing home at least a small slice of the bacon."

❧ Who Says Practice Makes Perfect?

"DON'T WORRY," they tell the child who's just wobbled his bike down the sidewalk and crashed it into a tree, "it'll be easier next time."

They say the same thing to the bride who's burned her first dinner. And because it sounds like a marvelous piece of advice they repeat it off and on to parents who are muddling through the twenty-five or so years it takes to raise their children from infancy to relative maturity.

"Don't worry, after you've had one child break his leg...go off to camp...flunk finger painting...pick all the neighbor's tulips...or call his brother an asshole, you'll learn to relax with the rest of them."

I suppose in a way they're right. After spending days, weeks, even months sitting on the edge of a cold bathtub waiting while David fiddled around and meandered his way through potty training, I simply shrugged with the others and said, "Oh, well, as long as they're out of diapers by the time they go off to kindergarten."

I also tended to agonize less every time I found myself,

on a bright September morning, standing at the school bus stop with a six-year-old who was scrubbed, combed, dressed in brand new everything from underwear on out, and anxiously waiting to join the ranks of the big kids.

Eventually I even got used to the fact that you can feed a Guatemalan orphan for a year on what it costs to buy one pair of track shoes.

But I also discovered that some things never get easier.

Two o'clock feedings, for instance, don't improve with time and repetition. I've never managed to reconcile myself to the fact that children are physically incapable of putting their laundry in the hamper rather than on the lid. The hours behind the grocery store with a neophyte driver who's learning to parallel park never seem to get shorter. The seven minutes it takes everyone to wolf down a meal I've worked all afternoon preparing never extends to ten or twenty. And when it's midnight and there's someone who still hasn't checked in, I'm never able to tell myself, "There's nothing to worry about," and believe it.

I also have problems with graduations and trips to deposit children at institutes of higher learning. But then I'm an incurable sentimentalist. I'm someone who worries that the old car out in the driveway senses it's about to be sold. I'm someone who cries at tree fellings and whose interior décor includes a felt banana, a large ceramic volcano, and a plaster handprint, all because they were gifts from the children.

Of course, I realize that sentimentality is out these days. In a world full of plastic Christmas trees, palimony suits, "shoot thy neighbor," winning through intimidation, and ostracism for anyone caught scratching his head, it's considered bad form to get a lump in your throat or a tear in your eye.

Nonetheless, all you have to do is seat me in a gymnasium, hit the first notes of "Pomp and Circumstance," and parade a group of capped and gowned graduates past me, and I'm a mass of handkerchiefs and wadded Kleenexes.

I expected to choke and snuffle when David graduated. After all, he was the first, and everyone's allowed to come apart at the seams when the first swallow flies. I also expected to use up two rolls of film. I expected to ignore the principal's plea that in the interest of time, we save our applause till the end. And I expected to rush outside after the ceremony and, whether he liked it or not, embrace my high school graduate.

I expected to, and I did. I swelled with pride at the baccalaureate when David introduced the speaker: "Ladies and gentlemen, may I present my grandfather, the Reverend Vincent H. Gowen." On graduation night I swallowed hard as the procession filed by and David nudged me and whispered, "Hi, Mom." I stood briefly and had to be hauled back down when the president of the school board announced that David had won a National Merit Scholarship. And when it was over and the graduates had trooped off to their all-night celebration cruise, I dabbed at my eyes, took Joe's hand, and sputtered, "Wasn't that beautiful!"

The unexpected came three months later, when we loaded up the station wagon and I delivered this same graduate, now a lowly freshman, to the indifferent arms of the University of Washington in Seattle.

It wasn't a move of transcontinental proportions. Where I'd traveled on the train for three days and three nights to get to Smith, he was separated from home and family by only a brief ride and twenty minutes on the freeway. Where my calls home had meant that the operator in

Northampton had to contact the operator in New York, who rang up the operator in Minneapolis, who signaled the operator in Seattle, who rang Mother's number on Bainbridge Island, he had only to pick up the receiver and dial home. And where I'd had to fit all my belongings into a trunk, a footlocker, and a couple of suitcases, he could simply balance his lamp on his bean-bag chair and stuff all his books into a couple of cardboard boxes.

So, when the appointed Saturday arrived and Joe had to work as usual, I didn't launch into a diatribe of "But how can you work when your son is heading off to college?" and "How can you ignore the fact that your first-born is leaving the nest?" and "Don't you realize it'll never be the same again?" I merely shrugged and said, "Oh, that's all right. We can manage, and it's not as if he were going away forever."

But my nonchalance ebbed slightly as we took the Forty-fifth Street exit off the freeway and inched our way through the university district traffic. And it faltered when we finally pulled up in front of Lander Hall.

It was a perfect fall day. The sun was out. The leaves had started turning gold and orange. It was warm, but there was a bite in the air that whispered, "Don't be fooled. Summer's finished." And there was the faint smell of autumn smoke in the breeze.

Activity was fierce in front of the dorm. Cars stuffed with stereos, plant stands, boxes, coats, skis, and an occasional rubber plant jockeyed for position in front of the main entrance. Fathers loaded down with garment bags and enormous stuffed animals wedged themselves into the lone elevator and pleaded with their daughters, "Wait till we get all this junk upstairs before you run off with your friends." Mothers tugged at suitcases and tried to prop open the front door. Boys shouted to each other from upstairs windows. And girls embraced and shrieked, "How was your summer? Tell me all about it."

Suddenly I remembered exactly how it is to be new, on the outside and one of the uninitiated, and I felt a twinge of pain for what David would be going through in the next few weeks.

I think he felt it, too, but he hid it nicely. "OK, Mom," he said when we'd parked the car as close as we were going to get, "you wait here while I check in. Then we'll unload."

So I waited...and I waited...and I waited. And after I'd seen three cars unloaded, read two chapters of *Watership Down*, and completed the crossword puzzle, he came back.

"Well," he said, more cheerful than I felt, "it's all set. Now let's get all this stuff up to my room."

It sounded easier than it was. For one thing, David's room was on the sixth floor. For another, the elevator, in considerable demand, seldom came when called. Because David was impatient, he suggested we take the stairs. I should have expected it. Everyone in the family is always suggesting, "Hey, Mom, let's take the stairs" and "Forget the bus, Mom, let's walk. It's only fifteen blocks" and "Why bother with the gondola, Mom? We can walk to the top of the mountain." Since I'm one of those people who don't like to admit they're lazy, I reluctantly agree.

So we took the stairs. I tottered after David with a suitcase in one hand and a couple of pillows in the other. On the next trip I huddled against the wall whenever a herd of students thundered by. I took the third one very slowly, and when the strain of carrying a load of books, David's tennis racket, three pairs of shoes, and a poster had me panting like an asthmatic mountain goat, I leaned against the railing for a while and rested. Eventually we got everything moved.

His room was small, small, and stark with about as much warmth as a roomette on the New York Central.

"My," I trilled (as a voice inside me screamed, "Oh, my God, what am I doing to my poor baby, leaving him here in this cell?"), "isn't this nice? You have your own desk, your own phone...and just look at that view."

Then, because I had to do something, I opened up one of the boxes and took out some sheets. "Here," I said, "why don't I make your bed up for you?"

"That's OK, Mom. I can do it," he protested, though I noticed he let me go ahead and seemed to appreciate the effort.

But when I finished, there was nothing more to do. I couldn't very well whip out a pair of scissors and start cutting off lengths of shelf paper. And I didn't think he wanted me to arrange his underwear drawer. So, since I also couldn't bring myself to say, "Well, so long, son. Have a nice school year," I picked up my purse, handed David his jacket, and reached for the door.

"Come on, honey," I said. "Let's go get some lunch and drive around to see what the campus is like."

As it turned out, it was a good idea. There was an excitement and an air of expectancy in the crowds of students that bustled up and down "The Ave.," milled in and out of coffee shops, and wandered through the bookstore, where textbooks were stacked up like office buildings in downtown Manhattan. And I felt less and less like someone dropping Junior at the orphanage.

We walked around. We got a hamburger and something to drink. Then we drove through the campus. It looked the way all campuses should look in late September.

Huge old trees stirred in the autumn breeze. There were couples walking along the paths that wound in and out between the buildings. Squirrels scampered across the grass, stopped, then scampered back the way they'd come. And a couple of boys pedaled past us on their bicycles. In the distance we could hear bursts of cheering as the fans watched the Huskies score against Navy in the first game of the year.

"Well," David said after we'd made the tour, "I guess you'd better drop me off at the dorm and get on home."

I swallowed hard. "Are you going to be all right?"

"Sure, don't worry about me. In fact, I'll call you to-night."

"Well...all right." I pulled up in front of Lander Hall and he got out.

"See ya, Mom," he said, and that was it. He disappeared into the building, and I headed out to the freeway. I made it clear to the boat. But once I was safely parked on the car deck and the ferry had pulled away from the dock, I burst into tears. But then, as I said, I'm a sentimentalist and sentimentalists always cry when their firstborns leave home.

Most of them regain their control, however, when the second, third, fourth, fifth, and sixth depart. Not I. At Jenny's graduation I wept and spluttered and kept nudging Joe to say, "Isn't she lovely?" At Geoffrey's commencement I gulped and dabbed and pretended I was having an allergy attack. And they'll probably have to carry me out on a stretcher when the twins march up to get their diplomas. They'll also have to sedate me when the twins head off to college.

I thought, after making it through David's launching without permanent emotional damage or a noticeable tic, that I'd be impervious to further wrenchings of the Evacuating Nest Syndrome. "After all," I told myself, "this is the natural order of things. Children are born. They grow up. They become so impossible you can hardly wait to see the last of them. And then they leave…at least they leave for extended periods of time so you can let your nails grow out again and get off the sauce. Besides," I added, "David wasn't swallowed up by the big, bad world. And Sylvia in her own way has survived. So why agonize over the fact that the rest of them will leave eventually?"

It was all very logical, and I shared my theory with anyone who'd listen.

Then it was Jenny's turn to flee the scene. She'd decided, because of its music department and because she'd have a chance to study with a particularly gifted piano teacher, to go to Whitworth College in Spokane, a good six- to seven-hour drive from home. This put Joe in the driver's seat and spared me from having to go the last mile with her.

Not that I wouldn't have. There simply wasn't enough room. I think it's because something happens to a girl when she's going clear across the state to college. Suddenly she's consumed with the notion that she's never going to see the inside of a store, or more precisely, the inside of Daddy's checkbook again. So she stocks up. She buys half a dozen tubes of toothpaste, two hundred yards of dental floss, Scotch tape, thumbtacks, bath powder, and deodorant. She loads up on laundry detergent, tea bags, cream rinse and shampoo. She buys enough pairs of panty hose to outfit a covey of secretaries. She corners the popcorn and the aspirin market. And she strips her room of everything but the rug and ceiling light.

So unless I was willing to ride shotgun on the fender, I had to stay home. This is not to say I was exempted from the rites of parting, however. For Jenny is not the

sort that tiptoes quietly out of town with only a brief and
silent wave at those she's leaving behind. Not at all. She
wails. She howls. She sighs. In the middle of the night
she flings herself on my sleeping form and sobs, "Oh,
Mother, what if my roommate hates me? What if I can't
do the work and flunk out? What if the dogs die while
I'm gone?" Then, when there's no turning back, she bids
an emotional farewell to everyone and everything.

She made the rounds on the morning she left for
Whitworth. While Joe and I struggled in and out of the
house with boxes and cartons and blankets and shoes,
she said good-bye to her room, to the cat, to the bay out
in front, and to the meadow behind the blackberry bushes.
While we stuffed pillows around her stereo and settled
her guitar on top of her quilt, she threw herself into the
arms of her startled brothers and Joan and swore she'd
think of them every minute she was gone. And while Joe
leaned on the horn and yelled, "Come on...come on.
We're going to miss the boat," she embraced the dogs
and even gave me a quick hug.

Then she was gone. Gee, it won't be the same without
her, I thought. There'll be no one practicing the piano
at eleven o'clock at night. Joan and I won't have anyone
with whom to sob our way through sentimental movies.
On Saturday mornings I won't hear anyone holler, "Who
wants pancakes?" I'll even miss the shriveled tea bags
she used to leave on a saucer by the stove.

As I wandered around the suddenly quiet house, picking up a stray sock here, retrieving a glass or an empty
cereal bowl there, I worried. What if her roommate does
hate her? What if she can't do the work and does flunk
out? What if she gets sick or hates her classes?

By noon I'd started pacing. By midafternoon I was on
my second pot of coffee. And by late afternoon I was
waiting by the phone, expecting any minute to hear that

she'd changed her mind and that she and Joe were on their way back.

Finally it rang. I snatched up the receiver. "Hello?"

"Hi, Mom," the poor pitiful daughter I'd sent off that morning chirped. "Boy, this place is neat. I've got a fabulous room. I love my roommate. I met a gorgeous hunk when Daddy and I went over to register, and I can't talk now 'cause we're all going out for a pizza. See ya later. Bye."

"That's it," I said to the cat after I'd hung up. "That's the last time I'm going to agonize over the fate of a child who's going off to college."

The cat stopped cleaning herself and stared at me, unblinking. Obviously she didn't believe me. Why should she? I didn't believe me either. And by the time another year had rolled by and it was Geoffrey's turn to depart, there I was again with a lump in my throat, a hollow feeling in the pit of my stomach, and a box of books under each arm.

With Geoffrey, however, things were different. For one thing, he'd decided to go to Western Washington University in Bellingham, putting him only two hours away. For another, it seemed as if half the 1980 class of Bainbridge High School would be joining him there, so I knew he wouldn't be lonely. As an added bonus, he'd have Jenny, who after one year on the frozen plains of eastern Washington, had decided to transfer west. I even had visions of transporting them both up together with one giant truckload of belongings.

But it was not to be. Geoffrey and his friend and fellow freshman Toby were going out for cross country. This meant they had to report early for a preliminary week or so of ten-mile runs, biathlons, jaunts around Lake Padden, and other leisurely training workouts.

The exodus was scheduled for a Sunday, the first Sun-

day of the pro football season, Joe noted with dismay.
But when I launched into my annual "There is life be-
yond football" lecture, he cut me off with a "Don't start.
I didn't say I wasn't going. I am. In fact, we both are."

"We are?" This was a surprise since we now had a
Honda station wagon and since Geoffrey was taking the
usual "whatever the traffic will bear." "How?"

"Oh, didn't I tell you? He's riding up with Toby and
the Smiths. We're simply the pack mules."

That sounded like Geoffrey, cool, casual, unsentimen-
tal. Why should he suffer through two hours of "Are you
sure you have enough socks?" and "You know the cat's
going to be lost without you, don't you?" when he and
Toby could spend the time sneering at the high school
students they'd left behind and imagining the women
and parties that lay ahead?

Of course, as a sentimental mother I chose to think
he'd given up his seat so I'd be able to go along and see
him in his new environment. I didn't come right out and
say I thought he'd miss me and wanted me there to help
launch him on his collegiate career. But a mother knows
this sort of thing, and even when it's not true, she clings
to the myth. She has to. The evidence to the contrary is
so overwhelming it would destroy her if she didn't.

So once again we loaded up. Because Geoffrey inherited, undiluted, his uncle Geoffrey's tendency to catch
ferries with only thirty seconds to spare, to do his Christmas shopping Christmas Eve, and to start packing on the
morning he's due to leave, we all joined in.

I went through the house:

"Are these sweat socks in the dryer yours or Robbie's?

"Where'd you put those towels I got you? I have a stray
washcloth here.

"Did you remember to pack your clock?"

Joe manned the car:

"Wait, don't put that there. It'll fall over.

"Here, give me that pillow. I'll stuff it in here.

"You'd better hurry. The ferry leaves in less than an hour."

Robbie and Joan played the part of customs agents:

"Hey, how come you're taking the sleeping bag? It's not yours. We need it.

"Boy, you sure have a lot of pictures of Carol. I thought you said she was just a kid.

"Can I use your desk while you're gone?"

Finally everything was loaded. Toby came, and we moved the wagons out and headed for the boat. We barely made it, and while everyone else went upstairs, Joe and I stayed in the car.

"You can go on up if you want to," Joe told me. "I'm just going to see if I get the game on the car radio."

"No, that's all right," I told him. "I'll stay down here with you. If I go up, they'll think I'm hovering, and hovering, as you know, is not cool."

So we sat in the car while the boat churned across the sound, avoiding autumn sailors out to take advantage of what could easily be the last glorious day of the season. We heard the Seahawks elect to receive. At least I think that's what they did. Once the radio waves had worked their way down to the car deck, past the U-Haul truck in front of us, and around the van beside us, they were faint and less than steady.

The reception did improve when we pulled into Seattle and headed north. Unfortunately the Seahawks didn't, and by the time we'd reached the outskirts of Bellingham they'd lost.

"Oh, well," I said as I spotted the parking lot in front of Fairhaven Hall, where we'd arranged to meet everyone, "we'll get 'em next week."

Joe mumbled something, but I didn't hear him. I was

looking for the Smiths' car, but it wasn't there. In fact, the only sign of life was one man sitting on a large rock next to the road. He, it turned out, was the coach. And I used the time before the Smiths arrived to grill him— discreetly, of course—on what was going to happen to my poor baby in the next week.

I was careful. I didn't disgrace myself by making him promise to see that Geoffrey ate properly and got enough sleep. I didn't even whimper when I heard how many miles they'd have to run every day. So when they all arrived and Geoffrey shot me an "Oh, no, what have you been up to?" look, I had a clear conscience.

I also had the familiar twinge of sadness as I watched the two boys trying to look nonchalant in their new surroundings. They weren't very successful. Where two hours before Geoffrey had swaggered around the house like Attila the Hun, ordering Robbie to do this and Joan to bring him that, now he hung back, and he and Toby conversed in low mumbles. When we all grabbed a box and threaded our way up the back stairs to their room for the week, he didn't vault past me, taking the steps two at a time, and Toby didn't yell out the window at him. They didn't even complain about their room, and everyone knows you have to complain about your room.

When we'd finished unloading the cars, we all stood around saying things like "Well it certainly is a lovely day" and "That's an interesting tree over there. I wonder what kind it is" and even "I think I got a paper cut from one of the boxes back there. Isn't it odd how much a tiny cut like that can hurt?"

That's when I knew it was time to go. So, after forcing the most casual of hugs on Geoffrey, Joe and I walked back to the car. We got in, waved good-bye again, and headed for the freeway.

Two and a half hours and a handkerchief later we arrived home. Joan was waiting for us, and the minute we walked in the house she rushed up.

"Guess what?" she said. "I've been reading some of Geoffrey's old catalogues, and you know something? I think I know where I want to go to college. Isn't that great?"

❧ Did I Just Hear Someone Go Out the Back Door?

I HAVE A MESSAGE for all those kind people who used to look at me piteously and say, "My God, woman, how do you do it?"

"Tell me folks, how do you undo it?"

Once you've mastered the art of driving Joan to the orthodontist at two, getting Jenny to her piano lesson at three-fifteen, picking up David at four, being at Geoffrey's ball game at four-thirty, meeting Joe on the five-fifty boat and starting dinner somewhere in between, how do you get used to the idea that come next year, the car will simply sit in the driveway for days at a time?

Once you've resigned yourself to seeing the living room constantly strewn with stacks of books, basketballs, some leftover lumber, a skateboard, two backpacks, and eight or ten coats, jackets, parkas, T-shirts, and sweaters, how do you deal with the fact that it's been three weeks since you've had to pick up so much as a pencil?

And once you've trained yourself to double the ingredients for every recipe you come across, how do you manage to remember that if you make the standard two meat loaves for dinner tonight, you're going to be eating leftovers till a week from Thursday?

I didn't really notice the change till after Geoffrey went away to college. Not that I wasn't aware that we were setting fewer places at the dinner table when David, Sylvia, and Jenny made their separate exits. I was. But I've always maintained that the difference between having two children and having three is the same as the difference between having two and having six. And this was my theory in reverse. When you have six, saying good-bye to one is the same as saying good-bye to three. Nothing changes till you're back down to two again. And it wasn't until we were down to Robbie and Joan that I suddenly realized we were no longer running out of peanut butter two days before I was due to go to the store, we weren't having to drink out of the cream pitcher because all the glasses were dirty, and at midnight the washing machine wasn't still grinding its way through a last load of gym shorts and underwear.

True, Sylvia's and Jenny's separate departures had left us with more bath towels in the cupboard. I could also count on there being mayonnaise and cucumbers in the refrigerator since they were no longer using the former to condition their hair or the latter to erase nonexistent shadows under their eyes.

When David graduated from the University of Washington, packed his bags, and went off to be a computer engineer in California's Silicon Valley, I had to buy a pocket calculator so I could balance my checkbook on my own. But his departure did present us with a guest room. Joan had already turned Sylvia's room into a sewing center, and Jenny kept coming home and reclaiming hers at vacation time.

But not till Geoffrey headed north to spend his academic year under someone else's watchful eye did I suddenly realize that Joe's and my tenure as active, on-duty parents was almost over. Not till then did it hit me that there is life beyond motherhood.

It took awhile to adapt. For the first month of Geoffrey's freshman year we were awash in extra portions of macaroni and cheese and beef chow mein. Half gallons of milk stood in the refrigerator and soured before Robbie and Joan could gulp them down. Hamburger buns bred in the freezer.

I found myself with a mild sense of unease if two days passed without at least one load of laundry being rushed through its paces. I constantly marveled at the fact that a clean room stayed that way for more than twenty-four hours. And when whole evenings went by without a single "Hey, you kids, hold it down up there. I can't hear myself think," I had to force myself to stay put and not rush upstairs to make sure both Robbie and Joan were still home.

Gradually, however, we adjusted. I gave up the twenty-year-old *Parents'* magazine-approved tradition of setting the alarm for five-thirty so I'd have time to get up, get dressed, make everyone breakfast and pack all the lunches: six bologna sandwiches—one on white, five on dark; two with mustard, two with mustard and mayonnaise, one plain—six apples; six packs of potato chips—not the barbecued kind, they taste yucky—money for milk; and one note saying, "Please excuse David early. He has a doctor's appointment at 1:30."

Instead, I lay in bed till Joe came in, poked me, and said, "Come on, honey. It's time to drive me to the boat." And I shrugged off the news that without my "Don't you want an egg?" and "Why don't you wear your jacket instead of that horrible sweater?" and "Just an apple's not a proper lunch," things were far less hectic.

After the exodus to school I made the beds, loaded up the dishwasher, generally straightened up the house, and sat down at the typewriter, confident that I probably wouldn't have to take a forgotten lunch to school. I definitely wouldn't have to bake a dozen cookies or a chocolate cake for the latest bake sale. And I most likely wouldn't have to pick anyone up after school, at least not till after cross-country practice.

The afternoon hours stretched out silently and crisis-free. When it came time to get dinner, I no longer had to work around bodies that were permanently stationed in front of the open refrigerator. I didn't have to drop everything and rush to the drugstore because "Mrs. Blakeslee says if I don't have a protractor by tomorrow, she's going to flunk me." In fact, if I was short of mushrooms or found I needed another can of tomato sauce, I could usually persuade Robbie or Joan to take the car and run down to Winslow and get them for me.

Suddenly I found I was hearing the evening news in its entirety. There was no more "And on the local scene, Superior Court Judge…" "Hey, Mom, where are my sweats?" "…sentenced prominent businessman…" "They're still in the dryer." "…to fifteen years in the federal prison at…" "No, they're not." "…for the brutal slaying of…" "Can you look for them, Mom? Can you, huh?"

I even caught sports reports and was able to tell Joe, when I picked him up at the boat, that the Sonics, playing in San Antonio, were ahead by six in the second quarter.

As time went on, I started taking things for granted. I no longer checked to see who planned to take a bath and who was going to wash her hair before I dared step into the shower. And I didn't put off running the dishwasher till morning "because all the hot water's gone anyway."

When the heel fell off my shoe or the stitching around the toe unraveled, I didn't dig around in the back of the closet to see if I had an old pair I could wear till after we'd paid for all the school clothes. Instead, I strode into the shoe store and selected the nicest pair I could find— on the sale rack. After all, Robbie and Joan still had feet at home.

I made an appointment with the dentist and belatedly had him bring my teeth into the late twentieth century. The car no longer turned into the orthodontist's parking lot. And our checkbook no longer automatically transferred its funds to the orthodontist's account.

We stopped buying peaches by the crate, cheese by the wheel, soup by the case, and milk by the cow. Phone conversations held in the privacy of the closet so nobody could hear dwindled down to a precious few. And arguments over who's the tallest, who has the smallest waist, and who can make it out to the mailbox and back in under thirty seconds disappeared entirely.

Joe and I suddenly found ourselves going out to dinner together even though it was no one's birthday or no one's anniversary and neither of us had got a raise. It was euphoric.

There was no "We can't. I don't have a baby-sitter."

There was no "We can't. I have to make caramel apples. I promised Jenny."

And there was no "We can't. Robbie's studying at Mike's and needs a ride home at seven-thirty."

Baby-sitters had faded into history when David and Sylvia entered their teens. Jenny wasn't home to volunteer to cater the fifth-grade Halloween party. If Joan agreed to bring refreshments to the class picnic, she was capable of making her own potato salad or her own

Chinese chews. And Robbie, now a licensed driver and a friend of licensed drivers, could always prevail on Mike to bring him home if necessary.

I didn't even have to cook them a full meal before we left. Both Joan and Robbie knew how to scramble an egg, fry a hamburger, or thaw and heat some of the soup in the freezer. And Joan's pizza was better by far than any I ever made.

Of course, summer vacations and Christmas were another matter entirely. We still didn't need a baby-sitter. Piano lessons and Little League games were still a thing of the past. And I still didn't have to make a casserole or cook a stew if Joe and I were going out.

But the confusion remained. Summer mornings dawned with three impassioned pleas for use of the car. There was a note on the bathroom mirror saying, "Please put my clothes in the dryer." The sink was full of the dishes left over from last night's late snack. Bath towels became a precious commodity again. Shirts and shoes, like Hansel and Gretel's cookie crumbs, trailed around the house and up the stairs again. And groceries once more disappeared almost before I'd had a chance to put them away. With Geoffrey home, the phone tripled its jangling, and any chance the call would be for Joe or me diminished even further. And clean, unfolded laundry on top of the dryer resumed its climb up the wall.

By now Jenny and Sylvia had their own apartments. Jenny, at the end of her sophomore year, had totaled up the cost of higher education and decided to get a job and go to night school instead. Though she made I'll-live-at-home noises, we discouraged it and reminded her that it was not the Empty Nest Syndrome that caused tremors and a gnashing of teeth, but rather the prospect of re-filling the empty nest with grown-up and independent birds. So she took a small apartment a mile from home and across from the high school.

Sylvia had settled into a third floor walk-up in Seattle, where she constantly put me to shame by being an immaculate housekeeper, an efficient manager of her own finances, and a frequent and imaginative hostess.

But she and Jenny came home often. Sometimes it was for the weekend. Sometimes it was for the day or just for dinner. Sometimes Jenny simply dropped by to do her laundry. And whenever they came, the clock turned back a bit:

"Say, Mom, whatever happened to that green sweater of mine? You know the one I mean. It had long sleeves and a cowl neck. You didn't throw it away, did you?"

"Can I try on your earrings and see how I look in your gray jacket?"

"You know what you should do, Mom? You should wear more make-up. And why don't you get a permanent? You'd look good in a permanent."

When they weren't improving me or telling me I ought to bleach the bathtub and sprinkle wheat germ on everyone's cornflakes, they were taking inventory and deciding I was overstocked:

"Can I have this little teakettle? It's just what I've been looking for."

"No, that was a wedding present."

"But you never use it."

"That doesn't matter. It was a gift to me, and I'm keeping it."

"How about one of these piepans? After all, you have four of them, and the last time I made a pie I had to use a casserole dish."

"Oh, all right. You can have one. Now shut the cupboards and leave things alone."

At Christmas things regressed even further since everyone came home at once, each bearing a favorite tradition we had to follow. I'd tried quietly to drop a few of the more time consuming rituals, but they protested:

"We have to have bubble cake for the Christmas brunch."

"When are we going string the popcorn?"

"Didn't you pick out the tree yet? It's supposed to be up by now."

"Where's the Advent calendar? Don't tell me you forgot to get one."

"You can't leave out the stockings. We've always had stockings."

"But you're all too old for fuzzy pencils, trick store puzzles, and another pair of mittens," I argued.

"That doesn't matter. You can get Geoffrey some film for his camera, a couple of tapes for Robbie, and I know where there's a pair of earrings Sylvia's dying to have."

"But—"

"Aw, come on."

"But I don't have as much time to shop around for clever stocking presents as I used to."

"We'll help, Mom...really we will."

I'd heard that story before, with puppies and kittens and impromptu picnics at the beach. But they were older now, I reasoned, and since mothers get smarter as the years go on, I took them up on their offer. I even improvised. I assigned the stockings to Jenny and Geoffrey, who were the most anxious that this particular tradition continue. I offered Geoffrey, whose funds were continually low, the chance to make wrapping all the presents his gift to me. I let Joan have as many wreaths, garlands, strings of lights, and candles as she wanted so long as she put them up and took them down again. I said whoever wanted bubble cake could make it. And I, who detest Christmas and look on it as another little something invented to keep wives and mothers occupied, marveled that I was actually beginning to enjoy the holidays.

"That's because the children have grown up," Joe said. "But don't worry. You'll get used to it."

He was right. They had. True, Robbie and Geoffrey still held wrestling matches in the kitchen, and David and Jenny still sniped at each other. But no one called Joan Whinella anymore. No one "dibsed" anything anymore. No one gagged on mushrooms or complained that he or she had been given the smallest pork chop and the largest helping of broccoli.

On occasion they even volunteered their services. Sylvia cleaned up the kitchen and mopped the floor for me. Geoffrey put gas in the car and paid for it himself. Joan trimmed the Christmas tree. David ran errands and cleared away the breakfast dishes. Robbie filled the woodbox. Jenny brought over some Christmas cookies she'd made.

I tried to get used to it. But it was like trying to get used to not having a toothache anymore. You have trouble enjoying the relief because you're afraid the pain will come back.

Then, on Christmas morning in 1981, they proved once and for all that Christmas isn't always for children.

It was when we all were gathered around the tree. Instead of the usual "Hey, let's get this show on the road" and "Come on, let's pass out the presents" and "Boy, I better have gotten what I wanted," the children handed Joe an envelope.

"Here, Mom and Dad," David said. "Open this first. This is for you, a combination Christmas and twenty-fifth anniversary present, and it's from all of us."

Joe looked over at me. "Do you know anything about this?" he asked.

I shook my head. "Not me."

He studied the envelope.

"Come on, Daddy," Jenny urged. "Come on. Open it."

"Yeah." They all joined in. "Open it."

Joe opened it. He read the enclosed letter. He read it again and looked at me open-mouthed.

"Read it out loud," Sylvia told him. "Hurry."

"OK." He cleared his throat. "It's from a travel agency," he said to me. "And it says, 'Merry Christmas. Arrangements are being made for you and your wife to travel from Seattle to Banff, Alberta.'"

"I don't understand," I said.

"It's a trip, Mom," David said. "We're sending you and Dad on a trip to Banff."

"Really?"

"Yeah," Joan explained. "It's all arranged. First you go from here to Victoria on the Princess Marguerite. You stay in Victoria overnight. Then the next day you take a bus and a ferry to Vancouver. There you get on the train to Banff. We know how you love trains. And," she added, "you can take it whenever you like."

I was stunned. Try as I might, I couldn't think of anything to say.

"Hurray." Sylvia cheered. "Mom's crying. That means she likes it. It also means we surprised her. We did surprise you, didn't we?"

"Surprise me? I'm flabbergasted." I blew my nose, wiped my eyes, and blew my nose again. "I simply can't believe it."

But it was true. They'd gotten together, some with a little more urging than others, and bought us a trip.

"We wanted to send you to Hawaii," Geoffrey explained, "but we couldn't afford it."

"Boy...couldn't we not afford it," said Robbie, whose part-time work as a dishwasher had yet to buy the hang glider he was saving up for.

"Do you like it?" Sylvia asked.

"Like it? I love it."

"In fact," I told Joe later, "I can't get over it. Who'd have thought that bunch of unruly, rebellious, cantankerous children would actually do a sweet and generous thing like that?"

"Well," he said, "apparently when they get older, they start appreciating good old Mom and Dad. I know I certainly appreciate them more now that most of them are out on their own."

"And just think," I added, "another year and a half, and they'll all be gone."

Joe sighed. Then he brightened. "Good Lord, I remembered something," he said.

"What?"

"Well, do you realize what's going to happen when Robbie goes off to college?"

"We won't have to nail his door shut when guests come?"

"No."

"There won't be anyone drinking out of the milk carton anymore?"

"No."

"I won't find shoes and belts and still-folded clothes in the laundry chute anymore?"

"No."

"What then?"

"Well, when Robbie goes off to college you and I are going to be able to get in the car and turn the key

without having a shot of rock music blast us into the back
seat."

"I don't know," I said. "I don't think I'll ever get used
to that."

❧ There's Always Someone Who Blinks First

THERE'S ALWAYS someone who blinks first.

When the party's finally going well, when Marty has his coat off, Scott's loosened his tie, Karen's sitting in the big overstuffed chair with her stockinged feet tucked under her and you can see the firelight reflected in the brandy, there's always someone who says, "Well, George, I think it's time you and I headed on home."

And when the evening sun is down behind the trees and the swallows are climbing higher and higher to catch its last rays before they swoop to earth again, there's always someone who says, "I'm beginning to get a little chilly. I think I'll go inside."

At our house Jenny blinked first. On July 8, 1982, the same day Lee died, she came over after dinner and announced, "Guess what, Mom and Dad? Carlos and I are engaged."

It wasn't a surprise. I'd expected it and welcomed it. Carlos, a gentle, loving man with a sense of humor that slipped into a conversation quietly, then crackled

310

with delight, was already an adored fixture in the family, and obviously he loved and understood our mercurial Jenny.

But at the time all I wanted was a chance to grieve for Lee. I needed time to get used to the idea that there'd be no more long phone calls discussing everything from local gossip to the Flat Earth Society, and the fact that when Democrats make their fortune and are no longer struggling, they tend to turn Republican.

I wanted an opportunity to absorb the fact that I wouldn't hear, "God, kid, I'll have to get a hundred-foot pole to touch you," whenever I sold an article or a book. There wouldn't be any more calling her up on a Saturday night to say, "How about going out to dinner with Joe and me?" I wouldn't hear brakes screeching in the driveway as she barely missed the garbage cans. The back door wouldn't open any more to the sound of "Hello, anyone home? I've got some cheap champagne." And I needed time to whisper, "Why couldn't you have lived a day or two longer? You would have enjoyed hearing about the intruder in Queen Elizabeth's bedroom."

I hadn't had a chance to grieve four years before, when Mother died suddenly. I'd had to take over: to make all the arrangements; to sort through a lifetime's accumulation of letters, pictures, recipes, clothes, and the like, deciding what to keep and what to throw away. And I'd had to see that Daddy, eighty-five, partially blind and helpless and spoiled the way only an English vicar who's spent thirty years in the Orient can be helpless and spoiled, had someone to care for him, cook his meals, and feed his dog.

So while Jenny trilled excitedly and spilled her plans, her hopes, and her dreams into our laps, I wondered, though I knew life had to go on, why it had to go on so quickly.

The weeks that followed were a jumble. One minute it was: "Now what do you think about this, Mom? We'll have a small wedding here and a big one in Pasadena."

"How's that again?"

"You know how it is. Carlos says he doesn't know if his parents can get away long enough to come up here. And I want my friends to be able to come to my wedding. You yourself said that was the one thing you regretted about getting married in Texas. You said you wished you'd had someone besides Grandmother, Granddaddy, and Uncle Geoff there."

"But two weddings. I don't mean to be crass, but who's going to pay for all these weddings?"

"Well...the one here would just be little. In fact, if you want, we could get married in the courthouse and then have a small party for my friends."

The next time I saw her it was: "We've decided to have one wedding. We'll have it here and have a small reception. Then we'll have a big reception when we get down to California."

In between there were noises about "bands" and "dancing" and "I just saw a picture of the perfect wedding dress. Of course, it costs twenty-four hundred dollars, but maybe we could find one like it."

With Geoffrey still in college, with Robbie and Joan queuing up for their turn, and student loans a thing of the past for those in our supposedly adequate income bracket, I had visions of Joe and me sitting, sharing a can of cat food, warming ourselves over a candle flame, and saying, "Well, at least it was a beautiful wedding."

And though I mentioned that while Princess Diana was to be admired, she was not necessarily to be emulated,

I didn't get very far. But then Jenny and I are alike, and because we're alike, we snarl at each other a lot, and while I was muttering, "She thinks we're made of money. She thinks we're simply made of money," she was saying, "Boy, if Mom had her way, I'd pick up a dress at the Goodwill and we'd serve peanut butter sandwiches at the reception."

Finally Joe took charge. "Just leave this to me," he announced as I spluttered and fumed.

Then he took Jenny aside. "All right, honey," he said, "I'll tell you what I'll do. I'll give you twenty-five hundred dollars to pay for the whole thing. Whatever you have left over from the wedding and reception here, you can use for a party when you and Carlos get to Pasadena. Does that sound fair?"

Apparently it did, or if it didn't, the chance for any further negotiating was obviously slim. So she agreed. And suddenly we were saving money:

"You're right, Mom. Your wedding dress does look good on me. Besides, Carlos likes the hoops.

"I have this neat friend who said she'd make my wedding cake and only charge us for the ingredients. Isn't that great?

"Why don't we leave the nuts out of the nut breads at the reception? Walnuts are terribly expensive, you know."

I balked at that. In fact, I did quite a bit of balking. But then the whole process of putting on a wedding terrified me. It was a holdover from other weddings I'd been involved in during the 1950s, when my contemporaries and I were taking turns marching down the aisle.

I remembered months and months of preparation: showers; dinners; fittings for the bridemaids' dresses. I remembered invitation parties like quilting bees, where four or five of us got together to address invitations. And when we were all finished, someone found a printing error and we had to send the invitations back and restuff all the envelopes.

I remembered Geoff's daughter's wedding just two months before. It had been a full year in the making. I had only till September eighteenth, and in between I had weekly deadlines at the paper and at least five chapters on my book to finish.

"I don't know how we're going to do it," I groaned, wringing my hands and running my fingers through my hair.

"What about the photographer?

"And the punch? I don't know how to make a decent punch.

"What do we need in the way of flowers? Do we have to have little bouquets in the church windows and sprigs of something on the ends of the pews?

"How about the rehearsal dinner? Someone has to host the rehearsal dinner, and if Carlos's parents come [the latest word was that they would be able to make it after all], they won't have time or a place or anything to do it.

"And then there's the guest list. I know I promised myself that this wedding would be Jenny's wedding and not Jenny's mother's wedding. Still, I'd like to ask a few of my friends, and I can't. I think she's already invited more people than the church and the parish hall will hold. In fact, I half expect her to say, 'Oh, yeah, Mom. I forgot to tell you. I've asked Idaho and western Montana.'

"Damn I wish Lee were here."

Finally Joan took pity on me. Of course Joan is organized. In fact, I have no doubt she'll one day run General Motors. And when she does, she'll say, "It all started with my sister's wedding."

"OK, Mom," she said one day when I was sitting at the kitchen table, guzzling coffee and wondering if Queen Elizabeth had ever said to Philip, "And then there are the gold carriages. They have to be polished. Frankly I don't see why they don't just live together and let it go at that." "Here."

She handed me a sheet of paper. On it, neatly typed, was a list of everything that had to be done. I looked it over:

Church...Joan
Organist...Jenny
Invitations...Jenny and Carlos
Flowers...Jenny
Tuxedos...Dad
Bridesmaids' dresses...each their own: Joan, three
Nut breads for reception...Mom, Dad, Joan

"See," she said, "I've put the name of who's responsible by each thing we have to take care of."

"How'd you get stuck with making three bridesmaids' dresses?" I asked.

"Well, I offered to do Julie's when I took the pattern over to the diner to get Jenny's approval and Julie said she didn't know how to sew. And Sylvia asked me to do hers."

"You're a good girl, Joannie," I said, giving her a hug.

She sighed. "Now about the tuxedos," she said, "I called four places in Seattle, and this one here offers the best deal. For every four tuxedos you rent they let you have a fifth free."

"Hey, that's great." I counted up. "There's Carlos, Carlos's father, Carlos's brother Jose, Daddy, David, Geoffrey, Robbie, and two of Carlos's friends from the Navy. Good Lord, that's nine."

"Yeah, maybe we can get two free."

"I doubt it, but we'll let Daddy worry about that."

The rest of the list was just as explicit. She'd even included the cost when she knew it.

"Now, about the rehearsal dinner," Joan said, "what do you plan to serve?"

"I don't know. How many people are there going to be?" We totaled up the wedding party, added spouses and dates.

"Don't forget Granddaddy and Auntie Sylvia," Joan said.

"Oh, yes, and Aunt Beth and Uncle Dan. They're coming up from Salem."

Uncle Dan was Mother's youngest brother, and he'd always been my favorite uncle.

"And of course, Carlos's family." I added in my head, no mean chore for me. "Yikes...that's about thirty people, give or take a few. That means it'll have to be a buffet. Why don't I cook a ham, make that cheese-spinach rice everyone likes? Then we can have a salad and a light dessert."

"Great." She wrote it down. "Now don't you feel better?"

I had to admit I did. But then I always feel better when I have a list in front of me and can look forward to the pleasure of crossing out each job as it's done.

My euphoria, however, would be short-lived, for the next step, after Joan had taken my wedding dress down to be cleaned and David had sent up his measurements, was that Joe, Geoffrey, and Robbie would go into Seattle to reserve the tuxedos and I would tag along and would be dropped off to look for a mother-of-the-bride dress for me.

They let me off downtown, within walking distance of three main department stores and untold dress shops and boutiques. And with the innocence of a small child whispering, "I believe," to Tinkerbell, Joe said, "Have a good time. Pick out something gorgeous, and we'll see you in an hour and a half."

"Right," I told him grudgingly. Then I shut the car door, watched them drive off, and headed into the first store. "Right," I muttered to myself as I marched past better jewelry, scarves and bags, and a truncated male mannequin in a pair of red briefs and got in the elevator.

Women's dresses were on the sixth floor, and the minute I stepped out of the elevator, I sensed I was in trouble because the "in" color that season was black, and the "in" look was tuxedos for women. I could just see myself going down the aisle on an usher's arm while members of the congregation whispered, "Who's the short, chunky fellow?"

"May I help you?" asked a saleswoman, who couldn't have been more than a size three.

I sighed. "Yes," I said. "At least I hope you can. I'm looking for a mother-of-the-bride dress. I want something simple, something I can wear again...there's nothing worse than paying a fortune for a one-event dress. I want something that doesn't make me look matronly and something that isn't in menopause blue."

She blanched slightly. "Menopause blue?"

"You know what I mean. It's the color all mothers of the bride end up wearing."

She shook her head, and I could almost see her thinking: Wait till I tell the girls about this one. They'll never believe it. Then she took a deep breath. "All right," she said. "Now when is the wedding?"

"Oh, in about six weeks."

"Six weeks." She gasped. "And you're just starting to look for a dress?"

"That's right." I didn't follow her reasoning, but I could see I'd been remiss, so with appropriate feelings of guilt I explained, "I've been busy, and we live over on Bainbridge Island." That usually works since people who live in Seattle think that we on Bainbridge have to crawl over the Olympic Mountains and swim Puget Sound to get to civilization, and they're also convinced we can find nothing more elaborate than a print housedress on the island.

"Oh," she said. Then she squared her shoulders and braced herself for the task ahead. "Well, let's see what we can find over here in Special Events." And she headed off.

I followed. Obviously there was no shortage of selection. I saw long dresses, short dresses, and slinky black dresses with sequined jackets. There were silk dresses, satin dresses, chiffons and failles; V necks, scoop necks; ruffles and bows. And not one looked as if it would suit me.

The saleswoman was more optimistic. "Don't worry," she said. "We'll find something...somewhere."

She whipped aside a row of hangers and hauled out a silky beige number. "This, for instance. This should look lovely on you. Try it on."

I glanced at the price tag that dangled lazily from the cuff. It was $250. "I don't know," I said.

"Go ahead, try it on."

I'm easily cowed. So I tried it on. Luckily it drained all the color from my face and made me look as if I'd been drinking embalming fluid.

"No, I don't think so."

"How about this one?" she asked.

It was fuchsia with ruffles around the neck, ruffles around the cuffs, and tiers of ruffles on the skirt. Now I looked like a Shirley Temple lampshade.

"No, that's not really my type either."

"Then there's this." She sighed. "At least the color's good on you."

The color may have been flattering, but the material was draped this way and that, and I felt like Julius Caesar's mother-in-law.

"I...don't...think...so," I said, trying to sound as if I'd actually considered it.

She nodded, massaging her forehead with the tips of her fingers. Finally she brought in a two-piece affair. It was sheer, shapeless, and the color of wet bark.

"This is it," she said, shaking her head and raking the hair out of her eyes. "This is the only other thing I could find."

I tried it on. Now I looked like a chiffon truck.

"No," I said. "It's just not quite right. I guess I'd better go somewhere else."

She tried unsuccessfully to hide her obvious relief. And as I left and the elevator doors were closing behind me, I heard her saying to a fellow clerk, "Thank God that's over. She should have started months ago. She'll never make it now."

But she was wrong. Two days later I went into a tiny store in Winslow and twenty minutes after that I walked out with the perfect mother-of-the-bride dress under my arm. It was short, raw silk, and not even close to menopause blue.

"Well, that's that," I told Joe that night after I'd crossed "Mom's dress" off the list. "But," I added, because I'm ill at ease when there's nothing to worry about, "I've been thinking about the rehearsal dinner, and it suddenly occurred to me. The dinner's scheduled for Friday night and do you suppose, since Carlos's parents are Roman Catholics, that they can't eat meat on Friday?"

Joe doesn't ruffle easily when it's my problem. "I don't know," he said. "Why don't you ask Carlos?"

So I did. And I was right.

Carlos was apologetic. "I'm sorry," he said.

"Oh, don't worry about it," I told him. "I can just as easily have a salmon."

But the more I thought about it, the more a salmon seemed like a bad idea.

"For one thing," I told Joe, "it'll have to be huge if we're going to serve thirty people."

"Oh, I don't know," he said in that patient "Now, now, don't worry, everything will be fine" voice that drives me crazy when I'm in a tizzy about something.

"I mean it," I barked. "It's going to be loaves and fishes time."

"Then have something else."

"But what?"

"How about clam chowder?" his sister Marie suggested.

"Clam chowder?"

"Sure. You can make it ahead of time and just reheat it."

I thought for a minute. "You know," I said, "you're right. I can make it that morning...or even the day before. It'll be perfect."

But in the days that followed perfection disintegrated into visions of thirty people milling around with thirty bowls of soup perched precariously on dinner plates.

"It won't work," I told Joe bare minutes after he'd come in with a gross of canned clams. "It just won't work."

He sighed. "Well, then," he said, "what will?"

"I don't know. But there has to be something."

And with that I started my search. I asked everyone: friends, relatives, the girl at the post office, a man in the bookstore, even strangers standing in line with me at the bank. "What am I going to serve at the rehearsal dinner?"

Finally Scotty, a friend to whom having thirty people for dinner is almost a vacation, rescued me.

"It's simple, girl," she told me. "All you have to do is make a whole bunch of little cream puffs. They're easy to make, and you can do it a week before and freeze them. Then, on the day of the dinner, stuff them with crab and shrimp fillings. Stack them up on a platter. Serve them with an assortment of raw vegetables and various chips. Then have fresh fruit and cookies for dessert. It's all finger food, so you won't need any silverware. And people can help themselves whenever they want."

"Oh, Scotty," I blathered, "you've saved my life."

And the next Sunday found me sifting, stirring, dropping by teaspoonfuls, making batch after batch of cream puffs.

"My God, Sunday at the stove is getting to be a family tradition," said Joe, who had spent the week before whipping up a dozen fruit cakes for the reception.

"How about Saturday at the stove?" Joan added. "It took me all Saturday to finish up those eight loaves of zucchini bread."

"You're right," I said. "In fact, it'll probably be October before the oven cools down."

"And if I don't get upstairs and work on Sylvia's dress, it'll also be October before I finish it."

But it didn't take her till October. She put the last stitch in the hem the morning of the wedding.

By then we'd all put in our last stitch. Carlos's family had come in Tuesday night after thirty-six hours on the road. We'd all met, found we liked each other, and had dinner and too much wine on Wednesday. David had flown in Thursday. Geoffrey, already back at college, was due to arrive early Saturday afternoon.

Joe had all the tuxedos hanging in a row from a high shelf in the library. He'd carted the champagne and the breads, the nuts, the mints, and "Oh, Lord, don't forget the guest book" up to the parish hall. And I'd polished whatever silver had to be polished, ironed the table-cloths, and set out the punch bowls and glasses.

The rehearsal dinner had gone well. The cat was now eating a sardine filling I'd made early, tasted, and wisely decided not to use. And because I always end up with too much food, bags of cream puffs were back in the freezer, waiting to serve as casual snacks and after-school tidbits.

Jenny was a bundle of nerves, but she brightened con-siderably when she learned the band had found a bass player and would be there as promised. Robbie, just for the fun of it, threatened not to shower or wash his hair. Sylvia had called from work to say she'd be on the four-thirty boat and ask if someone would run to the store and get her a pair of panty hose. Joan practiced walking up and down in heels.

When it came time to get ready, I could hear Robbie upstairs grumbling about having to wear a tux. I could hear Geoffrey and David mumbling, "How do you adjust these cummerbunds?" and Sylvia laughing, "You cinch this up, silly." But gradually, as each piece went on, they began to enjoy themselves. And I heard, "Say there, you don't look half bad," and "You know, Joan, you did a good job on these dresses."

Then there was nothing left to do. It was time. I'd left Jenny in the church nursery. She was nervous but dressed and in the able care of her bridesmaids. I was safely in my place in the front pew. David had brought me down the aisle, though I'd threatened, with all my sons as ushers, to sneak out, run around, and come down three times.

Then suddenly the music began. We all stood, and as I turned and watched the procession of bridesmaids, each on the arm of an usher, begin, I felt an unexpected lump rising in my throat. For here were all our children, grown and together for the last time as "the Combs kids." David was the first to go by.

Good grief, I thought as he gave me a quick smile, he's so tall, so slender and distinguished-looking. You'd never know that I used to have to plead with him to change his socks or that I thought I'd go crazy when he was learning to parallel-park.

Next came Sylvia and Geoffrey. She was poised and elegant in raspberry and lace. He, in his ruffled shirt and bow tie, looked positively dashing.

I can't believe it, I mused as they strode by. I remember when they hated each another. Now look at them. They're actually smiling at each other. And who would suspect she once seemed determined to be the black sheep of the family? Who would believe that it took me three years, when he was building his boat, to get him to move his lumber out of the living room?

When Robbie passed, he grinned. He knew he looked splendid in his tuxedo. This can't be the boy who almost died as a baby and who had open heart surgery when he was nine, I thought.

I expected that Joan would be a lovely maid of honor, and she was. But as she and Jose passed and she winked at me, I couldn't help remembering that this was the girl who as a toddler had turned up at the local elementary school in nothing but a T-shirt and a pair of training pants.

There was a pause. Then Jenny and Joe appeared. I'd seen Joe looking proud before, at birthdays and graduations and at the finish line of marathons. But never had he looked as proud as he did now. Jenny, as radiant as any bride I'd seen, smiled up at him and tugged on his arm to keep him from rushing down the aisle, leaving her in the wake.

That's amazing, I thought as tears welled up. There goes the girl who once fed Joan Tabasco sauce. She's the one who played the *Moonlight* Sonata for me as a Christmas present one year. It was she who spent her teen years insisting, "You don't understand, Mother. You just don't understand." And now she's a bride.

Finally they all were lined up at the altar. Joe had given his daughter away. He was back in the pew, sitting next to me. And as the service continued, as Carlos, his voice strong and steady, promised to love, honor and cherish and Jenny softly promised the same, I took his arm and gave it a squeeze.

"You know something?" I whispered. "I think we raised a pretty marvelous bunch of kids."

He nodded. "You're right," he whispered back. "And every now and then it all seems worth it."